LITERATURE AND RELIGION

A STUDY IN CONFLICT

LITERATURE
and
RELIGION

A STUDY IN CONFLICT

Charles I. Glicksberg

1960
SOUTHERN METHODIST UNIVERSITY PRESS
DALLAS

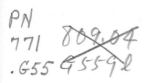

*Published with the Assistance of a Grant
From the Ford Foundation
Under its Program for the Support of Publication
In the Humanities and Social Sciences*

Library of Congress Catalog Card Number: 60-8675
Printed in the United States of America at Dallas, Texas

TO STEPHANIE

ACKNOWLEDGMENTS

VARIOUS PARTS of this book originally appeared as articles in a number of magazines.

"Literary Existentialism" and "The Myth of Nothingness" were first published in the *Arizona Quarterly*.

"The Literature of Death" appeared in the Summer 1956 issue of *Prairie Schooner*, Volume XXX, Number 2. *Prairie Schooner* is published by the University of Nebraska Press.

"The Religious Problem in Modern Poetry" was printed in the Spring 1958 issue of the *South Atlantic Quarterly* and is reprinted by permission.

"The Religious Revival in Contemporary Literature" and "The Literature of Absurdity" were first published in the *Western Humanities Review* and are reprinted by permission.

"The Paradox of Religious Poetry" appeared first in the *Bucknell Review*.

"The Modern Playwright and the Absolute" appeared in the *Queen's Quarterly*.

"The God of Fiction," combines two articles which appeared in the *University of Kansas City Review* and the *Colorado Quarterly*.

"The Lost Generation of Literature," "The Spiritual Quest in Eliot's Plays," and "Camus's Quest for God" appeared originally in the *Southwest Review*.

The author hereby renders grateful acknowledgment to the editors of the above-named periodicals for permission to reprint these articles.

C. I. G.

CONTENTS

PART FOUR
The World of Fiction

PART FIVE
Conclusion

PART ONE

THE SEARCH FOR MEANING

I

THE CONTEMPORARY
LITERARY LANDSCAPE

IF WE ARE to view in proper perspective the spiritual and religious conflicts of our age, as these are reflected in drama and fiction and poetry, then we must endeavor at the outset to understand the nature of the relationship between literature and belief. Nothing is more drearily ineffectual than aesthetic theory that seeks to cut the writer off from the social and cultural roots that nourish him, the viable meanings of the immanent world that establish his horizon of vision. No one denies the writer the fundamental right to create in the image of the truth as he sees it, but even as this concession is made a number of basic questions arise that clamor for an answer: how does the writer exercise this right, out of what material does he compose this bafflingly complex testament of truth, his interpretation of life? What is more, to grant him this fundamental right is not the same thing as to attribute to him some mysterious potency of spirit, a quality both transcendental and ineffable, which lies beyond the scope of analysis. Certainly the poet or novelist or dramatist is not to be judged by the validity (how, after all, is that to be measured?) of his *Weltanschauung*. We treasure and are deeply moved by the mighty contributions of men as diverse in their world outlook as Sophocles, Lucretius, Shelley, Dante, Donne, Gerard Manley Hopkins, Dostoevski, Dylan Thomas, Eugene O'Neill, Albert Camus.

Only the dogmatic religious-minded critic would venture to grade them according to theological co-ordinates of orthodoxy.

It is, then, not the conclusions these writers draw that prove, aesthetically speaking, so meaningful and moving. A poem, for example, is uniquely what it is. It does not achieve a measure of greatness because it grapples with a lofty subject like God or Heaven or Hell or immortality. Whether a novelist writes about a village in Italy or a plague that has broken out in a nameless city on the north coast of Africa or three cities in Russia or a house with green shutters or a sanatorium on a snow-clad peak in the Alps, whether a poet writes about a nightingale or Prometheus unchained or a Grecian urn or the west wind—what in each case makes the work live is the vividness and depth of perception with which the experience has been grasped and projected in imaginative terms. It does not matter if the poet is a Catholic, an agnostic, a humanist, an Existentialist, or an atheist. It is not, in short, the doctrine he embraces, be it religious or metaphysical, that makes the writer what he is.

Yet no writer, however independent in spirit, can hope to escape the psychological climate and cultural compulsives of his age; for every writer is an integral part of his world, participating in its crimes and crises and sharing inevitably its burden of collective guilt. The "horror" of our time—the horror of unconscionable mass violence and cruelty piled upon the horror induced by the empty spaces that so affrighted the mind of Pascal—has crept into the marrow of his bones and infected the substance of his private nightmares. Though he seeks to speak out, he cannot often rise to the heights of the tragic. Because of the critical human situation in which he is involved, he has suffered a marked lowering of creative vitality. The possibilities of creation are still endless, but he does not know what to do with them. Unable to commit himself with passion or finality to any cause, he wanders about lost in his own personal hell. The world seems to have fallen apart; men have been cut off from their organic relations with society in its time-ordered continuity, from the eternal sources of mystery, the numinous in nature, the symbols of the absolute. All this forms the cultural soi! from which the writer must draw his vital nourishment. It is out of this ferment of clashing ideas in his age, this sense of spiritual lostness, that he develops his "themes," his "philosophical" insights, his conception of character and destiny.

What then are the ideological forces which, for better or worse, have shaped the body of contemporary literature? First of all, science, technology, and industrialism have reduced the individual to insignificance and dwarfed the dimensions of the autonomous personality. In an age of conditioned reflexes, electronics, brainwashing, and hydrogen bombs, how can one continue to believe in freedom of will? How can one still cherish the illusion that he is responsible for mastering his fate? The protagonist of *Death of a Salesman* is Willy Loman—the name itself symbolizes his diminished stature. The hero of *The Adding Machine* is an unregenerate Mr. Zero. The central character in modern "tragedy" has lost his greatness of soul; he is a robot incarnate, a mechanical nullity, a thing to be bought and sold in the labor market. Society, as pictured by John Dos Passos in *U.S.A.* and by John Steinbeck in *The Grapes of Wrath,* has become vastly efficient, monstrously impersonal, and anonymous. In his despair, the hero of *Invisible Man,* by Ralph Ellison, tries to go into hiding, to withdraw into schizophrenic isolation. The human, organic community has given way to a mechanized antheap. In such a regimented environment, the human being is wretchedly alienated and impotent. Here we behold the dilemma of modern man: he remains alone and apart, marching without a sense of God or direction on a journey the meaning of which he cannot comprehend.

The severest blow he has suffered is his realization that, in point of time, his stay on earth is but a brief interlude. How can he feel at home in a universe, instinct with energy, which has no place in it, so far as he can make out, for moral values, the sense of justice, purpose, the presence of God? A metaphysical orphan in space, he regards himself as but a gratuitous biological accident in the magnificent but blind process of evolution. Why should he deserve a special degree of eminence not accorded to the worm? Now the supreme illusion—the belief in his own importance—has been taken away from him. With blinding insight he perceives that even if humanity as a whole should perish in an atomic holocaust, the disaster would not greatly affect the economy of the universe. This traumatic awareness of his nothingness in the space-time continuum drives him to despair. How can the myth of nothingness save him? Colin Wilson, in *Religion and the Rebel,* describes how at one point in his youth he was overcome by the shattering knowledge that life has no ultimate meaning. He had reached the ultima Thule of nihilistic unbelief. "It was not just *lack* of belief in anything—it was an active *belief in Nothing.*" For a time he contemplated suicide.

Is the naturalistic interpretation of life responsible for this outburst of nihilistic despair? Has the advance of science caused the death of the gods? If the intellectuals of today are engaged in a furious quarrel with God, it is because contemporary civilization has lost its traditional faith in religion. Some writers are satisfied with neither the conclusions of science nor the dogmatic theology of the church. A number of religiously oriented writers insist that the distinctive feature of being human lies in man's unique faculty of transcendence, his capacity to reach beyond himself, to outsoar his physical limits. In his aspirations, man enters the realm of spirit, pursuing ideals and striving for goals that cannot be summed up in naturalistic terms, establishing relationships and accepting responsibilities that are supremely human, not to be identified with the "natural" sphere. Other writers seek to find the abiding truth of all religions in the recognition of the intrinsic worth of every human being, which means recognition of man as made in the image of God and, therefore, potentially a son of God. Still others, taking refuge in the theology of crisis, reaffirm the reality and truth of the doctrine of "original sin." Man must punish himself without end in order to expiate the burden of guilt he must carry as the price of existence. Despite the revival of religious feeling in some literary quarters, the majority of writers in our time would agree with

Ludwig Wittgenstein that it is essentially meaningless to talk about immortality, eternity, and God.

The problem of the intellectual in a God-abandoned universe is that he cannot take refuge in the traditional teachings of religion. He is convinced that the anthropomorphic conception of God will have to go. Modern man must make his peace with a naturalistic universe which gives no hint of a providential purpose at work behind the scenes. He need not cling permanently to illusion, even if he should finally conclude, as Colin Wilson does in *Religion and the Rebel,* that the scientific pursuit of the truth is in itself an illusion. But as this young writer makes clear, a religion based on the idea of prayer and propitiation, of sin and punishment, of hell and heaven, is now out of the question. The religious hunger persists strongly among the writers of our age, even those who are rebels and blasphemers, but it cannot be fed with the old formulas.

If man is today a victim of cosmic alienation, that, according to the Existentialists, cannot be helped. To be alienated—that is to be human. Confronting the prospect of annihilation, modern man is forced to come to grips with the problem of the meaning of his existence and his relation to God. Frightened by the loss of those moral values that once held together the fabric of society and by the realization of his utter isolation in the universe, he desperately seeks a way out. Whereas believing man in the past was terrified by the thought of the torture awaiting him in hell, the present anxiety that springs from the perception of nothingness is even more demoralizing. From Heidegger the modern intellectuals derived their myth of nothingness and their obsession with death. Nothing is more striking in contemporary literary metaphysics than this monomaniacal emphasis on the inevitability of death. Each one is mortally stricken by the knowledge that he must die, and each one must die his own death. Can the threat of death, courageously faced, serve to emancipate the self and render possible a more authentic life? If death means a plunge into the void, can man affirm his own moral values in the world? How can he assume responsibility for his actions if he knows, as he does, that there is no justification for his existence? Can this vision of nothingness make for a literature that is tragic in content? We shall see later on how the fear of death, the primal fear, deepened by the loss of the religious sense, is at the root of everything on the contemporary cultural scene that is productive of anxiety.

The "alienated" writers become rebels, but they cannot play this role without experiencing a profound feeling of guilt. If the universe is without a moral pattern or ultimate purpose, then what duty remains to which they can give their allegiance? Since man stands alone, does the human being represent the highest value? How can the writer overcome the moral paralysis induced by a realization of the meaninglessness of life? How can he wrest out of despair the courage to be? Is the anxiety voiced so poignantly in Existentialist literature an attempt to derive some meaning from the meaningless? Can the contemporary writer transcend his negations, and if so, how? How can he find a home for his alienated spirit and "justify" his existence? How can he give imaginative expression to the storm and stress of doubt and denial, his search for the hidden God? What shall, what can, he do without betraying his artistic responsibility? Shall he, even as the atomic and hydrogen bombs are about to spell out the apocalypse of doom, continue to prophesy that the Second Coming is at hand? Is it his function to point out, if he can, the road that leads to salvation? What of his obligation to be unswervingly true to the imperatives of his vision? Where, in this ruined ideological landscape, shall he find the material for building with his fellow-men the Jerusalem of the spirit that William Blake envisaged?

The most pressing problem for the modern writer, regardless of the terms he may use in formulating it, is to determine the relation of religion to culture. How is he to establish his relation to the absolute, especially now that he is convinced God is dead? He cannot abandon the pure heritage of Christianity, which has shaped the past and made a precious and enduring contribution to human culture. Even if he abandons the theistic faith, he need not, like Nietzsche, engage in a bitter feud with the Christian outlook. He is torn between the two alternatives: either God is all-in-all or there is nothing. Though he cannot subscribe to the Christian creed, since he believes that nature is the sole locus of value and that human culture is all he possesses, the conflict within him nevertheless persists. If he rejects the ideal of divine transcendence and the kingdom of eternity, then how is he to face the truth of the human situation, the knowledge of his own imminent death? He hungers for a God, a force, which will symbolize a purpose that goes beyond the purpose of any single person, but he balks at accepting a historical savior. As an Outsider he strives to perfect himself, to make the Life Force flow through him and fulfil itself creatively in him, to become like God. Perhaps the new religion in the making will be proclaimed by the spiritual rebels of our age. In facing the truth of Being with unfaltering courage, in fathoming the abyss of terror that is the theme of Heidegger's metaphysical discourse—it is thus that a number of writers and intellectuals have sought for a means of reconciling the relationships, always ambiguous and paradoxical, between literature and religion. The vitality of the religious quest has not diminished; it goes on under new auspices and in terms of a radically revised vocabulary. That is why the "religious" literature of the twentieth century often seems "irreligious" or "blasphemous" in content.

II

THE SPIRITUAL CRISIS
OF THE MODERN WRITER

NO AGE can continue to live fruitfully without a sustaining sense of faith that it believes to be true and universal in its implications. But if there are no collectively sanctioned "religious" values to which the writer can confidently refer and to which he can give his assent, then he is bound to feel "lost," for his very means of communication seem to be cut off. If his creative work is to be more than ephemeral, he must know inwardly the purpose of his life, and of all life, past, present, and future. For why struggle desperately through the years to create a body of work that will endure the envious teeth of time, if life is but a hideous mistake, a tale told by an idiot, signifying nothing, a biological experiment devoid of all sense? Those writers who take their calling seriously must face the ultimate issues of existence; their spiritual dilemma is sharpened at present by the realization that they must face these issues alone. Here is the source of the sickness from which they suffer so cruelly, the dizzy affliction of metaphysical dread, the intolerable feeling of "nausea" or vertigo as they face the discovery that life is a useless passion.

These experiences are, of course, not peculiar to the writer, or to the writers of this age. In the life of every thinking man there comes a time when he must confront the ultimate meaning of his existence. His early years may have been spent in exploration, enjoy-

10

ment, and instinctive spontaneity, when the sounding cataract, the colors and forms of mountains and woods, the shows and splendors of the visible world, haunted him like a passion, and the living of life was all in all to him. But finally, in maturity, he reaches— most sensitive men do—a period of crisis when he hears the still, sad music of humanity, when he must take on himself "the burden of the mystery" and shoulder the heavy and weary weight of this unintelligible world. Now he perceives the threatening reality of death, and he knows of a certainty that he will die. What is he to do about this newly-won and frightening insight? He must find some satisfying answer to the existential questions his mind has begun to ask. But what he seeks is not a refuge from the storm of doubt and dread but the integrity of truth, the light that will pierce the universal darkness and reveal either the night of Nothingness or the face of God.

This is the "mystical" experience that many writers pass through, usually after they cross mid-channel; the seeker is driven to come to terms with himself the future, his existence on earth, the ultimate meaning of the universe. The first reaction of the writer caught in the grip of this crisis is one of dismay. As he looks about him and discovers nothing to which he can cling, he is overcome by a sense of deep anxiety. As he flounders in dark swamps of uncertainty, he feels no firm ground under his feet. Whether he knows it or not, he is undergoing what is in essence a "religious" experience, even when it does not culminate in the acceptance of God. Early in life, Pascal was obsessed by the misery of man without God. Small wonder he found intolerable the work of the skeptical Montaigne, who was indifferent to the drama of salvation. How could one face the prospect of annihilation, Pascal asked, without experiencing the shudder of fear and without the urge to repent? In the nineteenth century, Dostoevski declared that if he had to choose between Christ and the truth, he would prefer to stay with Christ. In the twentieth century, Karl Jaspers, in *Tragedy Is Not Enough,* makes the point that only by courageously facing the tragic situation can man hope to rise above it. Redemption is to be achieved through the stoical confrontation of ultimate failure; it is when man suffers shipwreck that he perceives the true nature of reality. The forces that man fights against are strange, not to be named, enigmatic. Everything, according to Jaspers, is questionable. Like Dostoevski, Kierkegaard, who plays an important role in the spiritual struggle for meaning on the part of the modern writer, cast off the bondage of logic and the tyranny of science. By means of the dialectic of "the leap," he attempted to transcend both the aesthetic and the ethical stages. Completely alone, cut off from his fellow-men, the individual realizes his own nothingness as the preliminary condition for embracing the truth of God. Only when man becomes aware of his own non-entity—an experience that is purely subjective and incommunicable—does he recover his real self and stand in the presence of God. This is the mystique which has been rediscovered by twentieth-century man, the leap from outwardness to inwardness, from rationalism to subjectivity, the revelation, that is ineffable, of the reality of the Absolute.

Tolstoy, too, in the middle of his life's journey, struggled furiously with the problem of God and immortality. Filled as he was with an abounding sense of life, he was haunted constantly by the thought of death and decay. This at last reached a point where he had to find a way out, some justification for the finality of death. In his *Confessions,* he describes how pointless life seemed and how moods of dread would overcome him. What was life for? What was its aim and end? The only truth he could embrace was that life was meaningless. He had come to the edge of a precipice, as it were, and ahead of him lay nothing but destruction. He could not stop or go back, nor could he avoid the devastating knowledge that real death meant complete annihilation. There was no reason for anything he did or for his whole life. Why had he not caught this shattering and universal truth before? Since death will come soon and nothing will remain but putrefaction, then why make any effort? Why go on living? The truth was inescapable, and the truth was summed up in death. Finally he found a solution, a "religion," in living for others, in loving them to the exclusion of self, to the point of total self-effacement; but the cruel tensions of his spiritual battle continued until the end.

Like Tolstoy, a number of contemporary writers suffer from a paralysis of the will, an inability to believe or create or even to function productively; they go on suffering until they have found some solution to the mystery of existence, some insight or provisional faith that will render their life and their work meaningful. Others, like Eugene O'Neill, become convinced that the destiny of meaninglessness is not to be avoided and that men must learn to live with the myth of nothingness. But how? That is the question which dominates their life and which constitutes the seminal principle of their art.

Many of the writers of today are unable to frame a satisfying answer to their "religious" questions. For they eliminate, to begin with, the traditional religious solutions. Heirs of the Age of Enlightenment, they cannot return to the cult of the supernatural, the mysterious reality of a God beyond human understanding. That road is closed to them. Yet the spiritual situation in which they are caught is not to be borne. Their worst predicament, apart from the torment of being thrust into a life that has been drained of ultimate meaning, is that they cannot determine their own identity. They do not seem to know, and cannot affirm, what is authentic in their own existence. The only thing that buoys them up is the biological will to live and the inexplicable urge to create, but neither is enough to satisfy their metaphysical hunger. Hence they are repeatedly brought to a halt; like Tolstoy, they stop what they are doing and begin to take stock of themselves. They ask themselves the age-old questions: "Where am I going? What is the meaning of death? Why was I born? Who am I? What is the purpose of human existence?"

For the religious believer, these questions pose no problem; God exists, God is real. The believer's commitment is total, not to be shaken by rational analysis. How can anyone doubt that God is the ground of Being, the reality behind all phenomenal realities? The believer knows God exists without any need for *adventitious* proof. But literature, of necessity, does not deal with ideas or doctrines or absolute certainties; it is not a mystical revelation, a transcendence of the relative and problematical and contingent. It portrays the arena of struggle, the scene of conflict, the battlefield of opposition between belief and doubt, affirmation and negation. It is concerned invariably with the individual and the concrete. Can the modern writer overcome his difficulties by arguing, like Keats, that the poet has no identity and can contemplate without distress the dark as well as the bright side of life? Can he cry out for a life of sensations rather than of thoughts? Is the man of letters, unlike the philosopher, sustained by what Keats calls "negative capability," the power of remaining fixed in uncertainties and mysteries, without irritably reaching out after reason and truth?

From the beginning of time, man has made the effort to impose some order on chaos, to understand and control the welter of forces into which he is plunged, to discover a meaningful and enduring pattern in the flux of phenomena. The search would not be so difficult or so painful if he were not surrounded by mysteries that baffle his understanding. Like primitive man, he finds himself threatened on all sides by a Nature that is supremely indifferent to his aspirations and his needs. A sensuous poet like Keats may be unaffected by the specters of metaphysical doubt, but the modern man cannot shut out the fear of the night, the terror of darkness. In addition, he is smitten with the terrible suspicion that all his absolutes are but ineffectual verbal incantations in the face of nothingness. It is precisely because he is infected with this dread of a meaningless universe that he labors so persistently to transcend the void and fill the darkness with light. In one sense, the literature of our time may be said to represent an engagement with the implacable forces that push mankind toward the abyss of nothingness, an attempt to transcend the demoralizing experience of being spiritually "lost," an effort to discover and affirm some kind of order in the universe, so that human aspiration and human existence will be justified.

The trouble is, the modern writer must take up anew the stupendous task of determining the meaning of life, the values men can live by, for the old schemes of salvation have been discarded as no longer true; a new dispensation is feverishly being sought. The contradictions remain. The lessons of the past cannot be ignored; the irony of the human predicament is a constant reminder that this spiritual quest may be entirely in vain. Other ages, faced with more or less the same challenge, framed answers which we now feel were woven on the loom of illusion. Rebellious in their outlook, the moderns refuse to walk in the footsteps of their forebears and repeat their mistakes. The metaphysical pilgrimage, like life itself, is a dangerous gamble; there is always the possibility that man may fail. Perhaps there are no answers for the ultimate questions he perversely continues to ask.

This, in brief, is the crisis at which modern civilization has arrived, a crisis which, according to some contemporary prophets, is not temporary but permanent, since all human life is problematical and precarious, essentially tragic in character. This sums up the frightening dilemma that modern man faces: he cannot go back to the divinely revealed certainties of the past, yet before him lies an abyss of nothingness and despair. This state of mind reflects the anguish of a fairly large group of intellectuals. The cancerous feeling of purposelessness gnaws at their vitals, and they seize upon recurrent symbols of alienation, catastrophe, and doom. In Merle Miller's 1948 novel *That Winter,* one character who is typical of the rootless postwar generation, a writer who has lost his ideals, his faith in everything in which he once believed—democratic capitalism, Soviet Russia as the fatherland of the proletariat, the war to end all wars, the crusade against fascism—declares that he can discover no purpose in life. The purpose, he says, is "purposelessness. That's the slogan of our age.... The purpose is purposelessness."

The writers of the past were at least borne up by a common conviction that man must rise above the flux of change and the pull of instinctual desire; the ultimate reality, they were convinced, did not consist of animal impulses and the preoccupations of the moment. Somehow they felt themselves to be in touch with a higher reality in whose existence they steadfastly believed. The modern writer, however, is convinced that he must strive to solve his problems within the dimensions of time. He must perforce seek his salvation in the realm of nature—or not at all. Carried along inexorably by the river of time, he struggles to find some substitute for the lost God, some secular order that can overcome chaos, some naturalistic principle that will justify life. Unfortunately, out of his prolonged struggle with the problem of human destiny has come the sobering realization that there are no short cuts, no scientific miracles that will bring him peace of mind, no technological magic that will establish the Kingdom of Heaven on earth. Every conclusion he arrives at is shot through with uncertainty; every utterance of faith is hedged round with doubt. The human situation remains inscrutably complex. It is man's craving for eternity that makes for tragic frustration, since he is caught fast in the trap of time.

In addition, modern man suffers from a sense of cosmic alienation. The discoveries of science—Kepler's laws, Darwin's theory of evolution, Freud's explorations of the unconscious—gradually made him realize that he is but an infinitesimal fraction of the energy that flows through the universe. Perhaps his quest for ultimate meaning was conditioned by anthropomorphic illusions; perhaps he continued to read his subjective needs into the fabric of the universe. He came to perceive that it is indefensible to interpret reality as an extension of himself and resolved henceforth to ask nothing of life or of the physical universe that they are powerless to give him. If he is but a biological creature, then, instead of spinning metaphysical cobwebs and straining after mystical absolutes, he would confine himself to the task of making life on earth more tolerable. Long before Sartrean Existentialism burst on the international scene, V. F. Calverton, in *The Passing of the Gods,* boldly declared: "Instead of pampering himself with the belief that the evolutionary emergence of man and the earth's coming to consciousness through the mind proves that there must be purpose in the universal design, he will reject all such assumptions as the futile inventions of anthropomorphic conceit."

Carrying this process of alienation much farther, the Sartrean Existentialists announce that failure is the fate of man and that every human project is doomed. Action is futile and aspiration absurd. Existentialism thus gives eloquent expression to the current metaphysics of despair. As Emmanuel Mounier points out, a civilization is ripe for the philosophy of Existentialism when it ceases to have confidence in the purpose for which it exists and loses its capacity for action. The Existentialist hero, introspective, irrepressibly subjective, tormented by doubt, is the representative par excellence of the "lost" intellectual. He is like the neurotic characters in Kafka's novels whose vicissitudes of spiritual suffering exemplify the destiny of man, a destiny without direction or meaning or purpose.

Having killed off God, the Existentialist finds himself alone in the universe, plunged in a solitude from which there is no possibility of escape. If God does not exist, then there are no absolute values and man must create his own meaning. He is now on his own. The world of existence is not informed with logical necessity. The problem is how to escape the horror of pure contingency, the absurdity of existence. One is born and lives and dies fortuitously, without reason. Man is superfluous on earth. It is the mark of the free man that he clings to this knowledge and, determined to question all categories, refuses, like Karl Jaspers, to commit himself to anything.

It is this rooted inability to give a direct, positive answer to the enigmatic questions that life hurls at man which has proved a source of distress to a number of writers. They cannot resign themselves to a philosophy of absurdity. Is not a literature dedicated to nihilistic principles a contradiction in terms? How can a writer undertake any serious creative project when he has no faith in it or in himself or in life? How can he create out of a mood of unrelieved despair? He has gotten rid of the old traditional faith, but can he find solace in the new scientific dispensation? In his autobiography Edwin Muir, formerly an embattled disciple of Nietzsche, describes how he suddenly came to believe in immortality and discovered that

at heart he was a Christian. That was how he freed himself from
the notion that religion was only a tissue of illusion, a mirage,
an opiate.

But those writers who cannot, because of their persistent skepticism, return to the fold of faith remain permanently exiled from
the state of grace. They know that their condition is not to be cured
by theological prescriptions. Faith is not something handed down
from on high. Each one makes "the wager" on his own account.
Does the dominance of doubt and despair in our culture help to
account in large part for the comparative sterility of contemporary
literature? Is it naturalism, the recognition of the animal nature
in man, that is at the bottom of the modern spiritual sickness? Or is
it the failure to go beyond naturalism to the creative affirmation
of life? For the naturalistic writer, as soon as he deals with values,
cannot help but trespass upon the metaphysical domain. Even a
scientific humanist like Julian Huxley imports metaphysical concepts into his writing. He believes that though man, having shed
his anthropomorphic illusion, stands alone, life can still be worth
living, and he speaks of such ideals as beauty and truth.

That is the heart of the matter. A number of religious prophets
inveigh furiously against literary naturalism on the ground that it
has degraded the character of man, but to what degree are such fulminations justified? Are the "truths" of science that many contemporary writers have assimilated to be cast aside simply because they
are difficult to live with or injurious to human pride? If man stands
alone in a universe that is indifferent to his spiritual needs, is the
writer incapacitated from affirming those human values which make
life worth living? If the meaning of life is to be found in life
itself, can the naturalistic writer give birth to a literature that will
highlight the grandeur and misery of man? What counts in the end
is the depth and intensity of the vision the writer beholds, the com-
prehensiveness and complexity of his interpretation of the world
of experience.

But try as hard as he will, the modern writer cannot muster
the energy to create, as Shakespeare did, characters who are capable

of dramatically embodying the greatness of the human spirit. Even if he possessed the creative energy, he lacks the faith which this energy could inform and render meaningful. Perhaps the two, energy and faith, are one and inseparable. If today's writer has no underlying faith in his art, how can he carry on? It is this lack of a viable faith which is his undoing and which intensifies his feeling that he is "lost." He cannot, by simply taking thought, hope to remedy his condition. That is the measure of his spiritual dereliction. He is aware of the vital values that supported the mind of the past, the noble ideals his predecessors cherished so steadfastly, the moral discipline to which they willingly submitted, the eternal verities (as they thought) which they so inspiringly proclaimed. Steeped in skepticism, he is unable to take himself or his creative mission seriously.

Suffering from the infection of doubt, he is no sooner attracted to a belief than he begins to suspect its validity. For example, in the symposium *Religion and the Intellectuals* James Agee voices his hope that religion may serve as a last line of defense to preserve the precious virtues of individualism against the steady advance of totalitarian tyranny, but in matters of religion he cannot take the plunge blindly. He is still torn "between belief in God, non-belief, and a kind of neutrality." But the writer who remains irresolute in this no man's land of noncommitment cannot function fruitfully. He cannot honestly say "I believe in God," but he is reluctant to abandon the idea of God, an idea which, is after all, a potent and enchanting myth. Since it can neither be proved nor disproved, why not entertain it as a vital fiction? The concept of immortality is intellectually absurd, yet surely there are ways of interpreting it——Nietzsche's faith in eternal recurrence, the biological continuity of the germ-plasm—which make it seem eminently respectable. Man is derived from lower forms of life in an evolutionary process, but he is also spirit incarnate, a metaphysical rebel, a restless pursuer of the dream of divinity. Matter alone exists, but how can one omit the element of aspiration, the influence of ideals, the spiritual component in man? The writer today would like, if it were possible, to have it both ways. These are the games of myth-making he indulges in, but he cannot get himself to choose between conflicting perspectives.

Victim of the damage inflicted by *folie du doute,* the modern writer thus cannot take himself, and consequently his life or his work, seriously. He would fain work out a *Weltanschauung* which will lend a sense of meaning and purpose to his life, so that he will be able to overcome this insidious feeling that all his activities are aimless. Even when he strives to conquer this debilitating metaphysical malaise, he cannot compose with the *élan* of a Shakespeare, who believed that neither marbles nor the gilded monuments of princes would outlive his powerful rhyme. For the modern writer continues to suffer from the suspicion that literature is all a form of make-believe. In his posthumously published autobiography, Leo Stein describes how, severely addicted to the mania of self-analysis, he could not take himself seriously. He resolved to escape from a world of self-induced illusion, yet he could not entirely quell the suspicion that others did not exist or, even worse, that he did not exist while others manifestly did. These are precisely the symptoms of the disease of alienation, the sense of being "lost," from which a number of other intellectuals in our time suffer.

The acids of skepticism have worn away the body of faith, and the writers are today left with nothing but a sense of irreparable loss. What is to be done? Unsupported by any genuine belief in the future of mankind, some contemplate the possibility of suicide. In facing the possibility of dying at their own hands, they are rebelling against what they consider an intolerable situation. If they decide finally to live on, it is because of their need, irrational but nevertheless irresistible, to affirm life at all costs, to rebel against a condition of life that is not to be endured. Whereas in the past men fought against poverty and hunger, injustice and oppression, today they rebel against life itself. Thus modern literature, even as it portrays the despair of a "lost" generation, has become vitally concerned with the metaphysical and moral problems of human existence.

The Victorian men of letters, for their part, worked in earnest, dreaming nobly and building solid foundations under their dreams, taking it for granted that life had meaning and that the meaning as well as the race would endure. But a drastic change came over the literary landscape with the dawn of the twentieth century. As D. H. Lawrence discovered, the modern writer is driven by the absolute need for formulating some satisfactory attitude toward himself and the universe. Lawrence knew that though literature is the product of pure passionate experience, it cannot be divorced from some justifying metaphysic—even if this is not expressly stated, so long as it pervades the writing. This vision of life is implicit in all art. Since the metaphysical foundations of modern life have fallen apart, Lawrence hoped that a new redemptive vision would be born. Each one, he insisted, must come to terms with himself and decide what goals he wishes to strive for, what he finally believes in, and belief must fulfil itself in both life and art. That is what makes Lawrence, as Father William Tiverton demonstrates in *D. H. Lawrence and Human Existence,* a "religious" writer; but his was a voice crying in the wilderness.

What we are witnessing today is a progressive deterioration of religious faith. What modern literature reveals is largely what sensitive men are everywhere thinking and feeling. In the past, the human personality could adjust itself to the various blows delivered by new scientific discoveries about the physical world and the nature of man. Renaissance man was not crushed by his vision of a heliocentric universe, since it afforded him an enlarged opportunity to control the forces of nature. The doctrine of evolution, though it administered a severe shock to human egotism by picturing man as not a divinely created species, did not result in moral confusion or despair. In most cases, the nineteenth-century writer could still retain his faith in God and his belief in the dignity of man, his purpose on earth, the transcendent significance of his ethical strivings. It is the introduction of technological warfare on a global scale, with the grim prospect of wiping out the whole of civilization, that has made a hideous mockery of humanistic ideals. To be consistent today, Albert Camus argues, one must be a nihilist. But why should literary nihilists take the trouble to write and publish their work? Why this last infirmity of noble minds? Why do so many writers today dwell in a spiritual vacuum, without a sense of order or purpose? Why are they so hopelessly lost?

III

THE LOST GENERATION
OF LITERATURE

THE YOUNGER GENERATION of
writers in our time are convinced, as we have seen, that they live
in a present which has no future. Aldous Huxley, after his conversion to a syncretic type of mysticism, insists that time must have a
stop. For the younger writers of our day time has come to a dead
end. Confronting the incomprehensible and absolute injustice of
death, deprived of God and the consolations of immortality, they
are not weighed down by the burden of tomorrow and tomorrow
and tomorrow. Much of their strident pessimism finds expression
in the writing of the forties and fifties. Everywhere in philosophy as
well as in belles-lettres there is the same oppressive refrain of futility, the same swan song of doom. The disturbing feature of the contemporary cultural crisis is that many of the intellectuals, dragged
into the destructive element, are beginning to feel there is no way
out. Though they refuse to give up the creative quest, the best
they can produce is a cry of anguish, a confession of defeat, a prolonged howl of disgust.

It is consoling to view the major clashes and crises of our age
in the long perspective of history, for then we are able to perceive
that our forefathers endured conflicts as crucial for the future of
humanity as any we face today. The dissolution of the Roman
Empire, the fanatical resistance of the Jews in Jerusalem before

their Temple was destroyed and they were dispersed over the face
of the earth, the struggle for survival of the city-states in ancient
Greece, the brutal persecution of the Christian martyrs, the bloody
Civil War in the United States—at the time these events took place
people were filled with dire forebodings, disaster loomed in the distance; and there have been many periods in history when prophets
felt the end of the world was nigh.

But historical parallels of this kind are impressive precisely
because they tend to leave out of account the depth and persistence
of the feelings that men have, their subjective, existential interpretation of the character of their age. It is for this reason that the
parallel with the past, however striking in some respects, breaks
down. In past epochs there was still some degree of faith in the
future of civilization and the continuity of culture. No matter who
won the war, the race would carry on its mission. Today that dimension of faith has been shattered. There is the haunting fear, despite
all propaganda to the contrary, that if war should break out tomorrow, civilization might be utterly wiped out. Those who have read
Hiroshima, or scientific accounts of the damage that the atomic
and hydrogen bomb and fallout can inflict, know that mankind
has gone berserk with the mania of destructiveness. How can
reason prevail? International co-operation, for all the conferences
staged and resolutions drawn up by the United Nations, is a myth.
The literati, traumatically shaken by these developments, ask themselves: Why be concerned right now with the communication that
art strives to achieve? Why create at all? That is the question Albert
Camus seeks to answer in *The Myth of Sisyphus.*

Our initial assumption is that literature, like life, cannot be sustained at its highest potential, if at all, without implicit faith that
the race will not only survive but continue to flourish. The ideal of
progress, even though it has been vigorously attacked of late as a
relic of romantic utopian thinking, seems to be a precondition of
striving, creating, living. What makes life in the present decades
nightmarishly difficult is precisely this perception that the sense of
historical as well as phylic unity has been annulled. For many people,

the fear of death, born of the myth of nothingness, has become an intensely real, demoralizing experience. It is as if this age—so poignant is the reaction—were the first to discover the metaphysics, nay the actuality, of death. Death is no longer an abstraction, a remote eventuality, but imminent and frighteningly personal—and final! An age of increasingly destructive wars has served to deepen the contemporary awareness of death until it has become a veritable obsession. Overwhelmed by a feeling of his own insignificance in a world ruled by malign atomic energy, the individual concludes that life is without purpose or pattern, an ephemeral and idiotic episode. The living presentness of the past is canceled by the knowledge that a rain of atomic bombs may blow our vaunted civilization to smithereens. It is this pervasive mood of futility which explains the rapid growth of the myth of nothingness and the paradoxical emergence of a literature of death which has nothing in common with the products of the eighteenth-century school of graveyard poets.

Everywhere we turn we are assailed by evidence of this metaphysical neurasthenia and alienation, this compulsive thanatophobia. André Malraux, who has abandoned his former devotion to the dogmatic absolute expounded by communism, points out, in *The Twilight of the Absolute,* that our civilization is the first to be blind to the transcendent principle of communion which binds each man to his fellow-men. Hence the conception of Man has been radically altered. God is dead, and now there is the crushing suspicion that Man, too, is dying or dead. Few writers of our century have been so tensely aware of the disintegrative flow of time and especially of all the forces that drive home the knowledge of our nothingness. What man has lost is the secret, once possessed by the great arts of the past, which mediated between man and the infinite and enabled him to feel that he was vastly more than an accidental by-product of mechanical forces in blind interaction. The trouble with contemporary literature is that it is incapable of spontaneous, affirmative expression. The best the writers can do is to ask questions, and they continue to ask questions because they cannot find an answer and because they have lost confidence in the future. Art dies not because its potentialities are used up but because faith begins to wane. Though man has conquered the world of things, the nature of man himself is called in question; but as Malraux asks, can a culture continue to exist that is based solely on interrogation?

The long, melancholy, withdrawing roar of the sea of faith has been heard for the past hundred years, and even before Darwin published *The Origin of Species;* and the twentieth century witnessed manifestations of nihilism before the Existentialist movement made its official European debut. Dada, for example, represented an unconditional revolt against the past, against civilization, morality, conventions, and taboos of any kind. Dada—which, literally, signified nothing—could not be defined because it had no plan, no program, no aesthetic philosophy. A systematized expression of the essential idiocy of the world, it sought to make a creative virtue of the absence of meaning. Dada, despite its large element of wilful mystification and propagandistic expediency, was actually "meaningful" in its very apotheosis of the meaningless, as Marcel Raymond indicates in his brilliantly written *From Baudelaire to Surrealism.* Vastly more than a species of exhibitionism or sensationalism, it marked a violent repudiation of the old dead world and its traditional moral values. World War I led inevitably to the realization that civilizations, like individuals, could perish and leave not a rack behind. Most significant of all, in the light of the problems writers face today, was Dada's "affirmation" of the meaningless. Nothing mattered, all human effort was futile, there was no point to existence. Though the contemporary writer perceives that a consistent adherence to this "philosophy" of the meaningless would result in the death of literature (or in a literature dedicated to the dialectics of death?), some intellectuals have been infected by the "metaphysics" of Dada, its revolutionary nihilism.

What is responsible for this mad dance of death, this obsession with absolute negation? Some seriously contend that science, by undermining the foundations of religion, destroyed the very possibilities of faith. Once the belief in God was scrapped, human values were inevitably subjected to a process of dissociation and revealed as fictions, perhaps consoling and beautiful but not borne out by the nature of empirical reality. Biology discloses that man is a part of nature; psychology reveals that man is certainly not a special creation. Increased insight into the unconscious mechanism of the mind, its irrational and instinctual forces, indicates that man is not master in his own house or architect of his destiny. Hence the conception of man as a pre-eminently rational creature, the lord of all creation, is punctured, and twentieth-century man, Freudianized, sees himself as a bundle of conditioned reflexes, galvanized by emotional desire, at the mercy of instinctual compulsions and binding unconscious energy. He is burdened with the stupendous task of salvaging values in a world that appears completely indifferent to his salvation or survival. That is why modern man is so skeptical, so nihilistic in outlook.

The contemporary sense of nothingness paralyzes the capacity for action as well as utterance. Hamletism lives again, but endowed this time with a new, neurotic twist. It is not merely the inability to resort to decisive action that plagues the young intellectuals and is at the root of their "neurosis"; essentially it is the realization that all action, whatever its motive, is equally tainted and equally useless. Hence, by a desperate paradox that is not at all hard to resolve, they defy death; they court danger; they make a ritualistic cult of bullfighting and of hunting big game in Africa; they commit "gratuitous" crimes; they experiment with suicide. It is all done in order to convince themselves that there are no moral absolutes, no categorical imperatives.

But no matter what these young intellectuals did, they could not drive out the sense of being lost, the belief that man is an inexplicable joke. Where in fiction can one meet more pathetically disoriented, neurotically alienated, and hopelessly damned characters than in the novels of Céline, Henry Miller, Sartre, Paul Bowles, Camus? Suffering makes them come alive; their suffering at least is real, but it only renders more full of anguish their fruit-

less quest for a meaning that will impose order on the contemporary
chaos and redeem them from the nightmare of nothingness. For
there are no traces of justification in their suffering and no values
to which they can honestly devote themselves. Here is the ironic
apotheosis of the romantic hero—the man without faith, without a
sense of purpose, lost, and doomed.

Inheriting the nihilistic outlook, the novelists of the forties
and fifties are, like their heroes, pathetically lost, searching for
values in which, alas, they do not believe and which they are
convinced do not exist. Isolated from life and devoid of faith,
living in a civilization about to fall apart, the writer is no longer
satisfied with the religion of art. In *After the Lost Generation* John
W. Aldridge comes to the disconsolate conclusion that the writers
of our time can assert the need for belief "even though it is upon
a background in which belief is impossible and in which the symbols are lacking for a genuine affirmation in dramatic terms."
Which is like offering medicine to a stricken patient with the
assurance that he is beyond help.

What is significant in Aldridge's analysis of the cultural situation is that the young writers still cling to the conviction that life
is meaningless. The generation that came of age during World
War II felt they had lost their individual identity; alone in an
indifferent and therefore hostile universe, with no one to give
them hope for ultimate salvation, they were bowed down by an
oppressive sense of cosmic nothingness. It is these husks of spiritual
nothingness that the modern writer feeds on. In his diagnosis
Aldridge declares:

The nothingness in which all things are unimportant has no value. It is,
in fact, a condition in which values have never existed. It is impossible,
therefore, for a writer to give it dramatic significance, since to be dramatic a thing must possess a value by which we recognize and accept
it as worth while. The best a writer can do if he finds himself dedicated
to spiritual nothingness—and he will be if he is at all sensitive to the
conditions of our time—is to seek in raw violence and direct sensation
that drama of shock which will always have a value to all men in all
times.

What is the source of this spiritual nothingness from which the young writers of today are suffering so dreadfully, the sense of loss and alienation, of being left without resources to cope with the fact of disaster? Shipwrecked and disillusioned, without a sense of dedication to a cause or even an artistic ideal, they lack sufficient spiritual vitality to keep themselves creatively alive in the fullest sense. Thus far the attempt, in spite of everything, to create what Van Wyck Brooks calls a vital, affirmative literature has failed dismally. The nihilistic dissociation of faith has brought about not only a loss of faith in man but a corresponding loss of faith in the creative life. Now that the fear of death is obsessive and the myth of nothingness has supplanted the consciousness of God, the writer wonders what standards he shall abide by in a relativized universe. What commitments, if any, shall he make during his precariously brief pilgrimage on earth, and what responsibilities does he bear toward his fellow-men?

Against such a background of ideological futility, with what significance can the work of the writer be invested? He is no longer the prophetic spokesman of his people, the conscience of his race. Face to face with the prospect of a civilization that may go up in atomic smoke and flame, he ceases to believe that his creative work has any effect in shaping the minds of men. Furthermore, there is no court of last resort, no posterity, to whom he can appeal, confident that it will vindicate his claim and grant him the vicarious immortality of fame for which he secretly longs. Together with the rest of doomed mankind he feels he is staggering down a dark road toward the end of night.

The great fear that oppresses the heart of the modern writer is, as we have said, the fear that a huge joke has been perpetrated upon mankind; the visible universe offers no support for the man-made beliefs and values that are part of the cultural tradition. It was in one of his agonizing moments of doubt that Tennyson cried out that the stars in their courses blindly run, but with us this knowledge forms our habitual frame of reference. The most unsettling influence on the modern mind is this very suspicion that our metaphysical and religious systems are but empty fictions. Even those have who arrived at bleakly negative conclusions and, like the atheistic Existentialists, play variations on the theme of nothingness, are stricken by the skeptical fear that these conclusions, too, are a bit of histrionic mummery and brave attitudinizing in the face of the infinite nothingness. Unable to bear his loneliness, the uselessness of his passion, in the cosmic float, man resorts to magnificent phrases, invents philosophies and theologies, ordeals and martyrdoms, and uses them ingeniously as perspectives through which to view the world reassuringly and to justify his life. But the elaborate strategy of this struggle, the underlying meaning of this debate with death, illustrates how, perhaps for the first time with such intensity and completeness, man has come to realize that he is an alien on earth, that the universe is indifferent to his existence. It is this growing conviction that man has no particular business on earth which the writer finds so deflating, morally and creatively. The old absolutes have crumbled under the attrition of the skeptical modern temper induced by the scientific outlook. Despite the return of some influential writers to the church, religion and the categorical imperative can no longer command instinctive belief.

There are no absolutes to take their place—that is the unfortunate aspect of the contemporary cultural situation. The conclusion that all mental constructions—philosophy, art, mythology, religion, and even science—are as-if fictions, symbolic ways of dealing with an intolerable situation, is one which but poorly satisfies the needs of the creative situation. If the suspicion that aspirations and ideals are but man-made illusions serves to weaken the life-instinct, it does equal harm in damaging the creative instinct. Since the writer has no faith in man or in the future, since he cannot get himself to believe that culture will somehow survive miraculously when the cataclysmic plague of atomic bombs is unloosed upon the world, he sees no cogent reason why he should continue with his work. If he nevertheless persists in it, he does so principally because he cannot help himself; and the absence of all values, the inner feeling that mankind is lost and doomed, infects everything that he produces, if it does not in the end reduce him to impotent silence.

It is clear that modern man has lost his goal, the purpose of his life, the faith that once fueled his vitality and justified his creative enterprise. Whereas in the nineteenth century the abandonment of supernaturalism represented a positive gain, an advance in knowledge and insight, the contemporary picture is one of confusion, uncertainty, and demoralization. Can modern man face the world without illusion and yet affirm the faith that he is going to live by? What tragic insights will the new literature of crisis produce?

IV

THE MYTH OF NOTHINGNESS

MANY CONTEMPORARY WRITERS, as we have noted, are suffering from what Jung calls "the general neurosis of our age": namely, the feeling that not only their own life but all life today is senseless and aimless. Nietzsche's life illustrates most poignantly the tragic consequences that befall the artist who embraces the nihilistic outlook. Nietzsche went mad. Suicide or madness: these are the only avenues of freedom open to those who, seeking to transcend their human limitations, cut themselves off from the rest of humanity. Confined in a madhouse, Nietzsche sounds this maniacal cry of alienation from the depths: "God is dead, Christ is a myth, and man stands alone." Because he chose to live alone without God or man, he was thrown back upon himself and confronted with the dreadful specter of nothingness. He could find no refuge from the storm of metaphysical despair that was sweeping across the West, but he had himself helped to generate the storm. His autobiography, *My Sister and I,* describes how this chained Zarathustra, shattered in body and mind, remains immured in an insane asylum while lunatics howl around him, and faces in his loneliness the God of Nothingness.

This was the cross on which he hung in agony. He beheld the awful abyss that yawns beneath man. If he rejected the myth of humanitarianism, the illusion of progress, the cult of redemption, what could he cling to in the flux of phenomena? Furiously he sought to rise above the horror of contemplating, and living in, a meaningless universe; but after casting aside as spurious all that men cherished and believed in, he was left with nothing to which he could give his allegiance. The madhouse was the only place of refuge from a civilization that had gone bankrupt. That is why Nietzsche, long before the advent of concentration camps, crematoria, atomic weapons, and global wars, prophetically declared: "If God were actually alive He would not allow the twentieth century to happen."

But the twentieth century did happen. It is here, and the writer, caught squarely in the midst of it, must make up his mind what to do with his life, what values to affirm, what faith to live by. What makes his position at present not only precarious but desperate is the militant skepticism which not only questions but categorically rejects all things. The temper of our time, on the literary front, is one of neurotic negation. Heidegger, like Nietzsche, has become the spokesman for many of our latter-day intellectuals. Obsessed with this vision of Nothing, they have not led a more "authentic" existence or become more productive. Burdened with this sense of aloneness, without roots or responsibilities, wedded to no viable principle of faith, how can they continue to be creative? Like Nietzsche, they move in a cosmic phantasmagoria, spooks and shadows in an unreal universe. Since they can accept neither God nor Devil, they cannot believe in life and must therefore preoccupy themselves with the horrifying phantoms of futility conjured up out of the void.

Hawthorne, in the nineteenth century, at least knew what the Unpardonable Sin was; it consisted in a want of love and reverence of the human soul, the separation of the probing intellect from the heart. Ethan Brand, who had discovered the Unpardonable Sin in his own heart, realized that this was the one crime for which Heaven could grant no mercy. What was this monstrous sin? "The sin of an intellect that triumphed over the sense of brotherhood with man and reverence for God, and sacrificed everything to its own mighty claims! The only sin that deserves a recompense of immortal agony."

Some modern writers have caught a taste of this spiritual agony. They have found that it is impossible for them to work creatively in a climate of metaphysical dread and denial. The fearful suspicion that at the heart of the universe there is nothing but illusion, that life is but a thing of sound and fury, signifying nothing, that man projects his own grandiose meanings and values onto nature—all this has tormented many thinkers of the past, but our forebears courageously faced the powers of darkness and formulated their interpretation of the tragic sense of life. Instead of surrendering to despair, they passionately affirmed the things they believed in. For ages, the generations of men labored earnestly to discover the buried secrets of nature and to advance the cause of truth. Gradually they succeeded in establishing a measure of control over nature and thus vastly enlarging man's scope of freedom. Were all these leaders of mankind misguided idealists, the blind leading the blind? Are we to accept the conclusion that the adventure of man on earth is but a miserable farce, a comedy of illusions, an obscene failure?

It is clear that the artist today has lost faith not only in his creative mission but also in himself and in humanity. It is no accident that the collapse of faith in art came soon after the twilight of the gods, the disintegration of the religious synthesis. How can the poet take his calling with high seriousness if he has no strong belief in the continuity of mankind? Whatever beliefs he does have are darkened by the shadow of imminent catastrophe. Yeats accurately described this state of affairs in "The Second Coming":

> Mere anarchy is loosed upon the world,
> The blood-dimmed tide is loosed, and everywhere
> The ceremony of innocence is drowned;
> The best lack all conviction, while the worst
> Are full of passionate intensity.

Anarchy has been loosed upon the world precisely because the best, the artists and creative prophets of our age, lack all conviction. Convinced that the end of the world is nigh, they do not, like Yeats, believe that the Second Coming is at hand. They see no sign of redemption on the horizon of history.

The spiritual sickness of the intellectuals today springs from their obsession with the cult of Nothing. Since God is dead, death is feared today as it never was in the past. The enormous black shadow that death casts has reduced existence to absurdity. But how can the creative spirit raise the sense of absurdity to the plane of the tragic? How can the writer utter the living word when he begins with the assumption that death will soon annihilate all meaning? He believes in nothing and hopes for nothing. He has gone —or so he likes to think—beyond the uttermost limits of tragedy. If he refrains from suicide, it is not because he knows of any good reasons for continuing to live but because he can discover no good reasons for taking his own life. That is why he lives on, but without illusions. At thirty-one, the hero of Sartre's novel, *Nausea,* declares: "I am free: there is absolutely no more reason for living, all the ones I have tried have given way and I can't imagine any more of them."

Man is saddled with a freedom that is dreadful because it rests on pure contingency. Reduced to a spectral shadow, man suffers from morbid seizures of doubt as to his own identity. Everything that happens is fortuitous and absurd. Whether man lives or dies—what difference does it all make? Yet how can man, and particularly the writer, live on in a world characterized by absurdity? That is the metaphysical hell in which the Existentialists must writhe. This is the spiritual crisis which culminates in despair. How shall the writer reconcile the world of consciousness with the alien, incommensurable world of things? How is man to *make* his own life if he is caught in this impasse of nothingness?

Existentialism gives heightened expression to a nihilism that is eating at the vitals of humanity. Existentialist man feels lost and alone in a universe that means nothing to him. All he is sure of is that death waits for him, but even death, the final ignominy, is meaningless. If there is no supernatural plan or celestial power, then what goals shall man choose? Infected by this ideological atmosphere, the modern writer has ceased to act or work with any measure of conviction. The world of man, like the world of nature, has lost its meaning for him. He cannot believe in himself because he cannot believe in the reality of mankind. Having lost his faith in humanity, he has no faith in himself.

Yet human beings cannot endure without some life-affirming faith. Not a "myth" served up specially for their consolation, not an as-if fiction whose purpose it is to soothe their restlessness and give them an outlet for their energy. Not that, but a vital faith in life. If the intellectuals of our time continue to embrace the cult of death and preach "the religion of nothingness," then the people will ignore them and turn to other forms of worship. The mass movements of our age, whether communism or fascism, are in a sense a feverish reaction against the sterile negation of leaders who proclaim that life is a journey to the end of night, a senseless encounter with Nothing. These mass movements, despite their intolerance and spirit of hatred, attract the true believer, whom Eric Hoffer defines as "the man of fanatical faith who is ready to sacrifice his life for a holy cause..." The doctrine of cosmic futility and despair is as self-defeating as the gospel held by "the true believer."

The crucial problem for many contemporary writers, who cannot identify the meaning of life with the full living of it, is how to discover a cure for what Jung diagnosed as the general neurosis of our age. How are they to neutralize the acids of despair generated by the belief that existence is purposeless? The aware-ness of the meaninglessness of the human situation in a meaningless universe drives them to despair, but it is out of this despair that they must wrest the courage to be creatively themselves. But how, if a writer recognizes the futility of life, is creativity possible? The answer is given with profound, if paradoxical, insight by Paul Tillich in *The Courage to Be:* "The act of accepting meaninglessness is in itself a meaningful act." Out of the ultimate of despair a constructive faith can emerge: the knowledge that man lives, not in nothingness, but in a meaningful universe, and that his life must therefore be rooted in a context of meanings, aesthetic, religious, and philosophical. The spiritual cannot be divorced from the aesthetic realm. If the writer is to give himself constructively to his work, he must, first of all, believe in its importance to the world of man. Literature must have a core of meaning that derives, in the last analysis, from the meaning that life has for the writer and the people for whom he is, presumably, the spokesman. His is not a solitary quest or a lonely pilgrimage. Nor does his sickness represent an isolated case. It reflects, in part, the malaise of a whole culture. The age is stricken with this plague of metaphysical despair. The trouble with the modern writer is that he cannot even affirm his negations. The infinite spaces frighten him to the point of hysterical inarticulateness. He cannot come to terms with himself and he cannot accept his own intellectual formulations. Though he suffers, he cannot believe in the reality of his suffering. He is no Ethan Brand.

Of only one thing does he seem to be certain: mankind has come to the end of the road. If there is neither God nor Devil, neither Heaven nor Hell, then there is nothing to live for and nothing, really, to write about. What incentive can he possibly have for going ahead with the creative enterprise? What point is there in composing plays and novels and poetry and philosophical tracts?

Moreover, try as hard as he will, he cannot break out of the prison of his isolation. Instinctively he realizes that so long as he remains in this spiritual state, he is doomed as a writer. No magic ritual of fertility will revive the parched earth of the spirit or bring the fructifying rain. So long as he is cut off from the magnetic chain of humanity, he will continue to be sterile. If he is to be saved, he must, like all the accursed heroes of myth, start out on a mental voyage which will lead him across lonely and stormy seas of suffering. Only then will he come to understand that he is organically bound to the fate of humanity.

The way out of his private inferno lies, not in schizophrenic flight, but in the brave acceptance of the tragic sense of life. The threat of world annihilation posed by the atomic bomb is not a new evil but a manifestation of the same evil that has dogged the race of man through the long ages of evolution as he struggled to rise out of the protozoan slime. The mass homicidal fury of our age is but another personification of the Devil that dwells destructively in each human breast, the Devil who must be fought and conquered if the God in man is to triumph. Once the writer ceases to pursue the vain myth of happiness, once he arrives at a more realistic conception of the nature of man, he has already been delivered from the dungeon of nothingness in which at present he is trapped.

In rejecting spiritual transcendence, the writer has plunged disastrously into the void. Since then his career has been either a fight against nihilism or a crushed withdrawal into what he considers a creative type of nihilism. Hence his resort to pseudo-mythical thinking and his desperate attempt to find justification through a cult of nothingness. But his dialectical process of compensation, his feverish quest of myth, are themselves based on illusion. As Jacques Maritain shrewdly points out in *Creative Intuition in Art and Poetry*: "The effort of a poet to create new metaphysical myths of his own invention, for the sake of his work as a poet, is self-contradictory, since, having invented them, he cannot believe in them." The will to believe is not enough to inspire and sustain the poet. If a new metaphysical myth is to infuse his work, he must give it complete faith, and how can he *believe* in the Myth of Nothingness? The faith must come first; then the poet creates and affirms. It is not the other way round. The poet needs the myth in order to work out his own destiny, not in order to produce satisfactory poetry. It is not for the sake of his art that he strives to order and unify his vision of the universe. At bottom, the modern search for new myths springs from a frantic desire to escape from the horror of the void, to throw off the neurotic burden of futility and absurdity, and to conquer the fear of death. The creative mind prefers the truth to illusion, but is the truth compounded of nothingness and death?

V

THE LITERATURE OF DEATH

THE ATOMIC ARMAGEDDON looms now as more than a biblical figure of speech, the symbolic rhetoric of Doomsday. It may actually happen—soon and without warning. Is it any wonder that in our time writers, convulsed with fear of the great god Thanatos, have joined in the collective *danse macabre?*

Never before in the history of the race have the intellectuals been so affrighted by the specter of non-being. What they behold is no longer an abstract, metaphysical vision of the inevitability of death. They go beyond that. They are terrified by the vision of nothingness; the kingdom of death reduces all their aspirations and activities to meaninglessness. If death threatens, then every ideal they cherish is stripped of content, and every affirmation they make is steeped in absurdity. Because death stands menacingly in the background, overshadowing every lived moment of time, fate seems not only inexplicable but utterly absurd. And if that is so, then how can man affirm his being and how can the artist seriously devote himself to his art?

What has caused this collective anxiety neurosis? For the truth is that men die only when they are ready to die. Man unconsciously consents to his own death. Those who have something meaningful and worth while to live for do not speculate endlessly about death and they do not die. They live on for the simple reason

that they have a constructive purpose which keeps them alive.
For the "will to live" is more—much more—than a matter of
simply staying alive and keeping off the inroads of death. It is
a forward-looking, dynamic, essentially creative process. Man is
not only profoundly concerned to preserve his identity and to
perpetuate the species; he is also bent on fulfilling his nature, on
achieving those goals which will help to make his life more meaningful. In short, the biological will to live, however deeply rooted
in the organism, must be sustained by moral and emotional energy
that makes the adventure of living immensely rewarding. What has
happened to modern man which has brought about this suicidal
impairment of his will to live?

Whenever man speculates about the nature of death, he is in
reality concerned with life. The contemporary attempt to formulate a philosophy of death, to work in terms of a "scientifically"
postulated "death instinct," is a revealing cultural symptom of
our age. But in whatever he thinks and says, in his metaphysical
and scientific preoccupations as well as in his literature, man confronts his life. Hence it follows logically that a generation obsessed
with the thought of death must be afraid of life. It must have suffered
what Dewey calls "a failure of nerve." The manner in which its
writers interpret the experience of death is closely connected with
their ontological anguish, their fixation on the fatality of time.

For the conception of Time as grim, irreversible, a sinister
figure of decrepitude and death, was not represented in ancient art.
On the contrary, it is represented as the divine principle of inexhaustible creativeness: a winged figure, without the traditional hourglass,
the scythe or sickle. As Erwin Panofsky points out in *Studies in
Iconology,* the ancient images of Time are symbols of power and
fertility, not symbols of decay and doom. In the Middle Ages, Time
is seen as a devouring force, the inexorable agent of King Death.
The graveyard school of poets in the eighteenth century fixed
their gaze with morbid fascination on the chemistry of the grave,
but they did not negate life. In the case of the Christian poets, the
promise of redemption is ever present, and it is the horizon of

eternity that makes this brief earthly pilgrimage and the prospect of dissolution bearable. Even in the Middle Ages, the Dance of Death was an artistic representation of the dual theme of man's reluctance to leave this earth and the grim inevitability of the call. Though Death included men of high or low degree within its impartial sweep, all of them hung back fearfully from the final summons. It was this clinging to life that made the art of the Middle Ages, despite its *memento mori* strain, so human and so moving. Finite and imperfect creatures, men still loved their habitation of flesh and the things of this world.

At present a small group of literary mystics are preoccupied with a dimension of time—eternity—that has no corresponding correlate in nature or in historic time. Whereas memory can lift a moment of experience out of its place in the order of the past and make it live vividly in the present, eternity takes us entirely out of the limits of time. It is timelessness, which has no relation to physical time. The nature of eternity that such literary mystics as T. S. Eliot, Aldous Huxley, and Charles Williams contemplate is an eternity not contingent upon the limits of memory. It shadows forth the ultimate truth of things, a timeless order of Reality. Eternity thus becomes a metaphysical essence, not to be disproved because it transcends the boundaries of the empirical. The mystical experience in its apprehension of God and eternity cannot be tested; it cannot even be communicated, for language belongs to the realm of the finite, the world of nature. Nature is a veil of illusion, a forest of deceptive symbols. Mysticism consequently involves, as Hans Meyerhoff makes clear in *Time in Literature*, "a denial of time both in experience and in nature."

Today it is not so much the fear of death itself which has mounted alarmingly; what is the cause of intense anguish is the loss of faith in life, the fact of the alienation of man from the universe, from the rest of mankind, and from himself. In desolation of spirit, modern man cries out: "We die and this renders life altogether absurd," when what he means is this: "Life appears to be inherently meaningless and futile and it is therefore absurd to die."

In Western culture, death is regarded as the worst of evils, the supreme calamity, the ultimate of misfortune, the fatality that reduces all other events to utter insignificance. Even though death is actually a part of the total life experience, a part of reality, most people today are terribly afraid of dying. The emergence of atheism has induced a state of metaphysical vertigo; many writers in our time suffer from the spiritual oppression caused by the triumph of nihilism. The Existentialists are motivated by a despair that springs from their perception of the nothingness that surrounds them. Death is their single-minded, delirious theme.

The question of time is, of course, intimately related to the modern approach to the ultimate of death. A psychology of death depends on a psychology of time, for death and time are interdependent in subjective experience. As K. R. Eissler says in *The Psychiatrist and the Dying Patient*, "If man could not experience time, he could never fathom death, which would then be as meaningless to him as it is to the animal." But what is time in literature, and how do our present-day writers envisage it? As Lawrence Durrell declares in *A Key to Modern British Poetry*: "If art has any message it must be this: to remind us that we are dying without having properly lived." Modern man, trapped in a world of nature that devours its victims, deprived of faith in God and the vision of eternity, feels terribly insecure. As Durrell goes on to say: "If time is, as I believe, the measure of our death-consciousness, you cannot revise your concept of it without affecting our ideas of death and life." What emerges from all this is certainly not a philosophy of time but a revelation of the death-consciousness that dominates the *Lebensanschauung* of modern man.

Unamuno knew that it was madness to seek to penetrate into the mystery of what lies beyond this world and to impose the desires of the heart on the stubborn facts of reality, and yet, in *The Tragic Sense of Life,* he insists on believing in a life beyond the grave, in the possibility, that is an object of passionate faith, of being joined with God. At least he courageously poses the problem and struggles with death in a spirit of heroic defiance.

What drives him in all his work is the urge to discover a meaning in life so that the gibbering hosts of futility will be exorcised. What impels him is not simply a fear of death but a desperate refusal to die and be turned everlastingly into the nothingness of dust. If death is certain, then what meaning can life possibly have? It is the Nothingness toward which death tends that he found so demoralizing, for he was consumed with an insatiable hunger for more of life. The essence of man, he therefore concluded, inheres in this irrational but unconquerable desire not to die.

The discovery of death is, after all, not a new thing. What is of singular interest is the way each generation symbolizes, in poetry and fiction, in drama and art, the universal experience of death. With the Nietzschean announcement, sacrilegiously celebrated, that God is dead, the advent of death lost its once sacred, supernatural significance. The Victorian poets, though shaken by the theory of evolution, refused to abandon their faith in personal immortality. Despite all the lacerating doubts he voiced in *In Memoriam,* Tennyson could still believe that he would meet his Maker face to face when he had crossed the bar. Browning, for his part, an invincible cosmic optimist, was convinced that he would be reunited with his wife in the hereafter. Thomas Hardy, believing that the First Cause was either blind and not aware of what it was doing or an automaton and hence not responsible for its actions, could find no solace in the grave.

When we read "The Love Song of J. Alfred Prufrock" we enter a new and bleak climate of thought, an atmosphere of derisive disenchantment. Here death is pictured as an undignified, precipitate exit, without the viaticum of dignity or beauty. The fountain of life has dried up. J. Alfred Prufrock measures out his life with coffee spoons. He is desperately trying, even as he ages, to escape from the relentless trap of time. The striking change of mood and meaning is illustrated by these lines from the poem:

> I have seen the moment of my greatness flicker,
> And I have seen the eternal Footman hold my coat, and snicker,
> And in short, I was afraid.

In *The Waste Land,* Eliot declares: "I will show you fear in a handful of dust." Life, it is clear, has lost its meaning as well as its beauty. Caught in the rats' alley "Where the dead men lost their bones," modern man is neurasthenically afraid to think, afraid to face the truth of nothingness.

Contemporary writers are haunted by this intolerable vision of the imminence as well as inevitability of death. Here is the inspirational, if morbid, source of their creative travail: a perpetual wrestling match, foredoomed to defeat from the start, with the dark angel of death. But though they know that all struggle is unavailing, they believe it is their duty to face the meaning of death honestly and unflinchingly. A special school of literary philosophers, drawing their nourishment from Heidegger, have been most influential in contributing to this literature of death. Their object is to gaze at death objectively, without drawing away from the unspeakable dread it induces. Philosophy, as they develop it, implies a kind of secular training in the art of dying. The authentically modern note they strike is that death ceases to be a strictly philosophical problem, obscured in abstract generality, and becomes an intensely personal, subjective experience. It is the individual who dies; each man is faced with the realization that he has to die, and this knowledge colors all of his life. Death sets the boundary of life and prescribes the goal toward which we move.

All of life is thus subject to the irrational tyranny of death. Everything else is illusory and vain; only death is ontologically real. But (to come back to the problem that oppresses the modern literary consciousness) how can a writer who embraces such a philosophy find the energy and the incentive to create? If he is doomed to die and death may strike at any moment, then how can he give himself to any project that demands time for its completion? If he is a child of nothingness, if God is dead, if there are no values that live beyond him, why should he put forth any effort to "immortalize" himself in art? If death dramatically highlights the fate of cosmic absurdity, then why live?

Though sustained by a mystical faith in the Absolute, even the religious Existentialists are not unaware of the tragic aspects of life. Indeed, Gabriel Marcel makes the observation that we have today entered upon an eschatological age; not that we are approaching the end of the world but that man, for the first time in history, perceives that it lies within his power to destroy the universe. In fact, most Existentialist writing, the philosophical as well as the literary, may be said to constitute an interminable dialogue with death. Whether the Existentialist affirms the Christian doctrine or rejects it, he knows that man can never hope to become the master of his fate, since he is being driven ineluctably toward death. We live for the purpose of dying, and that is the fate which is uniquely our own. But if that is so, then life is utterly absurd, especially when we consider that all through life we are involved in the process of dying.

Literary Existentialism gives memorable expression to this anxiety neurosis of our age. The Sartrean hero questions the meaning of existence and finds that it eludes his comprehension. Human existence is without justification. Reality dissolves into the nothingness of death that waits for all of us. Absurdity is enthroned as the idiotic God of the universe. The trouble with the Existentialists is that they fail to pursue their ontology to its remorseless, logical conclusion. Their fundamental error lies in seeking to build their life on a foundation of purposelessness, and failing to go beyond that. If nothing matters, if death is the end, then we are plunged in absolute darkness and all values are confounded in nihilistic chaos. Why should men like Sartre and Camus use up precious energy in this futile project of communicating their views about nothingness? Why take the trouble to pierce the veil which hides the abyss of absurdity? What value is there in a metaphysical doctrine which simply maps out the road to the end of night? If everything is absurd, then is not art, too, fatally tainted with absurdity? And if everything is absurd, then Existentialism is also an absurd error.

Existentialism has not discovered anything in the world of thought or experience, but it has feverishly reaffirmed man's perception of the horror of a life bounded on all sides by the infinite of death. Its distinctive note is its awareness of death as a tragedy of meaninglessness that befalls each man. Each man dies alone and the world then ceases to exist for him. But this preoccupation with the dialectics of death is paradoxically associated with the theme of limitless freedom. Since God does not exist and death is inevitable, man must shoulder the responsibility of creating his own values. It is the recognition of the ultimate power of death that adds a tragic dimension to his existence and gives him fulness of self-knowledge.

But what does this self-knowledge amount to? How does it help man to live his life more satisfyingly? How can he go on living if he has no sense of direction, no faith in the future, no faith in life itself? What is beyond comprehension is the denial of life itself. If the intellectuals of today have developed a mad fixation on death, it is because they have caught a terrifying glimpse of the horror of our time, its unrestrained indulgence in barbarism, its limitless capacity for murder. It is the political nihilism of our age that has helped to nurture the metaphysics of nothingness.

An age that specializes in wholesale political murders, an age of crematoria and genocide, must be understood before it can be repudiated. Who indeed can compute the number of those who perished in Auschwitz and Maidanek, Dachau and Belsen—and what do figures alone matter? If we know that seven or fifteen or twenty-five million victims perished in these hellish camps, it still fails to create the reality that the suffering and death of one man has the power to evoke. David Rousset, a former professor of philosophy and member of the French underground during the last war, describes, in *The Other Kingdom,* his experiences in the concentration camps at Buchenwald, Helmstedt, Neuengamme, and Wöbbelin. Though he attempts to be "objective" in his description, his vocabulary falters before the stupendous task of picturing these monstrous aberrations of human instinct, these cruelties more ferocious than anything that animals can devise. Only in brief surrealist flashes of exposure can he hope to reveal, fragmentarily, the nature of his experiences in this universe of horror, the ludicrous determination of these scarecrow inmates to cling to life, to survive the ordeal in hell. For there was always the crematorium. Hence they must strengthen their will to live. They must suffer rubber bludgeons cracking on cringing flesh and skulls, fists pounding sadistically into the face, kicks that cannot be resisted. Men murder each other for a crust of bread, they eat the flesh of bloated cadavers. "Amazing skeletons with empty eyes trample blindly over heaps of stinking corruption. They lean against a beam, heads sunken on their chests, and stand motionless and mute, one hour, two hours. After a while, the body has crumbled to the ground. A living corpse has become a dead one." This universe, "the weird kingdom of an unlikely fatality," is cut off from the rest of the world. The gas chambers get rid of as many as ten thousand victims every day. "And when, inexorably, the massive portals of the gas chambers close, the victims hurl themselves against them in such a mad stampede to live, that when they open once more, the wall of corpses, inextricably intertwined, spills in a cascade over the rails."

Nihilism in the end culminates in a philosophy of death and sanctions the necessity of murder. If absurdity is the rule of life, then what difference does it make if we live or die, kill or refrain from killing? Absolute negation results in absolute absurdity, for even as the intellectuals arrive at such conclusions they go on living. As Freud declared in 1915, in "Thoughts for the Times on War and Death": "To endure life remains, when all is said, the first duty of all living beings."

Lonely men, without God or a sustaining code of morals, the nihilists of our time seek for meaning and order in the universe and discover only a howling chaos of futility. Whether or not they know it, all their utterances are dictated by their hatred of death and their craving for life. They fight death because death nullifies all meaning. For all their perverse metaphysical disclaimers, they are fighting in behalf of life—of a life that is meaningful. Camus dedicated himself to the affirmation, through suffering and sacrifice, of a nature that is common to all men, and in this respect he parted company with the revolutionary nihilists.

It is ironic that a rebel like Camus came to a conclusion that is not far removed from the answer provided by the theology of crisis. The only way in which man can affirm himself is to live creatively and spontaneously within his age, within the context of his culture. But in order to live creatively, he must make his spiritual life a matter of ultimate concern. He is responsible—who else?— for the making of his life. Choosing himself and taking responsibility for his actions, he must affirm his life in the face of death. Only by being true to himself can he transcend the sense of meaninglessness and the paralyzing terror that the contemplation of death calls forth. That is the answer Paul Tillich gives in *The Courage to Be,* and it is substantially in agreement with the secular, humanistic answer that Erich Fromm gives in *Man for Himself.* Uncertainty must be borne. "If he faces the truth without panic," Fromm declares, man "will recognize that there is no meaning to life, except the meaning man gives his life by the unfolding of his powers, by living productively; and that only constant vigilance, activity, and effort can keep us from failing in the one task that matters—the full development of our powers within the limitations set by the laws of our existence." In short, the only sovereign remedy against death is life itself—a life that is meaningful because it is productive.

Having diagnosed the spiritual crisis of our time and analyzed the major motifs—the sense of being lost, spiritual nothingness, the obsession with death and doom—that appear in contemporary literature, we must now undertake to examine closely and critically how writers weave these motifs imaginatively into the warp and woof of their work.

VI

THE RELIGIOUS REVIVAL IN CONTEMPORARY LITERATURE

WE ARE NOW in a position to sum up the nature of the obscure but dangerous metaphysical disease from which the Western world is suffering, and to observe how it achieves symptomatic expression in contemporary literature. Many spiritual doctors, each one a specialist in his own field, have been rushed to the scene of the emergency. A number of the healers still maintain that scientific humanism provides an efficacious method of saving civilization from disaster. A few contend that the individual must recover his lost integrity of purpose by retiring within the sacred fastness of the self. Some urgently preach the need for a revival of religious consciousness. Others hold up the perennial philosophy of mysticism as the way and the life. In the meantime, the patient suffers acutely and is becoming steadily worse. What is the best cure for this alarming malady of nihilism, with its anxiety, anguish, spiritual fatigue and failure of nerve, existentialist dolor and despair? Modern poets, novelists, and dramatists have given a poignant description of this state of spiritual alienation, but they do not as a rule know how to overcome the sickness from which they suffer. The best they can do is to talk nervously about their own dereliction.

What is most amazing, when one proceeds to examine this human predicament objectively, is that many of these writers look upon their condition as if they were the first ever to face the dread sphinx of nothingness. Complaining about their woes as if they were utterly cut off from civilization and the magnetic chain of humanity, they do not seem to comprehend that their vision of doom has striking parallels in the past. They appear to have lost the power to think and act affirmatively. Inwardly they realize clearly enough that without this capacity for affirming life, without this faith in the destiny of mankind and their constructive participation in the forward march of culture, they cannot continue to function. This is precisely the curse that has fallen upon them, the sickness of soul that renders all effort futile and reduces their existence to a nihilistic nightmare.

If the writer is unable to discover a fundamental meaning and purpose in life, then his individual life is inevitably disorganized. Upon what unifying principle or ideal can he call to give meaning to his creative aspirations and to motivate his actions? Everything, including his artistic labors, seems senseless. Out of this has sprung the metaphysics of absurdity (and with it a literature of absurdity) that is so disturbing a manifestation of the loss of faith in life among contemporary writers. For their feverish indictment of the universe, their forlorn and hopeless alienation from the life of mankind, represents, as we have seen, a will to death. All their agonized struggles to choose their freedom are but ritualistic gestures of defiance born of absolute despair. A life that is rooted in negation and ruled by a sense of pure contingency cannot either affirm or create. Contemporary man has lost faith not only in God but also in his own reality. Out of this experience of dread, this perception of the utter meaninglessness of existence, this crushing knowledge of his own mortality, emerges the insight, which is strangely equated with freedom, that he must learn how to live with the bride of Nothingness. Man is born of Nothing and returns to Nothing.

Here is the dominant metaphorical perspective through which human destiny at present is viewed and evaluated. Here we are brought face to face with the crisis of our culture. The intellectuals suffer from cosmic fear, from the unspeakable dread that the contemplation of death induces. Discerning no sign of grace or good in the universe, they cannot believe in any promise of salvation. That concept has been abandoned, for the religious vision that made it so hauntingly real and alive in the past is now dead. Naturalism taught them that man is subject to determinism, that life is a trap. This was then the universal law of life; it was no longer a scientific abstraction but a profoundly felt belief. Man was the victim of his environment, surrounded by forces that were not only alien but hostile. The naturalists stressed the helplessness of man, his victimization by death, his sense of estrangement in a universe that he could not comprehend. Practically all those writers who accepted naturalism shared a common feeling of being spiritually uprooted and lost. Afraid of life, they devoted their writing to affirming the myth of nothingness, to exploring the state of spiritual lostness which had become their central theme. Having given up their belief in God and immortality, they could not find their way home again.

The Victorians, though they, too, had confronted the ultimate issues of human destiny, were at least able to formulate a positive answer. For them religion was of paramount importance. Not religion in the formal sense, religion as theological conformity, but religion as the earnest expression of what a man actually believed, the nature of his relationship to the mysterious universe. For they held that it is the religious outlook, the religious vision, which determines man's destiny on earth. That is why Carlyle felt that it is enough to know a man's religion to understand immediately the sort of man he is. That sums up the quintessence of man. It is also the motivating force of history, for what a man profoundly believes dictates his course of action.

But the age of heroes and hero worship is over. The Sartor Resartus of the twentieth century, unreconciled to life, continues to proclaim the Everlasting Nay. For what sort of religious consciousness do modern writers hold? Unwilling to compromise with the truth, they feel that Nature refuses to divulge its secrets. Iconoclasts at heart, they know that man knows, and can know, nothing of the absolute. Like Nietzsche, they wrestle with the horror of meaninglessness in the universe. Not only faith but reason too is impotent. No matter how great their distress, they will not make their peace with God. As Nietzsche phrased it with characteristic Zarathustrian pride: "I cannot let God transcend me; I can only transcend *myself* in infinite nothingness, in the eternal void of Not-Being, the ghost-land of shadows where the exiles from life float in the dark opacity of a blurred dream!" Thus, still unresigned, wrote the most militant prophet of nihilism from within the confines of a madhouse.

In continuing to struggle with this infinite nothingness, the writers of the twentieth century have again raised the question of the religious consciousness, which seems virtually to have disappeared. There are, it is true, signs of a religious revival in literature, but not in a doctrinal sense. Modern writers are not theologians, brooding miserably about their sins and anxiously examining their chances of salvation. At least, only the Catholic poets and novelists are thus preoccupied, those who behold life as a Manichean struggle between good and evil, between the animal and the angelic in man. In a world disrupted by revolutionary change, when all certainties are being challenged and overthrown, many writers feel the need for a spiritual place of shelter, preferably one that will stand up until the crack of doom. They wish to flee from the raging storms of doubt and denial and the desolating emotional imbalance that the loss of faith has brought about.

But it is exceedingly difficult, when the age is rationalist in temper and predominantly skeptical in outlook, to recover the habit of faith by an act of will. Though there have been ages of unbelief in the past, they were never marked by so extreme a crisis of alienation as exists today. Whereas the Middle Ages believed that faith was superior to reason, the present age has not only abandoned its faith but also jettisoned its extravagantly optimistic belief in the redemptive power of reason. The utopian dream of perfection to be achieved through technological progress and the implementation of the scientific method has been shattered. Thus we have a curious and disturbing dilemma: man cannot believe in a God that offends his reasoning powers, and he distrusts the very powers that lead him to deny the existence of God. Yet the tide of defection from religious orthodoxy, especially among contemporary writers, is still strong. How many today still believe that the world could have been created by an intelligent being or that morality is of universal validity or that the will is free to act?

What the religious synthesis can do for the writer is to offer him a meaningful interpretation of the universe, a number of conventions and symbols with which to work. Catholic writers, for example, are concerned with the theme of original sin, the motif of redemption, the concept of immortality and damnation, the Fatherhood of God. As Rayner Heppenstall points out in *The Double Image,* a brilliant study of a number of Catholic novelists in France: "Catholicism to-day is at once an answer to and symptomatic of the unbalance of the age." For the return to religion is not without perilous difficulties. The desire to transcend a skepticism that is sterile and suffocating—that is not enough. Faith cannot be won by an imperative act of will. One must genuinely believe if the faith is to be real. A lonely, unco-ordinated spirit, a born heretic, the writer must subject the religious experience to the same rigorous test that he applies to reality. Hence his writing is bound to reflect the never-ending struggle between belief and doubt. It is by no means an easy matter to shift over from a secular to a religious way of thinking and feeling. Brought up rigidly on the curriculum of rationalism, the writer finds that he cannot formulate his religious intuitions in rational terms, and he is foiled every time he seeks to express his faith unequivocally. An eclectic in his attitude toward existing religions, he takes from each what it has to offer, without trying too hard to integrate them into a coherent system. Yet he is not in a position to make affirmations on which he is willing to stake everything. Now that the collapse of revolutionary messianism has left him spiritually homeless and bankrupt, he must turn somewhere.

The writer must build on a foundation of faith, yet he must avoid the temptation of using this faith formally, as doctrine or philosophy, in his work. Whether he writes fiction or poetry or drama, he must beware of abstraction and formula, dogma and theology. Always it is the ineffably concrete experience that he deals with, the human soul in its immediacy, the feelings that are infinitely complex and not to be communicated as pure feelings. If he endeavors to translate his religious intuitions, his vision of the world in all its mysteriousness and numinous splendor, into theological terms, his art is bound to suffer, just as if he sought to make his intuitions conform to a philosophic or psychoanalytical or political system. He cannot afford to put an exclusive theological or ideological frame around the universe, though he must, of course, interpret it in the light of some perspective that will give it coherence and meaning. Essentially he must hold on to his vision as the alpha and omega of the creative process; it is the vision that is the secret of technique and the heart and lifeblood of form. It therefore follows that, whatever the theme the writer is led to develop, what gives it value for literature is the vision with which it is penetrated. Gerard Manley Hopkins, a Jesuit who constitutes as it were a test case, writes a poem about his agonistic struggle to find God and the poem bears within it the dialectical tension, the piercing doubt, the ironic negation, that is the glory of poetry at its most intense. He cries out in anguish to God: "Mine, O thou lord of life, send my roots rain." Francis Thompson composes "The Hound of Heaven," and the lyrical confession, soaring and haunting, communicates its "religious" motif: the effort to escape from the knowledge and presence of God and the impossibility of doing so. By the same token, a mystical confession like *I and Thou*, by Martin Buber, has been rightly called a lyric poem. By the proper extension of terms, and the elimination of formal theological categories, many of Wordsworth's and Emerson's poems are informed with the religious spirit.

Each age, as Emerson says, must write its own books, and our age is the age of tormented anxiety. Trapped in a blind alley of uncertainty that cannot be put into words, many contemporary writers experience a feeling of despair that is beyond their power to endure. The result of all this, as we have pointed out, is that they are stricken with what might be called spiritual neurasthenia, a metaphysical fear that is nameless, undefined, and for that very reason terrifying. This makes itself felt in every sphere of thought, not only in belles-lettres, but also in philosophy and in the theology of crisis. Here is the spiritual landscape of horror that the genius of Kierkegaard so clairvoyantly pictured for us. He became convinced, as he indicates in *Fear and Trembling,* that faith is to be achieved not by pride of intellect or the strenuous exercise of the faculty of reason, but only by virtue of embracing the absurd. In this Existentialist recognition of the paradox of the human situation, we get a new conception of the act of faith. Each individual must establish his own unique relation to God, without the mediation of corporate institutions. The human understanding, finite and fallible, must be given up. God must not be judged. The most challenging concept in the Kierkegaardian outlook is unquestionably the category of the absurd. (It is interesting to note that a mystic like Kierkegaard and a rebel like Camus both embrace the mystique of the absurd, but how different, as applied to literature and life, are the conclusions they draw therefrom!) Judged by the calculus of reason, faith held under such a condition seems the height of absurdity. Precisely! That is the ultimate basis of faith. The ways of God are beyond human comprehension. The individual gains the inaccessible peaks of faith when he has matured sufficiently, through suffering, to perceive that his weakness is the source of his greatest strength. Just when he is overcome by despair and ready to give up the struggle, he achieves the victory and miracle of faith.

It is not in the least surprising that a number of modern writers in England and the United States have traced in themselves the symptoms of the spiritual sickness described by the Danish thinker. Though his mind was God-centered, the account he gives of his perilous journey in search of God is imaginatively moving. Kierkegaard brings home to the modern mind the psychological reality of death. Here are the confessions of a religious sufferer whose cries of distress are painfully authentic to the consciousness of mod-

ern man. Rationalism is the enemy to be conquered. Humanism is
not enough; science is at bottom an expression of man's satanic
arrogance. He seeks to penetrate below the surface of the intellect
and listen to the voices that speak so compellingly from within.
That is his test of Existentialism: spontaneous immediacy, the vital
intuitions of his being, the "truths" that are subjective, intensely
personal, felt rather than cognized. That is why he willingly accepts
suffering as the price he must pay for the triumph of transcendence.
Nothing but God would satisfy him, no one but God could save him,
and yet what a God this is—sicklied o'er with the pale cast of doubt,
born of the agony of despair, conceived in the womb of death. It
is the experience of confronting death that, in his case as in that
of Unamuno, is the generator of faith. Faced with this final, intolerable mystery, his reason capitulates; he accepts the paradox of
the absurd and affirms the miracle of rebirth in the inferno of dread.

All this has an important bearing on what the modern poet
faces when he must choose between Nothingness and God and
give expression to the tensions set up by the struggle between doubt
and faith. Kierkegaard admirably illustrates how difficult it is to
sustain faith without falling into heresy. One is reminded of the
creed that Dostoevski formulated: "I am a child of this age, a child
of unfaith and skepticism, and probably (indeed I know it) shall
remain so to the end of my life. How dreadfully has it tormented
(and torments me even now)—this longing for faith, which is
stronger for the proofs I have against it." Both Kierkegaard and
Dostoevski, in their struggle to affirm the reality of God, show
clearly why the creative imagination cannot be made to follow
prescriptive commandments and catechisms. That is why institutional
religion finds the imagination so perversely intractable and therefore
suspect. The creative personality, heretical in its vision, cannot rest
in any dogma. It must have no intermediaries between its vision and
the reality it contemplates.

The advent of romanticism made the poet painfully aware of
the ambiguities and contradictions in his own self. He did more
than strip himself clean of all illusion; exploring, long before Sartre,

the terrifying relationship between self and the universe, he discovered that his existence was not in the least necessary to nature. The world of matter, without a soul or indwelling purpose, cared not a whit for human destiny. But in rejecting spiritual transcendence, the poet was forced into the void; and since then his career has been largely a desperate but losing fight against nihilism. In its spiritual ferment, modern poetry represents a struggle between negation and the renewal of the religious quest. In hating God, in hammering home the last nail into the coffin of the God-concept, the romantic poets revealed their nostalgic but inverted religiosity. In their diabolical worship of evil, in their frantic eagerness to be damned, they betrayed the extremity of their longing for the Absolute. Jacques Maritain, in *Creative Intuition in Art and Poetry,* sees in this frenzied appeal of atheism "an obscure, or reversed, longing for faith."

Hence the desperate resort to myth on the part of these poets in the hope of finding a respectable cultural surrogate for the lost God. But this process of compensation, as Maritain calls it, this search for the redemptive myth, was foredoomed to failure because it was based on a profound illusion. A myth is alive only when it is believed in. It is faith that quickens the myth; the myth that is *invented* to serve a special compensatory purpose is a contradiction in terms. The will to believe in a myth, whatever its nature or name, is not enough to inspire and nourish the poet. If a new metaphysical faith is to infuse his work, it must become the basis of a new and all-inclusive religious affirmation. The man believes, then the poet creates. Once he believes, he discovers within himself the mysterious incentive to create the universe anew, with its sun and stars, its earth and its satellites, its teeming humanity. Maritain's point is simply that while metaphysical myths are needed, they cannot be furnished by poetry but must come from life itself, from the spiritual resources of the poet.

The crucial question for the writer, one that we shall discuss more thoroughly in the next section, is how this religious consciousness, whatever its content, is to be related to his literary work.

It is a question that can be answered only in aesthetic, not in theological, terms. Just as there can be no science of poetry, so there can be no official religion designed to invigorate poetry. Poetry is essentially a poetry of the earth, the celebration of the world's body, frankly sensuous in its appeal. To love God with complete devotion means to shut out the distractions of time and matter and become ineffably one with pure divine essence. As Karl Shapiro states the opposition of forces in *Beyond Criticism:* "Some poets, to be sure, are men of God and some men of God are poets, but, in general, churches are weak in esthetics and the glory of this life, while most religious poets, so-called, are weak in talent.... The mystical is the opposite of the creative process...."

The religious vision may furnish the basis for a heightened poetry, but it cannot afford to be circumscribed or exclusive. It cannot shut out of its confines the elements of the ugly, the horrible, the secular, the evil. The poet captures a moment of timeless reality, but he is concerned with art, not with God. His song springs from his sensibility, not from his fidelity to dogma or formulated truth. Hence art cannot be a surrogate for religion. It has much in common with religion but it is not in partnership with a particular school of theology. The artist must keep faith with his vision; that is his whole system of "morality." To its making he must give all of his energy and devotion. It is T. S. Eliot who, in *Notes Towards the Definition of Culture,* has declared magisterially: "To judge a work of art by artistic or religious standards, to judge a religion by religious or artistic standards should come in the end to the same thing; it is an end at which no individual can arrive."

The unsettled condition of the world, the frightening threat of another world war, the bankruptcy of the Marxist eschatological vision, the revolutionary changes that have taken place in the scientific outlook, the splitting of the atom and the manufacture and use of atomic bombs, have been in part responsible for the present reversion to religion on the part of a number of intellectuals. Unable to reconcile themselves to the scientific picture of a world in which spiritual values are excluded as irrelevant and invalid, a number of contemporary writers, as is indicated in the symposium, *Religion and the Intellectuals,* originally published by the *Partisan Review,* reject a naturalism that would compel them to fashion their own gods. Though they turn to religion for reassurance, they cannot cancel out the preceding centuries of rational inquiry and skeptical criticism. Consequently, their religious belief is largely a matter of willed conversion, a deliberately intellectual assent for the most part, not something spontaneously experienced and organically felt. Despite all their desperate efforts to believe, they are infected with the plague of skepticism. They cannot drop their ironic reservations, their awareness of relativism in the naturalistic flux, without laying themselves open to the charge of harboring superstition and succumbing to mysticism. And if they lapse into dogma, they have betrayed their creative responsibility. They produce theology, not literature. Many of the intellectuals who have gone over to religion are actually incapable of the miracle of faith. For all their protestations of desire, they cannot believe in the reality of the supernatural. Their "conversion" has not significantly affected the quality of their creative contribution. At heart they are still, with but few exceptions, members of their disbelieving generation.

This tension between belief and nonbelief, affirmation and negation, cannot be eliminated, but if religion be interpreted as man's search for ultimate meaning, then even the metaphysical rebel in our age, despite his lack of orthodoxy, is "religious," for he protests against a universe and a type of life that he finds intolerable. He rebels, however confusedly, in behalf of a dream of order, a higher value. But the rebel, by overthrowing God, must assume responsibility for creating order and justice in the world. Thus emerges the crucial problem of the age: without God, what system of morality can man devise? On what foundations will he base his conduct? In the name of what ideal is he to act? Nietzsche, who denied everything, did not draw back from any of the damning implications of nihilism. He denied the very foundation of faith, namely, the belief in life. He declared that one can live, believing in nothing, if one is pre-

pared to accept and to act upon the final consequences of nihilism.
Here then is the high priest of negation announcing that there
is no need for God. The dream of heaven, the hope of everlasting
life, the categorical absolute—these fictions must be resolutely
abandoned. Nietzsche courageously states the problem: Can one
live, believing in nothing? That is the question which bedevils the
mind of contemporary man. If there is no supernatural power, then
man must create his own law of life or go mad. Henceforth he must
hold himself responsible for everything that takes place. It is then
he perceives the demoralizing truth of his condition on earth: his
cosmic alienation.

It is this state of anarchy that has driven a number of writers
to rebel in the name of a higher religious principle, a moral law.
Man cannot surrender abjectly to the dominion of blind chance. If he
does so, then he denies the possibility of judgment, he has no light
to see by, and everything stands horribly confounded. How can
he go on living, or creating, in a world that is lawless? The religious
writer sees the multiple dangers that today beset mankind, the
various kinds of temptation that beleaguer the soul, the triumph of
technological and political power untempered by a consciousness of
human limitations, the ascendancy of the scientific temper that dis-
regards the spiritual needs of man. Unfortunately, some of these
writers, in their alarm at the sick condition of the world, demand
an orthodoxy that is difficult to impose and for many impossible to
attain. Though the return to religion represents a significant and
vital movement in our time, the writer must finally come to the
sober conclusion that the quest for faith, the craving for spiritual
and creative integrity, will not and cannot take place under the
auspices of a single church.

The modern writer who believes, whatever his doctrinaire per-
suasion, is bound to be "impure," tainted with doubt, wounded
by the knife of skepticism. The emergence of Existentialism and the
theology of crisis is symptomatic of a profoundly changed spiritual
orientation. Religious writers are today impelled by a tense realization that the center of Western civilization cannot hold. If the col-

lapse is to be prevented, it must be by a prodigious and concerted moral effort. The religious writers are seeking to develop a sense of moral responsibility and to formulate a faith that will lead them out of the contemporary wasteland of denial and despair. The dialectic of nothingness is giving birth to the craving for the authentic religious vision; but the religious affirmation, in poetry, must be made in the spirit of creative freedom. The religious writer will inevitably share the doubts that surround the act of faith and yet be able to affirm his beliefs despite them. In ultimate issues of this kind, he knows that he can receive no guarantee of empirical truth. He clings to his belief despite all the evidence reason can muster to prove that God does not exist.

The writer, however, no matter what he believes, cannot be spared the duty of facing the ordeal of reality in all its refractory mysteriousness. A man who does not believe, at least in himself and his work to begin with, is not really alive and cannot be productive. If he does not believe in the reality of his own being, then he can have no organic relationship to life. He clings to biological existence, but he is always on the outside, a detached, bewildered spectator, a shadow in a phantasmagoric dance of shadows. As long as he remains uncommitted, not dedicated to an ideal that transcends the finite self, he cannot be truly creative. Even if he has the defiant energy to articulate the torment of his absence of faith, the best he can do is to utter a series of hysterical negations. How can nothingness find a voice? But as soon as he knows that he serves a purpose that outlives his limited existence, then life takes on meaning. Out of chaos he shapes a cosmos. He has found the vital symbol that will unify his life on earth. Literature in this sense springs from a comprehensive "religious" orientation, but it is a perspective that goes beyond any single creed.

The literature of theology is one thing, but poetry that is "religious" in spirit is something entirely different. A Catholic or Protestant theologian is committed in advance to a fixed, traditional body of doctrine. The poet, however, cannot hope to shadow forth the truth of reality by imprisoning it within some institutional dogma. He must communicate the whole of experience in all its baffling complexity, its irreducible contradictions and irrationalities, its ugliness as well as its grandeur, its boredom and evil as well as its beauty and holiness. He must reveal the doubt as well as the faith in the arena of the mind. The whole mind, the whole being, is active in the creative process: the passional self, the instincts, the unconscious; and the poet, though he obviously selects his material in accordance with his philosophy of life, cannot afford to impose a pattern that is restrictive in its effect. He cannot honestly leave out those elements in life and in his own personality which war against the faith and militate against his belief in God.

Whatever the faith which the poet finally embraces, literature must project the conflict that is at the heart of all life, the struggle between darkness and light, good and evil, purposelessness and purpose, affirmation and denial, the sacred and the profane, flesh and spirit, death and the hunger for immortality, God and nothingness. When the poet remains faithful to his calling, he will inevitably give expression to this enigmatic aspect of being. The religious consciousness is never a settled thing, something established with finality, never to be questioned or assailed. It is perpetually in a state of crisis and renewal. The poetry of our time must therefore reflect this crisis: the anxiety, the search, the metaphysical despair, the nihilism, as well as the counterpointing cry of affirmation and the triumphant discovery of faith.

PART TWO

THE WORLD OF POETRY

VII

THE RELIGIOUS PROBLEM
IN MODERN POETRY

IN *The Modern Writer and His World*, G. S. Fraser presents a cogent analysis of the paradoxical, and indeed desperate, situation in which the "typical young writer" of the past decade finds himself. He is pictured as

being driven in many cases from a secular to a religious way of life, and yet his whole intellectual training, which has probably been entirely secular, tends to make it impossible for him to formulate these religious intuitions of his in a coherent or rational way, or to make any outward act of faith and acceptance.

What is this but another way of saying that the writer of our time is in need of God and yet is either unable to find Him or unable to believe in Him? As a humanitarian agnostic, he is eclectic in his attitude toward existing religions, but he cannot work them into a consistent system and he has no confident, affirmative outlook of his own. Hence he drifts in uncertainty and often in dire confusion between the poles of rational skepticism and a faith that he embraces halfheartedly in a fit of irrational despair.

The twentieth century was born when anthropomorphism in religion received its deathblow at the hands of science. The power once attributed to God has now been transferred to the First Cause, the fundamental source of energy in the universe. The work of demolition really began in the nineteenth century, when religion, forced to accommodate itself to the new scientific dispensation, had to revise many of its assumptions and beliefs. Literature bore witness to the intensity of this ideological struggle. Browning remained relatively untouched by the revolutionary ferment set in motion by scientific inquiry. Not so Matthew Arnold or James Thomson or John Davidson. The issue was brought dramatically to a head in Thomas Hardy's poetry, particularly in *The Dynasts,* in which he deliberately refers to God as "It." God has become the symbol of a blind series of forces; man is no longer regarded as the king of creation, in direct communion with God or with supernatural realities. Hence the note of bitter pessimism that crops up in much of Victorian poetry. *The City of Dreadful Night* is a dirge of nihilistic futility. God is dead, and how is man to live in an inscrutable, meaningless universe? Hardy's "pessimism" perpetuated this tradition of man's agonized bewilderment and suffering in an incomprehensible world of brute energy.

A poet does not, of course, spend all his hours composing metaphysical lyrics on the nature of God, yet *implicit* in his poetry, in everything he writes, is his *Weltanschauung*—his ontological values, his attitude toward God. Hardy, for example, convinced that death ends everything, could not believe in the existence of God. What was God but the creation of man? His reason—reason was the acid that acted as a dissolvent on the traditional body of faith—effectually prevented him from remaining under the wings of a God that for him had no reality. Rejecting the anthropomorphic concept of God, he concludes that God, the creator, was ruled by blind necessity. The universe could not logically be said to carry out any rational plan. Is God then but an automaton? Hardy does not know the answer. All he knows is that we are born and that we die. There is no sense in brooding on the meaning of life, for nothing is gained thereby. In *The Dynasts,* the Semichorus of the Years sings:

> O Immanence, That reasonest not
> In putting forth all things begot,
> Thou build'st Thy house in space—for what?

Today the religious battle still rages fiercely, though the terms in which the debate about ultimate issues is waged are strategically different. Twentieth-century science has weakened, if not destroyed, the presuppositions of theology. The poet of our time feels lost, as if he had wiped the cultural slate clean of all past supernatural beliefs and decided to start anew. Everything is to be questioned and nothing affirmed. Consequently the modern poet has wrought semantic changes of vast significance in his interpretation of God. Though many writers continue to deny the reality of God, they cannot somehow refrain from dealing with him in some form or other. Regardless of their personal attitude toward Christianity, poets like T. S. Eliot, Auden, Robinson Jeffers, and Dylan Thomas have had to employ a radically transformed imagery when speaking of God.

For much of contemporary literature is not only secular in content but oftentimes divorced from the main stream of Christian belief. The forces that make for secularization have gathered increasing strength and become aggressively outspoken. Freud discovered the origin of religion in the child's fear of the earthly father, forbidding and all-powerful, the protector and the punisher. Moreover, he challenged the basic assumption that religion could afford man protection against the arrows of outrageous fortune. In short, he contended that human destiny did not conform to any overriding principle of justice. Religion, a form of animistic wishful thinking, was generally used as a means of gaining control over the world, but the attempt invariably failed. In *Moses and Monotheism,* Freud declared that he envied those who believed in the existence of God, but then he added with a note of finality: "We can only regret it if certain experiences of life and observations of nature have made it impossible to accept the hypothesis of such a Supreme Being."

That is precisely the state in which the secular poets of our age find themselves: certain experiences and observations and insights have made it impossible for them to accept the hypothesis of a Supreme Being. All that remains of the traditional concept of God is an idea, a metaphor, a myth. Some of the younger scientific humanists affirm that the only loyalty they will honor is that which keeps faith with the truth based on experimental inquiry, the truths warranted by the scientific method. Alex Comfort, for example, an English poet, novelist, and critic, insists that the Christian tradition has lost its appeal and its power, and that is because Christianity can no longer withstand the assaults of scientific inquiry. If Christianity has been abandoned, he argues, it is not because man has fallen on evil ways but because Christianity no longer seems true. The idea of a personal God—that is an assumption which must be subjected to the same battery of objective facts and tests as any other idea about "reality." It is not enough, he contends, to trump up the argument that the universe possesses design and intelligibility and that this therefore presupposes a creator or architect who is intelligent. Like Hardy, Comfort can discern no sign of moral meaning or purpose in the universe. The ineffable voice that is supposed to emanate from the heart of the universe is in reality the voice of man himself. God is but the echo of man's striving and spirituality. Henceforth, Comfort maintains, men are responsible for mastering their environment and shaping their own destiny. Man must learn to face reality and make the proper adjustment in his dreams, his expectations, his ideals.

Yet how can man endure without faith? Can one, like Nietzsche, live, believing in nothing? There can be little doubt that a number of modern writers are desperately in search of a faith that will make their life and work meaningful and sustain the integrity of their vision. They have lost their romantic ecstasies, their utopian ardor, their hope of a messianic fulfilment in their time through the combined instrumentalities of science and politics. Alas, they have discovered that the road to salvation is neither straight nor easy. Out of their inner struggle with the problem of human destiny has come the realization that there are no short cuts, no synthetic substitutes. They have come to the liberating, if paradoxical, insight that every conclusion they arrive at, like every commitment they make, is shot through with uncertainty. All faith is hedged round with the ambiguity of doubt; that is precisely why it has to be affirmed and reaffirmed. If there were no tensions and no contradictions, then faith would be a spontaneous and instinctive possession, a natural process like breathing. Herein lies the predicament of the modern poet: he feels the inner need to affirm a faith that his reason cannot accept. After a century of skepticism, modern consciousness cannot believe with wholehearted, instinctive assurance. As Sartre phrases it: "To believe is not to believe." That is to say, one believes and does not believe at the same time. "Every belief," according to Sartre, "is a belief that falls short; one can never wholly believe what one believes." While Sartre, in this context, is not referring specifically to religion, his formulation nevertheless reveals much about the psychology of belief today.

The advent of rationalism in all its diverse forms has seriously weakened the hold of Christian symbolism (as well as the faith out of which it originally sprang) on the poetic imagination. This creates a perplexing problem for the modern poet, since without the stay and support of some form of orthodoxy he is thrown upon his own resources. He can no longer take anything for granted but feels impelled to question everything. Christianity is no longer a potent creative force in the world. The poet is therefore driven, even if it lands him in heresy, to invent his own "mythology"—to build, like Yeats, a system of values intended largely for his own private religion. He must supply his own interpretation of life, his own gods. But such an attitude may fill him with a deep sense of guilt as well as dismay, since it seems to cut him off from the world of men. In his effort to achieve reintegration, he seeks in many cases to recapture the orthodoxy of the past, to slough off his intransigent individualism, to steep himself in tradition. Yet the motives which first led him to revolt still continue to be active. There is the contradiction that finds expression in modern poetry: the conflict between a romantic individualism that has proved self-defeating and sterile and religious orthodoxy that is repugnant to reason.

Can the modern poet resolve this dualism between external reality and his inner vision? Unlike Matthew Arnold, he can no longer believe that poetry provides a viable substitute for religion. He finds it hard to enter the church or accept its teachings, just as he cannot comprehend the meaning of those who speak of God and eternity. Freed from the bondage of God's will, the constraints of formal Christianity, he is at a loss when he wishes to write about God. But if God is dead, then how can he satisfy his profound need for transcendence? On the other hand, he cannot escape the contagion and corrosion of doubt. Karl Jaspers, who accepts nothing as final, makes the revealing confession: "I do not know whether I believe." This is not unlike the confession by James Agee, which we quoted earlier, that he was still divided "between belief in God, non-belief, and a kind of neutrality."

What some religious thinkers of our time view with alarm as an expression of relativism and extreme skepticism has always been the precondition of faith, which is, like truth, a precarious possession. Religious insight is born of the dialectics of contradiction. Religious affirmation seeks to reveal that which lies beyond the scope of definition and understanding. The human predicament is mysterious, baffling, beyond the grasp of discursive knowledge. The highest expression of religious thought represents a synthesis of the opposition between faith and doubt, negation and affirmation. It is Pascal, the mathematician and the seeker after the absolute, the philosopher and the mystic, who perceives the paradoxical nature of the life of man. "All things," he declares, "proceed from the Nothing, and are borne towards the Infinite." Like Pascal, Kierkegaard came to see that faith is a hazard, a poetic paradox, and it is this aspect of faith which has attracted a number of poets to religious Existentialism.

The virtue of the Existentialist religious outlook is that, in enthroning the category of the absurd and affirming the reality of faith, it does not destroy the cause of metaphysical anguish. Modern man still stands bewildered before the infinite, contemplating a universe that is denuded of meaning. The modern poet cannot solve his problem by coming to rest in God. Nor can he remain indifferent to and unmoved by the special challenge of his age if he is faithfully to discharge the responsibilities of his art. If in the interests of a special theological doctrine he shuts out aspects of modern experience that do not fit into his formal scheme, his work is bound to be limited in range and therefore, to that degree at least, unsatisfactory. If he seeks to do full justice to the art he practices, he must strive to encompass nothing less than the totality of human experience, even though he knows it is beyond his powers. Whatever his "religious" outlook, he must be free to speak out as his vision dictates, to omit no evidence that contradicts his faith. The best "religious" poets are those who, without benefit of dogma and without abandoning their faith, grapple with the tumultuous life of their age. Every poet who does this honestly, regardless of his views on theological issues, is to be considered "religious."

Why is this so? Because reality remains sphinxlike, unknowable, susceptible of a host of different interpretations. Each pair of eyes views it inevitably from a different perspective, and nothing must be left out of the total account that poetry struggles to render. The solution is never an easy one and never certain. The poet cannot conscientiously afford to censor any item of experience that works havoc with his particular "system" of salvation. So long as the element of uncertainty is not to be overcome—and how can it be in our life? —faith cannot be purged entirely of doubt. Art cannot therefore be identified with any body of theology; it must cling to the ambiguities that forever prevent it from achieving completeness of knowledge or completeness of expression. The Christian revelation offers a perspective, one among many, but the poet cannot root himself in it for the reason that it will strengthen his art and give him a firm, spiritual foundation on which to rest. As we have said, he must first believe in it.

Even faith, no matter how exalted, is ineffectual if the poet loses his grasp of reality in all its concreteness and complexity. If a mystic like Gerard Manley Hopkins is stung into expression by his glimpse of the ineffable beauty that God has wrought, he communicates this experience not only by a magically heightened handling of language but also by concentrating his gaze on the particular phenomenon he is reporting. For Hopkins, God was a real and living presence. His poetry is so meaningful, so moving, so vitally contemporary, because, instead of versifying the dogmas of the order to which he belonged, he gave voice to the agonizing struggle of the soul wrestling with God. If a professed "atheist" like Shelley can pour out his heart in impassioned and unpremeditated verse, why should it cause surprise that a Jesuit is capable of scaling the loftiest Himalayas of song? The expression of the spirit does not fit into any denominational mold. Because Hopkins never sought the vainglory of publication, because he wrote poetry solely for God's sake, his work preserved its purity of expression. Here is poetry that speaks for itself, restrained yet ardent, revelatory of his inner struggle to capture the assurance of faith. His poems are instinct with the tension of his debate with God, the unavoidable dichotomies of existence, the anxieties of the finite soul confronting the enigma of the infinite. He knows the depths as well as the soaring heights of the questing spirit, the abysmal despairs as well as heavenly visitations. Few poets have sounded more poignantly the note of metaphysical desolation the believer experiences as he questions why the thralls of lust and the wicked thrive more fruitfully than those who sacrifice everything for God, and then begs God to send his roots nourishing rain. Such lyrics are authentic in tone and universal in theme because they express so powerfully the dread and doubt that afflict the believer in his moments of darkness, when he is forsaken of God's presence. Hopkins possesses the courage to confess his uncertainties; hence the spiritual crises that inform his poetry rise above the theological plane. It is the pure religious consciousness that speaks out with such intense sincerity.

Hopkins, indeed, serves as an admirable example of the handicaps the poet labors under when he endeavors to force his creative vision within a religious framework. For the modern poet is not a Hopkins. He cannot hope to recapture the primary vision that haunted and sustained a Dante. He cannot approach his material with the innocent eye and enraptured mind of complete faith. For the scientific myths of today introduce a wedge of separation between knowledge and faith, belief and behavior, which were once joined together in inseparable unity. The poet who tries to utilize Christian myths and Christian symbolism as a means of vitalizing his poetry is doomed to disappointment. Having lost the mythopoeic perspective, the contemporary poet possesses a radically different outlook and sensibility. Steeped in the relativism of his age, how can he recover the overwhelming vision of the supernatural, the pervasive presence of the Wholly Other? While Yeats was strongly attracted to Celtic mythology, he had no conception of the universe as rooted in God. He resolved to dispense with theology as a source of poetic inspiration. The choice he made was a wise one. Art cannot express either the absolute or the eternal. The poet of today cannot engage in a quest for salvationary values that he does not believe in. How can he penetrate beyond the world of appearances and body forth a transcendent reality? If such a reality cannot be experienced, how can it be expressed? Art cannot go beyond the framework of experience, actual or possible.

The modern poet who believes that science is the only discipline which can provide reliable knowledge about the human condition replaces the consolations of Christianity with the bitterly disillusioning but objective truth. He understands that the world is not designed to satisfy his subjective wishes. The tragedy of life lies in its lack of meaning. Robinson Jeffers, for example, who has rejected all the traditional religious values, seems to feel that "salvation" is to be found in extinction. Nirvana has become God. This is the heart of Jeffers' negative preachment: humanity is to be denied; the ideals that mankind cherishes are lies and illusions. Christ, as portrayed in *Dear Judas,* sought to convince man that his destiny on earth is of supreme importance. There is the egocentric illusion that has plunged the race into a bottomless pit of introversion. If he wishes to free himself from the toils of this pernicious error, man must will his end: that of nonbeing. He must break out of the meaningless cycle of birth and pantheistically merge with nature.

Thus the poetry of the twentieth century has undergone a profound spiritual change. The use and interpretation of sacred symbols, the semantic implications of a term like *God,* the specialized vocabulary as well as the discoveries of science, the intensive study of the way meaning is communicated—all this has had a disturbing

influence on the structure as well as content of poetry. The chief
burden of T. S. Eliot's poetry, his central preoccupation, is the
nature of time and man's relation to time. Eliot is struggling hard,
as the poets of the past did not have to struggle, to impose form
upon the formless, order upon the destructive flux. As Josephine
Miles makes clear in her study, *The Primary Language of Poetry in
the 1940's,* Eliot is obsessed with terms like *time, end, future,* and
past, as he pictures a world that is elusive, phantasmagoric, insub-
stantial, fleeting. For Eliot could not continue to function creatively
in a world that is chaotic and overshadowed by meaninglessness. As
a means of opposing the forces that hasten the process of cultural
disintegration, he harked back to the past and rooted himself in
the main tradition. He sought to transcend the relativism and moral
confusion of his age by returning to the Absolute, whose home is
the church.

His later poetry, after his conversion to Anglo-Catholicism,
involves a rejection of the philosophy of humanitarianism, the cult
of perfectibility, the doctrine of evolutionary progress. Casting aside
all such optimistic illusions, Eliot bids man, a fallen creature, to
recognize his earthly limitations and to seek for redemption through
the available means of grace. Man must transcend his self-centered
will, his devouring egotism. In *East Coker,* Eliot tells man how to
face the inevitability of death:

> I said to my soul, be still, and let the dark come upon you
> Which shall be the darkness of God.

But he captures and communicates the tension of the never-
ending struggle for faith, the further union, the deeper communion,
that is to be found "Through the dark cold and the empty desolation." Man must abandon desire, even the temptation to glory in
his own martyrdom. As if aware of the insupportable burden he is
placing upon poetry in essaying to communicate the ineffable, the
perception of truths not susceptible of logical formulation, Eliot
confesses how words crack and sometimes break under the strain.
All about him he beholds the unending drama of decay, the tragedy

of change and corruption. Life is a ritualistic repetition of an ageless formula: "Eating and drinking, Dung and death." All this wearies him, the world with its mania for owning things, its mundane concerns, its trivialities. "The poetry," he concludes, "does not matter." His creative mission no longer satisfies him. The ultimate wisdom that man can possess is the wisdom of humility. Death covers all, and every moment is a time of death. In *Four Quartets,* Eliot declares that man must yield to "prayer, observance, discipline, thought and action."

In his criticism as in his poetry, Eliot sounds the same note of concern with eternity. Hence he condemns contemporary literature as being on the whole degrading, corrupted by the sin of secularism, completely incapable of understanding the meaning of "the primacy of the supernatural over the natural life." In "Catholicism and the International Order," he is explicit in his demand that Christendom be united and that humanity be considered always in relation to God. It is incumbent on every Catholic to aim at the conversion of the whole world to the true faith. What Eliot desires, in brief, is cultural unity in religion. What is more, he is convinced that religion can vitalize and fructify poetry. About a Catholic poet like Gerard Manley Hopkins he makes this revealing statement: "Hopkins has the dignity of the Church behind him, and is consequently in closer contact with reality." Here Eliot definitely betrays his hand, in his insistence that tradition and orthodoxy must guide and inform the poet's vision. Inspiration is therefore to be distrusted. The affirmation of the doctrine comes out clearly enough in his statement:

In an age of unsettled beliefs and enfeebled tradition the man of letters, the poet and the novelist, are in a situation dangerous for themselves and their readers. Tradition by itself is not enough; it must be perpetually criticized and brought up to date under the supervision of what I call orthodoxy....

It is the use of the term "supervision," as well as "orthodoxy," that carries with it the repressive and repugnant demand for doctrinal conformity.

Though there are no commonly accepted standards on which the writer can rely, the religious classicists are grievously wrong in their clamor for spiritual conformity. As D. S. Savage points out eloquently in his attack on T. S. Eliot in *The Personal Principle,* the religious classicist who seeks to unify society in the name of Christian orthodoxy replaces the commissar with the priest. Savage declares:

There is, indeed, little likelihood of a universal return to Orthodoxy, understood in the old, formal, conventional sense: no likelihood of a universal, traditional acceptance of Catholic Christianity with its external authority. That old kind of external authority, symbolized by the Pope with his dreaded power of excommunication, is gone for ever. Christianity itself is eternally true, but Christianity will have to be positively re-created within the lives of individuals in terms of personal experience, and this means going forward into creative freedom....

The accent here is on the precious principle of creative freedom. Regardless of the religious outlook a writer embraces—Buddhism, Protestantism, Judaism, Catholicism—he cannot, as a poet, sacrifice his creative autonomy to a set of orthodox doctrines. He must fight to discover his own truths, his own reality. It is not enough for him to acknowledge the externals of religion; he must undergo a spiritual crisis, a vivifying and transforming inner experience. The religious experience must be creatively assimilated before it can emerge in his work. In the case of Eliot, the religious propagandist has largely supplanted the poet, with the result that his writing, however mystically illuminated, has become speculative, abstract, vague, full of generalized imagery. In replacing art with supernatural morality as the standard of value, Eliot has submitted to a law which is the negation of creative freedom. In poetry, it is the vision, the creative insight, not the religious ideology, that counts supremely.

How different is the religious experience that W. H. Auden has undergone. Influenced by writers like Pascal, Kierkegaard, Kafka, and Charles Williams, he projects the sense of cosmic fear, the guilt that infects the present cultural situation. But his faith is never instinctive, rapturous, unquestioning; it is always in the process of becoming. He records his adventures on the long road to faith.

Auden has come far since the thirties when he preached a secular evangel compounded of Freudianism and Marxism. Now he maintains that one must do more than believe in original sin; one must also believe in Jesus Christ; otherwise Christianity is stripped of its essential content and meaning. One who believes in original sin without believing in the miracle of the redemption is using religion as an opiate. But religion in our time, if it is to be credible, must be invested with an existential aspect. Unfortunately, as Auden realizes, a purely existential attitude cannot be Christian. Only a madman, Auden declares, could seriously adopt atheist Existentialism. The logical outcome of such an Existentialist system is suicide.

In their return to the fold of orthodoxy, a number of contemporary poets go too far. The rediscovery of the values of Thomism is too often accompanied by a wholesale rejection of much in modern life that is spiritually vital and fortifying. The theology of crisis, as it is embodied in the work of some contemporary poets, represents a flight from life rather than a genuine transcendence. On many occasions T. S. Eliot writes as if history were a lost cause and secularism the road to damnation. Moreover, on what grounds can religious faith be formulated once and for all as a set of authoritative dogmas that must be universally accepted? If faith is not to become stagnant it must be perennially renewed, and that means opportunities for the expression of personal faith and vision, or of agnosticism, or of atheism even, must be kept open.

If the creative spirit of man is to find a voice, it is not necessary that it be tied umbilically to orthodoxy. Poetry, the expression of vision, is not doctrinaire in content. A poet may also serve creatively even if he fails to align himself with one of the institutional religions of the past. Heresy, too, has its uses, and even blasphemy may carry a message of profound spiritual import, as Eliot has himself conceded in his essay on Baudelaire. A writer who is alienated from formal Christianity may nevertheless express vital "religious" intuitions. Indeed, the most fruitful "religious" writings today are being done by men who are not inside the church, which has lost its position of prominence. As Amos N. Wilder, a Protestant critic, phrases it in *Modern Poetry and the Christian Tradition:* "The Spirit has continued to operate on the hearts of men outside the churches as well as within, through uncanonical as well as canonical channels." It is indisputably so. Here is a thoughtful critic who perceives the "religious" character of much contemporary literature, despite its seemingly nihilistic drift. Yet he fails to point out that while many poets outside the religious fold have come to grips with "theological" themes, they do so in radically untheological and untraditional ways.

This is not to say that poets who are still filled with the presence of God cannot continue to express that vision in their work. The vision of faith, if it constitutes a genuine spiritual experience, is as much an integral part of the substance of poetry as is the vision of the destructive element in contemporary life. But those writers who have abandoned the presuppositions on which Christian theology is based must of necessity reject the language and symbols of theology. Though poetry and "religion" are intimately related, the relationship turns out to be exceedingly complex. What we have been urging is that the imaginative power and aesthetic efficacy of a poem are not to be measured by its degree of doctrinal purity. Not that the poet, even when he seems to be iconoclastic, can throw off the cumulative impact of the past, the legacy bequeathed by his predecessors. Twentieth-century man is the end-product of a long process of cultural evolution, but he feels the full force of Arnold's conclusion in "Dover Beach," that he is on this planet as on a darkling plain "where ignorant armies clash by night." He has lost the language of faith, the language of prayer, with which to exorcise the demons of the Abyss. No longer can he worship the old gods or practice the rituals that were once so precious. Now he feels lost in empty space, a victim of time and death, cast out of eternity, chained to a life that does not seem to serve any meaningful purpose.

To be sure, even when the poet feels lost in the middle of life's journey, surrounded on all sides by darkness, he can communicate his "religious" apprehension of life. Poetry divorced from dogma can still voice this "religious" insight, even if it is only a perception of the numinous and the mysterious in life. It is when the theologian demands a type of poetry that embodies an orthodox view of salvation that he asks for more than poetry can legitimately give. For poetry cannot be specifically religious in content, for then it becomes moralistic, piously tractarian, and preachy. Poetry is alive and efficacious precisely because it cannot be confined within a narrow sector of doctrine. It escapes all categories of limitation, moral, political, or religious. Independent in spirit, it continues to explore the unknown and the deeper, refractory dimensions of the soul. It strives to give expression to the totality of human experience. That is how it manages to keep its vision of life fresh and uncorrupted.

Since he is neither a theological propagandist nor a priest, the poet instinctively rebels against any force which would exploit him for ends not inherent in his calling. His function is not to convert but to reveal. He writes not out of a body of fixed beliefs but out of his deeply felt vision of life. Some beliefs undoubtedly enter intimately into his perceptions, and he cannot very well keep them out entirely, but he struggles resolutely against the pull of theological doctrine. He does not wish to settle his accounts with the world and capture the secrets of eternity. On the contrary, he is enchanted with the phenomenal world, the flow of time, the stuff of human experience, human passion, human joy and sorrow. If in responding to the world of experience in all its immediacy and variousness he gives utterance to profoundly religious intuitions, these are not of an orthodox theological cast. Ingrained doubt as to the existence of God is today an inescapable condition of religious faith. The element of questioning intelligence, the note of challenging inquiry, the steady awareness of the complexity of experience, a knowledge of the revolutionary contributions made by a number of scientific disciplines—these must enter into the body of poetry if it is not to lapse into innocuous didacticism or sentimental religiosity. The modern poetic consciousness, as it unburdens itself of its charged sensibility, its deep sense of irony, its conception of change, cannot continue to exploit the myths and metaphors of a Christianity that is no longer relevant to the context of reality. The "religious" poet of our time must transcend the narrow limits of a creed and give free expression to his imaginative vision, even if this involves him in the dilemma of heresy.

Even the dedicated scholar who seeks to explore the realm of the invisible is "infected" with this germ of doubt. In *Studies of the Type-Image in Poetry, Religion, and Philosophy,* Maud Bodkin studies the dual image of God: Christ, the suffering savior, dying for mankind, and God the Omnipotent Judge and Father. But the images that man conjures up of the Divine are evidently not enough to save him from evil or spiritualize his life. Nevertheless, Maud Bodkin contends that man cannot live without the mediation of religious images, which will give expression to his relation to the invisible reality and to mankind. She discerns a divine plan that, despite all setbacks and frustrations, does get itself fulfilled. Hence there is a fundamental need for imagery that will give shape and substance to what may lie beyond the limits of life on earth, though she cannot get herself to believe that waking after death is a certainty. She thus arrives at the provisional affirmation "that the Divine source of our being is encountered by us through no single unique revelation, but individually by different modes of approach; and therefore the great need of our time, as concerns religion, is for sincerity in our faith, and, for the differing forms of others' faith, imaginative respect." The one thing to believe in is honesty of revelation, fidelity to the truth, however unattainable in practice. That is the only "faith" man can cling to in this dark hour when the gods are dethroned and the tables of old values smashed. Today man is faced with a crucial choice between a skepticism that remains sterile and absolute, incapable of rising to a dynamic affirmation of the creative potentialities of the spirit, but which nevertheless cannot be shaken off, and a skepticism that, after exhausting the possibilities of doubt, abandons the neurosis of denial for a faith that says Yea to life and that the mature mind can accept.

We must now examine more closely the nature of the paradox the poet faces when he attempts to compose religious poetry.

VIII

THE PARADOX OF RELIGIOUS POETRY

RELIGIOUS POETRY is actually a contradiction in terms, unless we mean by it poetry that is explicitly designed for purposes of indoctrination; but if that is the case it ceases to be poetry and becomes virtual dogma. Religious *poetry,* when the emphasis is placed on the noun and not the adjective (when, that is to say, poetry is cut off from the prescriptive requirements of dogma), communicates the depth and difficulty of the poet's struggle to achieve unity of faith in a universe that persistently balks such an effort. At the heart of the religious utterance, in poetry or drama or fiction of the twentieth century, is the awareness of the never-ending endeavor to hold on to a faith that is elusive and paradoxical, a faith that cannot be grasped cognitively or verified empirically, a faith that transcends the limitations of language—above all, a faith that must be perpetually renewed if it is not to perish. Strange as this may sound, the essence of the religious affirmation is best to be found in the conflict generated by the force of skepticism. Out of the dialectics of doubt, out of the crisis of negation in the dark night of the soul, rises the despairing or triumphant cry of faith. That is the process which lends tension and irony, ambiguity and complexity of insight, to its creative expression.

Was it otherwise in the past? Was the religious creative act one of pure devotion, a pious rehearsal of orthodoxy, an ecstatic commentary on divinely revealed texts, a series of hosannahs and hallelujahs, or possibly a versified exercise in homiletics? The dynamics of the creative process seem to point in an entirely different direction. In all literature that aspires to the universal and that seeks to bear the burden of the mystery, one discovers this ferment of doubt, this sense of fear and trembling before the hidden and inscrutable God, this tense awareness of the impossibility—and indeed absurdity—of the divine encounter, the despair of ever making clear in words the nature of the numinous experience. In the consciousness of man, the Devil forever challenges God to combat; Ormuzd and Ahriman are eternally locked in battle; good is arrayed against evil, light against darkness, heaven against hell. Ceaselessly the war continues between a faith that cannot be justified by reason and a lack of faith that cannot be lived.

What we must begin with, then, is the assumption that poetry, whatever its content, secular or sacred, must be approached primarily as poetry. That is the first essential criterion. Whatever other virtues it may possess stem from this fundamental quality: its incarnation as poetry. Hence adjectival qualifications, whether political or religious in nature, are alien to the consideration of poetry per se. It is possible, of course, to examine "scientific" poetry or didactic poetry or the use of the Eucharistic symbol or the image of the dynamo or the concept of relativity in poetry and emerge with some highly interesting correlations. But is there any justification for the study of religious poetry in any other sense except the poetic? Though a knowledge of the religious background does help to illuminate the meaning of the *Divine Comedy*, shall we judge the greatness of Dante's poetry by its degree of conformity to Thomistic doctrine? If Poe fulminated against the heresy of the didactic, against the attempt to make poetry subserve such abstractions as Truth and Duty, he would, logically, also have objected strenuously to the heresy of the religious. Hence the paradoxical conclusion that all religious poetry, despite its subject matter, is "secular" in meaning.

The paradox as well as the tautology of the above statement needs to be explained. The realm of "spirit" lies outside the reach of the creative imagination. If it is to be captured and communicated, it can only be done by means of dramatic suggestions, pregnant hints, audacious metaphors, sensory images, and a system of what Baudelaire called symbolic correspondences. The "spirit," in other words, must be brought down to earth, given flesh and blood, body and roots and a local habitation, before it can be comprehended. If this interpretation be correct, then dogma never makes its appearance in genuine poetry, or if it does it ceases to be dogma and becomes pure vision. For example, the Incarnation of Christ, the sacrifice of the body of the Son of God, has already become symbolically transfigured. The God is pictured as man and the dream of suffering and sacrifice is translated into mythic, poignantly human terms. It is no longer a question, on the poet's part, of remaining loyal to dogma; the symbolism the Christian poet uses implies a recapture of the original vision, the terrible re-enactment of the Passion, with all its haunting contradictions and tragic mysteries. Otherwise the poet is simply echoing an established but spiritually lapsed tradition.

Such an interpretation is challenged by those critics who treat religious poetry as if it were indeed a vehicle of religious values. Malcolm Mackenzie Ross, in *Poetry and Dogma,* a study of the transfiguration of Eucharistic symbols in seventeenth-century English poetry, frankly states his belief "that the dogmatic symbol may inform and sustain the poetic symbol as such without losing its proper dogmatic identity and without tyrannizing the specifically poetic process." In this statement, which is obviously intended to apply to all poetry, we behold a curious confusion of immiscible categories: the theological and the aesthetic, the dogmatic and the poetic. Let us grant for the sake of the argument that the Christian poet, whether of the seventeenth or the twentieth century, *believes,* but once he puts on his singing robes he is not concerned with the formally integrated body of his beliefs. He is not, after all, composing a tract. What is he doing? Whatever any poet does when engaged in the travail of creation. He is venturing into the unknown, seeking to body forth an experience in all its sensuous immediacy.

John Donne, despite the intense sincerity of the religious convictions which he took for granted, repeatedly questions the implicit truths of faith. He is tensely aware that the "new Philosophy calls all in doubt." When Hopkins composed "God's Grandeur," he was not thinking of the *Spiritual Exercises* of St. Ignatius. He was beholding a radiant vision of the world charged with "the grandeur of God." He was intoxicated by his mystical glimpse of the freshness that lives "deep down things," of "the last lights off the black West," and of the Holy Ghost brooding over the bent world "with warm breast and with ah! bright wings." If the affirmation rings out clear and deep, it nevertheless recognizes the distressing fact that men are not responsive to the divine beauty immanent in the universe. The undercurrent of despair in the poem lends poignancy and power to the poet's celebration of the glory and divine meaning present in all things. The second- or third-rate poet may play ingenious variations on the traditional dogmas that were once vital intuitions, but the major poet goes to the fountainhead of the living symbol, reaches out boldly to the vision of reality in all its refractory mysteriousness.

The poem as an organically complete and autonomous world abhors the intrusion of dogma. Certainly poetry is charged with vibrations of meaning that extend beyond the domain of the strictly aesthetic, but these are set in motion and achieve efficacy only through the poetic medium. The religious critic is therefore mistaken in seeking to judge poetry by religious rather than aesthetic standards. In *Poetry and Dogma*, Ross argues that Christian poetry is of necessity rooted in dogmatic religion—a point of view that is controverted by Amos Wilder's *Modern Poetry and the Christian Tradition*. Ross contends that "Christianity demands of the believer a certain precision of belief." But can it legitimately demand the same *precision of belief* on the part of the poet? Must the symbols he incorporates in his work bear this stamp of dogma? This is to confuse poetry with apologetics and to turn the poet into a kind of inspired but orthodox dogmatist. What this categorical demand leaves out of account is that every religious utterance, at least in poetry, is hedged round with doubt and besieged by the dangers of heresy. Primarily concerned with making a poem, the poet does not adopt symbols by first testing their degree of theological orthodoxy. The Christian critic who insists that religious poetry must achieve this precision of belief is not unlike the Marxist critic who maintains that poetry must remain basically revolutionary in orientation.

If the God the poet celebrates is a hidden God, then the poet can only resort to the language of paradox to suggest His being, and even so the divine essence is transformed into the humanly perceived. Such a transformation of vision beyond the power of words to express is inevitable—first, because words are neither things nor essences; and second, because it is the creative imagination, finite and earth-trammeled, that serves as the medium of expression. There again we behold the contradiction already alluded to: the poet fights a losing battle in seeking to give life and form to that which is spirit and consequently beyond conceptualization. He can do no more than stammer forth the few syllables that describe his ineffable experience with the divine. Between the human and the divine, between God and man, there is no ground of commensurability, no intelligible means of communication. Who, by means of language however soaring and inspired, can bridge the gulf fixed between heaven and earth, time and eternity?

Hence poetry and mysticism in its extreme form are actually incompatible. Blake, a supremely religious poet, worked without the support of a theistic tradition. Relying on mythology for his poetic vision, he pictured God in the image of man. According to Mark Schorer in *William Blake:* "Blake was the most thorough of anthropocentrists: heaven and hell and 'all deities' are within man; heaven consists in his capacities fulfilled, hell of his capacities denied, and God, created in man's image, is the sum of all his potentialities."

When the poet dispenses, as did Blake, with the traditional conceptions of God, he avoids one danger only to fall into another. The best example of the dilemma thus created—a challenge to the

poet's mythopoeic powers—is to be found in Hardy's curious decision to use the neutral "It" in order to designate the power that
runs through the universe. Obviously, this, too, is a symbol of
transcendence, though it has been shorn of all its supernal glory.
The image of God has now lost its archetypal appeal; it has been
turned into a scientifically neutral, disembodied term, a semantic-
ally sterile word, lacking in those overtones of suggestiveness and
unutterable mysteriousness and awe that reside in the image
of God. To transform God into an "It" is to strip God of his godhood. Science, the murderer of God, thus deprives the poetic enterprise of one of its most potent symbols, one of its most fruitful
archetypal images.

But the difference between addressing an It and a Thou is
radical and absolute. When Hardy speaks of God as It, he does
more than effect a transvaluation of values; he brings about a revolution of consciousness. Hardy is not even blasphemous; he does not
say that God does not exist; he is simply finished with all talk of
God. What he confronts is a blind force, a mechanical universe that
is informed with neither purpose nor consciousness. A seeker after
the truth, he concludes that God, the creation of man, is but a myth.
How could he take refuge in the traditional systems of faith or
console himself with belief in an afterlife? The First Cause, whatever its nature, was neither good nor evil but unmoral. It is these
obstinate and often despairing questionings of ultimate issues that
the poets of our time cannot escape.

That is why, in creating his work, the poet is concerned not
with dogma but with concrete, sensuous experience. Committed
to no rigid framework of religious or political or philosophical
values, he is free to respond to any aspect of life's infinite variety;
he does not exclude his reaction to the enigma of existence, his
perception of the sacredness as well as mysteriousness of the
energy pulsing in the veins of the universe. That is how he transcends the limits of his individual being and feels a kinship with a
power that is infinitely greater than the self. Yet some phases of
the religious experience present a formidable, perhaps insuperable,

difficulty for the poet, since that which lies beyond the apprehension of sense cannot be voiced in language that is sensory. How can the poet, no matter how gifted, give expression to the Absolute? How can man visualize the Wholly Other or sum up in finite and faltering words the nature of the Godhead?

Hence whatever religious symbols find embodiment in poetry do not achieve, and are not intended to achieve, a direct representation. No symbol can possibly furnish a literal picture of the unseen and therefore unprovable world. This explains in large measure why religious symbols in poetry are rooted in contradictions and ambiguity, both affirming and denying at the same time, remaining fluid, protean, never fixed, in meaning. What sustains these symbols, which cannot be taken literally, and gives them profound meaning is the vision that gave them birth, the mystical sense of union with the ground of all being, the immediate, overwhelming sense of Something There. What the symbolism attempts to do is to suggest the sense of transcendence, but transcendence here implies a numinous connotation, a feeling of reverence. Thus implicit in religious symbolism, in the lyrics of, say, Traherne or Donne, is an ontology, a basic metaphysical distinction between appearance and reality, the relative and the absolute, the finite and the infinite. What lends a specifically religious tone or atmosphere to this attitude is precisely this feeling of awe before the Wholly Other. Sartre, the philosophical atheist, calls this Nausea; Rudolf Otto describes it as the sense of the numinous; Hardy defines it as the impersonal It; for the religious poet it is a Thou, the radiant voice and visage of God.

The poet, however, is under the necessity of casting about for appropriate means of symbolizing that which does not lend itself to embodiment in words. The best he can do, as we have said, is to depend on analogy, indirection, suggestiveness, paradox, ambiguity, and symbolism. The creative problem is rendered even more difficult in the case of the modern poet who has lost the suffusing sense of the divine and can no longer, like Hopkins, feel God's grandeur, the reality of God's presence pervading all things. His faith, when he struggles to give it form, takes on the character of an existential contest, an experience that is paradoxical and essentially incommunicable. The religious experience is, by definition, ineffable. Was it not Kierkegaard who insisted that the finite can never be made into a vehicle for mediating the reality of the transcendent? How can man presume to commune with God? But if God is hidden, then how does he reveal himself and how can man penetrate the divine mystery?

The poet, we take it, is free to deal with any aspect of reality, psychic or material, external or internal, but this "reality" forever eludes formulation. If he perceives the world in the light of the "religious" vision, if he beholds symbols of the numinous in a flower rooted in a crannied wall, then his task is to lift that experience to the plane of poetry. But his poetry, however revelatory, will not take on the vestments of dogma. Blake is perhaps the best example of the truly religious poet whose purity of vision saves him from any trace of theological didacticism, the vice of mistaking bloodless abstractions for genuine experience. Thus he achieves lyrical moments of incandescent expression, poetry that is luminous and prophetic, when he discovers the mystery incarnate in a grain of sand and hears the music of eternity in the flickering passage of a second. That is the fundamental point: religion when it enters the body of poetry throws off the formal restrictions of creed. Since the poetic utterance is born of inner tension, the ambiguity resident in all experience, the poet is compelled to use the language of paradox, compose lines that both affirm and deny, doubt and believe. The Epilogue of *The Gates of Paradise* concludes with the lines:

> Tho' thou art Worship'd by the Names Divine
> Of Jesus & Jehovah: thou art still
> The Son of Morn in weary Night's decline
> The lost Traveller's Dream under the Hill.

In this quatrain Blake is saying that the idea man has of God represents only a projection of himself. Though it is called by many a holy name, Blake considered this projected image the enemy of man, an epiphenomenon of the mind, the dream of the traveler who has lost his way. In interpreting these lines, George Wingfield Digby, in *Symbol and Image in William Blake,* declares that Blake was aware "that reality, or God, is beyond idea and form. The projection, the Spectre, has to be realized and so overthrown.... This is the cardinal idea in all Blake's writing and in all his art."

This approach to the function of religious awareness is well stated by Philip Wheelwright in his article, "The Semantic Approach to Myth." Expressive language, unlike the language of logical discourse, is characterized by the quality of polarity; it attempts to do justice to the ambivalence of human attitudes. Here is the crucial key to the semantic complexity of poetic expression, since in every affirmation the poet makes there is implicit an element of doubt and denial. The same holds true of such "prose poems" as novels. In the world of Dostoevski, as Irving Howe makes clear in *Politics and the Novel,* the combination of skepticism and orthodoxy, mysticism and doubt, piety and atheism, constitutes a dynamic source of internal tension. For the larger affirmations, as Wheelwright points out,

touch upon the radical mystery of things, which forever eludes our intellectual grasp. There are two ways of affirming such a sentence as "God created the world." It can be affirmed dogmatically, as a declarative without any interrogative aspects; or it can be affirmed with a fitting intellectual modesty, in which case the declarative and the interrogative will be blended as inseparably as the complex and convex aspects of a single curve. For, to assert it as a pure statement is to imply, "There was a question, but the question is now answered, and there is no longer a question." But this can be the case only if the sentence, "God created the world," is essentially intelligible—that is, only if "God," "original creation," and "world" carry meanings that we can put the finger on and say, somewhere in experience, "That is it!" And since this condition—the adequate verification of a transcendental idea by the finite evidence of human experience—cannot possibly be met, it is equally impossible that the sentence, "God created the world," should be a pure statement. To assert it as such is therefore self-delusive.... Religiously considered, the sentence employs theological terms symbolically in order to express the radical inseparability of meaningfulness and mystery.

Though this is a general analysis of the problem at issue, it does apply strikingly to the poetic enterprise. For how is the poet to express this radical inseparability of meaningfulness and mystery, how fuse these disparate, contradictory elements into a single, organically fitting utterance that makes up a poem? How can he write symbolically and communicate the depth of feeling and commitment inherent in his faith without verging on the declarative and the dogmatic? In brief, how can he affirm meaning without denying mystery? This problem is treated at great length in Wheelwright's book, *The Burning Fountain,* in which he seeks to keep linguistically open the truth-possibilities of religion, metaphysics, and poetry. This enables us to get to the heart of the matter: is there a truth-function in poetry? What does "truth" mean in such a context? Suppose the poet believes in God and believes that his belief is a true one? He bases his belief on the evidence of his spiritual experience, though he knows that no laboratory technique can possibly confirm the existence of God. He is dealing with a kind of experience that is beyond operational measurement. Wheelwright is willing to take the moral risk of affirming that the statement, "God exists," is meaningful, even though the truth it embodies transcends the possibility of empirical verification.

An influential critic like T. S. Eliot makes the religious emphasis primary in his interpretation of poetry. Protesting against the tendency to make poetry a substitute for religion, he urges that religion has the power to vitalize and fructify poetry. In an age of unstable belief, the poet must come to the realization that tradition is not enough; "it must be perpetually criticized and brought up to date under the supervision of what I call orthodoxy." It is the use of the term "supervision" that strikes an ominous note. If Hopkins achieved a major accent in poetry, it is, according to Eliot, because he had behind him the authority of the church and was therefore in closer touch with "reality." How much truth is there in this point of view?

It should be no more a cause of surprise that a Jesuit is capable of reaching the highest peaks of song than that a Shelley or a Hardy could pour out his heart in impassioned but disenchanted song. If we are at all astonished by Hopkins' remarkable achievement, it is because we realize that as a Jesuit he was handicapped by the orthodoxies of his order. If he succeeds in his lyrical flights, he succeeds despite these limitations. One of the few truly religious poets who have profoundly influenced modern poetry, Hopkins left a body of writing which is drained of that which Eliot finds so objectionable, the element of personality, but his triumphs of artistry are displayed best in those poems that reveal his struggle to transcend the doubt and affirm the faith; they reflect the anxiety and agony of the lonely, finite soul confronting God. Hopkins knew that the mind has mountains and chasms, frightful "cliffs of fall," no-man fathomed. How heart-rendingly does the sonnet, "Not, I'll not, carrion comfort, Despair, not feast on thee," describe the poet "wrestling with (my God!) my God." Few poets have given more piercing expression to the metaphysical desolation of the believer as he struggles to overcome the radical incommensurability of meaningfulness and mystery. In describing these moments when he feels utterly forsaken, in recording his search for God, Hopkins rises above theological considerations. What speaks through him is the religious consciousness that suffers from a deep division of the soul. Whereas his soul sought to bind itself to the supernatural, his poetic instinct drew him like a magnet to the sensuous or natural order.

If we are justified in drawing a distinction between the religious experience (as described, for example, by William James in *The Varieties of Religious Experience* or by Rudolf Otto in *The Idea of the Holy*), then it follows that as soon as religion is formalized into ritual and dogma, it loses much of its original vitality. Theology codifies as Holy Writ what first came as personal vision and revelation. God cannot be imprisoned within theological walls.

As soon as he is fettered to dogma, he ceases to be the authentic God; his voice is silent. Religion thus begins in a mystery which in turn drives inquiring man, in co-operation with his like-minded fellow-men, to build a house of worship for the spirit, a sanctuary of hallowed meanings and sacred traditions. The believer seeks to translate this vision of the transcendent into some mode of worship whereby he can pay reverence to the holiness of the energy that runs through the universe. But this experience of transcendence is interpreted in a variety of ways by the spirit of man. Who shall say that one way of apprehending the divine ground of being is the truth and all other ways are forms of blindness and heresy? Certainly the poetic mind is not the dogmatic mind, for it responds to the world's body in all its varied forms of charged beauty.

Moreover, this world that the poet contemplates is a carrier of cultural meanings as well as sensuous beauty. When Nietzsche proclaimed the death of the Christian God, the unity of Western culture was disrupted, and new sources of spiritual integration had to be found. In literature this meant not only a severe break with the values of the past but also a revolutionary reconsideration of the metaphysical bases of the writer's vision. Deprived of God, the writer today must undertake his search for salvation under secular rather than sacred auspices, for he cannot cure himself of the pandemic disease of doubt. Once the Christian mythos loses its efficacy as an object of absolute faith, then the supernatural becomes for the poet merely a literary convention, a metaphor, a myth. No writer of our time who has been exposed to the teachings of Darwin, Freud, Dewey, Russell, Carnap, and Einstein can hope to recapture the medieval intensity of faith in the supernatural. The revival of interest in the work of Kierkegaard serves but to reinforce the impression that doubt in our age is universal. The foundations of religious faith have been sapped. The strenuous attempts of Christian apologists to revive the faith so that it will once more impregnate the body of modern literature have not borne much fruit.

We have thus far tried to show why modern as well as

seventeenth-century poetry, infected with the indwelling germ of doubt, has been gradually cut off from the traditional sources of belief. Today in particular the poet cannot depend upon a common background of spiritual values. That is one of the reasons why he feels so impoverished and why his utterances sound so ineffectual. If in the Middle Ages poets affirmed their mystical intuitions with passionate conviction it is because they believed in them profoundly; these represented a higher, absolute truth; whatever marginal doubts bedeviled their consciousness, they were inwardly convinced that their religious beliefs were more than psychologically consoling fictions or anthropomorphic illusions. But man today dwells in a mechanized universe, trapped in a nature that is alien as well as inscrutable. Moreover, the modern poet is bound to perceive that there is no correspondence between correctness of belief and the greatness of the literary product. Is Shelley an inferior poet simply because he rooted himself in science? Is Robinson Jeffers a lesser poet because he rejected the teachings of Christianity?

Yet how account for the fact that some poets, revolting against the scientific dispensation, have returned to orthodoxy? The old religious symbols were potent because they were active engines of influence and belief, whereas the disillusioned modern poet assumes that life, a mechanical nightmare, is played out and the death of civilization assured. For a time, to be sure, the motif of negation proved heartening since it meant the relinquishment of empty theological conventions, but the continued rejection of life culminated in a kind of spiritual suicide. One recalls the nostalgic but despairing quest of Henry Adams, after his disillusionment with a science whose symbol of force was the dynamo, to discover the secret of the energy called forth in the Middle Ages by the Virgin Mary. Hence some contemporary poets flee from despair by attaching themselves to some positive religious dogma, but they do so by progressively losing their grip on society. In *The Making of a Poem,* Stephen Spender rightly points out that the creative imagination cannot be restored to a position of prominence by the reinstatement of orthodox religion. For the world of science cannot be pushed aside by a mystical faith. Even if the poet returns to dogma, he must come to perceive that the dogma lies outside the province of poetry. "The really important distinction today," Stephen Spender declares, "is not between different creeds but between believing and not believing. Beliefs put man at the centre of his poetry; materialism makes him an illustrator of a system outside the poetry."

The spiritual dereliction of modern man, the distress he suffers because he is alienated from God, is best illustrated by a philosopher like Heidegger. His nihilistic ontology brings into focus the crisis of thought in Western culture. Night has fallen over the world and there is no possibility of a Second Coming. There is no god who can unite men and give the world the radiance of meaning. Instead of God, we are given the concept of Nothingness. Nihilism has thus become a sovereign power, a ruling principle of thought, the determinant of man's fate. How, under such intellectual auspices, can faith be maintained? Even though the poet tries to affirm his faith, the nihilistic infection persists. How can he tell that he genuinely believes? In *Reason and Existenz*, Karl Jaspers points out the interesting contradiction that though Kierkegaard achieved faith, his victory represented a negation of the world. Though Kierkegaard sought to breathe life into the dead bones of the old theology, his art, declares Jaspers, seems like that "of perhaps a nonbeliever, forcing himself to belief." An epoch of reflection was marked by an absence of faith: "Rejecting faith and forcing oneself to believe belong together. The godless can appear to be a believer; the believer can appear as godless; both stand in the same dialectic." And the dialectic is one of indefeasible doubt, one of incurable negation. Hence the difficulty, spiritual as well as aesthetic, the poet encounters when he tries to affirm a coherent religious outlook.

Nevertheless, modern poets cast about desperately for symbols which have sufficient life in them to replace the lost God. For what generative power can they derive from the Heideggerian myth of Nothingness? Thrown upon his own resources in an age that is badly fragmented, the poet must endeavor to work out his own values. The traditional Christian teachings no longer provide a solid foundation for meaning and are no longer containers of collective faith. The serpent of doubt has driven the children of Adam out of the Garden of Eden, symbol of the old instinctive and universal innocence of faith. Stripped of its efficacy, the Christian myth has lost its power of binding people together in the sacrament of faith. Consequently many writers in our age have become divorced not only from the church but from the Christian tradition as well. But they have paid a high price for this severance, for their world now lacks a central unifying principle.

Those who make the attempt to revive the Christian mythos do so, curiously enough, through the instrumentality of reason. They cannot infuse their writing with the spontaneous passion and immediacy of faith; their poetry, as is true notably of T. S. Eliot's writings after his conversion to Anglo-Catholicism, remains largely abstract and metaphysical. If the Incarnation, as Stuart Holyrod maintains in *Emergence from Chaos,* lies at the heart of the meditations in *Four Quartets,* then Eliot's effort to voice the mystery of the Incarnation is in vain. The words stumble and falter and lose form and precision:

> The hints half guessed, the gift half understood, is Incarnation.
> Here the impossible union
> Of spheres of existence is actual,
> Here past and future
> Are conquered and reconciled.

Yeats, however, rejected the Bible as a source of revelation and decided he could not use the Christian tradition in his work. He had to depend on his personal vision, his privately developed myth. This illustrates the frustrating position the modern poet finds himself in: deprived of a religious myth that can inform his work and command his assent, he must nevertheless continue his search for God. But the world he lives in is too chaotic to give birth to a unifying, salvationary myth. Though some poets continue to invoke the old sacred names and religious concepts, they incorporate them inevitably within ironic contexts. The religious experience has become intellectualized, a springboard for psychoanalytic specula- tion or metaphysical analysis. The poets cannot affirm their belief wholeheartedly, since their consciousness and their culture cut them off from all possibility of communion with God.

The demand of the religious-minded spokesmen for conformity on the part of the poets is bound to fail. That is not how creativeness will be restored to the ailing body of poetry. The church, whatever message of redemption it may offer its communicants, is not the home of the Muses; neither the priest nor the commissar can prescribe the cure for the sick arts and letters of our age. Authority in the realm of poetic art cannot be imposed from above. In the end, the poet must rely on his own sensibility, his own sources of experience, his personal vision. The only truth he can shadow forth is one that he has felt and lived. It is not enough for him formally to acknowledge or intellectually to accept the tenets of Christianity. The religious experience must be creatively assimilated and then imaginatively embodied. There is no substitute for the primary, inner vision. What is more, the will to believe is the very opposite of faith. It is manifestly dangerous for the poet to take his theology—or his philosophy—from some authoritarian source and give up the attempt to judge for himself in a spirit of creative freedom.

The religious vision needs no propagandists. It exists, and those who have caught this vision will speak out. But the truly religious poet of our time shares the doubts of his age and affirms his beliefs despite them. Transcending the Heideggerian myth of Nothingness, he can partake of the numinous experience of com- munion with Nature that is beyond the power of words to utter. He can voice hints of the mystery which clothes itself inevitably in the language of paradox. If this be a myth he embraces, it is for him nonetheless true, for it is by means of this affirmative faith, this mystical perception of the oneness of life, that he is able not only to live meaningfully but to create. In ultimate issues of this kind, he can hope to receive no guarantee of empirical validity. He clings to his belief in God despite all the evidence that reason can muster that He does not exist. The paradox of religious poetry is that when it is explicitly doctrinaire or dogmatic, it ceases to be poetry. The poetic essence is lost because the vision that should have nourished the expression has been left out. The best the poet can do, in endeavoring to communicate in language the nature of his religious experience, is to rely on paradox and analogy, metaphor and myth, ambiguity and indirection. That is how the Ground of Being, whatever be the name by which it is called, the eternally hidden and ubiquitous, the ineffable, enters into the rhythms and textures of meaning in poetic expression.

IX

POETRY, SCIENCE, AND RELIGION

OBVIOUSLY THE POET who merely appropriates the codified knowledge and dry abstractions of science is in as bad a situation as the one who devoutly versifies the dogmas of theology. If science is attacked, as it has been for the past three centuries, by literary critics, poets, metaphysicians, and theologians, it is because the world-view that science logically entails or seems to support is mechanistic. If man is part of nature, if he functions like a machine, then all talk of spirit or of God or of free will is so much nonsense. And how, in a nightmarish universe of energy, can the poet justify his creative labor on either prophetic or aesthetic grounds? Cut off from the realm of empirical truth, which is under the exclusive jurisdiction of science, he is restricted in his art to the lyrical utterance of pseudo-statements, vital fictions, and imaginative myths. If the scientific method is furiously assailed, it is because once it becomes the basis for a philosophy of life, it begins to generate the seeds of infidelity.

Not that the naturalistic explanation of the universe is without its limitations and even contradictions. No philosophy the mind of man devises answers all questions. A positivist like Freud could declare: "The moment one inquires about the sense or value of life one is sick, since objectively neither of them has any existence." But surely that is no answer. What does Freud mean by "existence"?

The poet is driven endlessly to question the value of life, and the prophets have done so consistently through the ages. The Christian heritage still lives on, and there are many who, under its influence, would vastly prefer to believe in divine revelation. A philosopher like H. J. Paton, in *The Modern Predicament*, declares: "Those who cannot base their morality on divine revelation seek to base it instead on scientific revelation. There is no scientific revelation; but if we have to choose, it is obviously more rational to believe in divine revelation." This at least represents a commitment of belief, but who is qualified to interpret the dictates of divine wisdom, the meaning of revelation? Even the theologians are agreed on one point: no finally convincing proof on rational grounds can be furnished for the existence of God. Today the tradition of skepticism cannot simply be dismissed as a sinful aberration.

If the assumptions of science have been repeatedly challenged by the poets, it is not because they are qualified to undertake the difficult task of refutation. If they were drawn inevitably into a battle not of their choosing, it is because they could not as poets reconcile themselves to living in a universe governed by mechanical laws. Here was scientism, a new secular "religion," which demolished the beliefs central to religion and shattered their faith in the autonomy, if not sacredness, of their calling. In turning against science, they rejected a fruitful source of understanding which could have given poetry a new lease on life. How can the poet be harmed by the new knowledge science provides about the nature of man? For what he deals with are not facts or theories but new ways of observing the phenomena of nature, new ways of arriving at a more enlightened understanding of human nature in all its baffling complexity. He is not called upon to embrace some system of scientific orthodoxy or even to incorporate its technical vocabulary within his work. In fact, he does not commit himself to any philosophy or faith; the materials of experience, of which scientific insight presents one facet, are imaginatively transmuted in his poetry. The consequences of such a transvaluation of values are now plainly visible in the writing of a number of twentieth-century poets.

For orthodox faith has been forced to yield ground. The modern poet can no longer root himself in a common faith, be an integral part of a collectively sanctioned religious myth. Now that religion has lost its traditional authority, the supernatural bases of morality are taken away. In *Science and English Poetry,* Douglas Bush points to the revolutionary transformation wrought in our age by the passing of the gods, the loss of faith in immortality and in the teachings of Christianity. If the natural man and the scientifically disclosed picture of the universe are the sole realities, then what is the heaven to which man, stripped of a soul, shall aspire? "The poet, and man in general," Douglas Bush writes, "might ask what, if the religious quest is not a main object in the human adventure, we are to go forward to—a utopia of gadgets, a heaven of abstract cerebration, 'a scientific morality,' or universal destruction."

The objection raised is a familiar one. What ultimate ideal shall replace the absolute values that orthodox religion once embodied? That is indeed the problem with which the modern poet has had to struggle. The intellectuals of our time suffer, as we have seen, from the Pascalian terror of the abyss, the Kierkegaardian "sickness of soul," the anguish which stems from confronting a nature that is neutral, mechanical, indifferent to their needs and desires. They have had to surrender their illusion of cosmic importance. They can no longer accept the religious ideals that their forebears believed to be eternally true. But if, as is often asserted, the poetic imagination requires a vital myth to sustain it, what is this myth to be? What are the spiritual realities which the poet can genuinely believe? Douglas Bush is perfectly correct in saying that "All modern poetry has been conditioned by science, even those areas that seem farthest removed from it." No poet can escape this conditioning; it is part of the air he breathes, the ideas that constitute the vocabulary of his mind, the life he lives from day to day. He may feel that scientism has reached a peak of unprecedented barbarism and is about to plunge civilization in ruins, but he cannot in this crisis seriously offer a solution by reviving a number of theological dogmas or seek, like Niebuhr, to rehabilitate the doctrine of Original Sin.

In the twentieth century, the conception of man as born in the image of God or tainted incurably by original sin has largely vanished. Stripped of his faith in immortality, modern man perceives that he is but an atom of energy in space; he knows for certain that the stars blindly run; he can appeal to no providential deity to justify all the terrible evils of existence. How different is this world-picture from the one which prevailed during the medieval period which relied on the purely religious method of apprehending the infinitely diverse phenomena of nature and of life, a method concerned not with scientific truth but with the salvation of man. The medieval poet could use religious symbols naturally and spontaneously, for these symbols then carried universal conviction. The Elizabethan age, too, clung to a faith in a presiding God from whom all things flow and who is the source to which all things return. Yet it was in the Renaissance that there first emerged with challenging distinctness the conception of a life rooted in this earth and measured entirely by this-world standards of achievement and fulfilment. Once some Renaissance writers ceased to believe literally in a system of rewards and punishments in a life everlasting after death, their attitude toward themselves and their culture underwent a drastic change. The idea of Kingdom Come was no longer situated in some heavenly aftermath, but within the confines of life in the present. Now that man knows himself to be alone, he feels the full force of the injunction that others be judged with boundless compassion, since all are leagued together in a solidarity of suffering, bound by the common destiny of death. Since he is now the measure of all things, he cannot trouble deaf heaven with his bootless cries.

This, as we have noted, is the problem that has beset writers for the past three centuries. How can man live alone, without putting his reliance on God? How can he proceed on his brief and perilous journey to the end of darkness, depending solely on his own resources? How can he dwell in a world that is full of contingency and uncertainty, realizing as he does that death is the final end? His reason tells him that he must make his peace with these intolerable conditions; but it is reason, as was the case with Pascal and Kierkegaard, that is aware of its own impotence. For good or evil, whether he likes it or not, modern man cannot go home again; he cannot recapture the spontaneous faith of the past. He can no longer cling to the myth of the fall of man nor can he look upon life on this minor planet as an epic struggle between the forces of good and evil.

He does not abandon the religious outlook without regret, for with its passing he has lost something precious and perhaps irreplaceable. For it made life seem meaningful, part of a universal design, and it affirmed the dignity of man. But this theocentric world-view has had to be abandoned, and man now stands alone. If he were free to choose a cosmology on the basis of its consolatory value, without regard to its validity, then the faith of the Middle Ages would seem to satisfy every human need and aspiration. It was certainly suited to bring out the full range of Dante's genius. But no such freedom to choose is at present available. Skepticism in our time is "normal" and inevitable. Today man cannot blind himself to the knowledge of his biologic origin, his organic relation to nature, his evolutionary past. Indeed, it is questionable if in any age, even during a period when theological absolutism prevailed, the foremost creative minds were entirely free from the germ of doubt. Wherever God has reigned in the Western world, the Devil walked the earth.

For every age, in its struggle to achieve order, is an unstable configuration of conflicting impulses. In the eighteenth century, when rationalism was dominant, the currents of irrationality flowed freely, and the abnormally acute sensibility of a Rousseau, for example, stands in opposition to the intellectual temper of the time. Newton had indicated that the cosmos was subject to universal, invariant laws, and the eighteenth century felt that this was a wonderful revelation, the manifestation of divine wisdom. The divine plan was confirmed by the scientific demonstration of universal law. But with the emergence of the romantic revolt, the conception of uniform laws and unalterable nature was given up, for the poets perceived that man is surrounded by mysteries which cannot be resolved by the aid of reason alone. Hence much of romantic poetry rebelled against the Newtonian universe and the tyranny of the laws of science. Science failed to exhibit the grandeur of man and the majesty of God's work. Mathematical formulas and mechanistic interpretations destroyed the sense of life's ultimate mystery. Hence the poets repudiated a mechanistic rationalism that meant the death of the creative spirit.

The twentieth-century poet has traveled far from the Wordsworthian or Tennysonian intimations of immortality. Even if he has not studied quantum theory, he tends to view the world through the perspective of the space-time continuum. He has seen how matter has been dematerialized, reduced to a phantom flux of energy. He is familiar with the theory of relativity which postulates a universe in which the observer is himself involved. Reality, when it is observed within the framework of time-and-space, thus takes on new configurations.

Let us see how a modern American poet, Robinson Jeffers, who is friendly rather than hostile to science, deals with the religious issue in his work. Because he repudiates the Christian God and the Christian hierarchy of values, Jeffers has been denounced by many critics as the voice of anti-Christ, though Radcliffe Squires, in *The Loyalties of Robinson Jeffers,* hails him as "probably the most deeply religious of all twentieth-century American poets." This is no display of paradox. The truly religious poet of our time is least of all orthodox. His religiosity comes out in the uncompromising intensity of his quest, even in the violence of his negation. He cannot resist the call of truth, however ugly and unpleasant it may sound to the ear of the masses. Jeffers early abandoned the Christian humanism of his father. In "Meditation on Saviors," he replies to those who turn to the Christian

God for salvation. "The apes of God," he declares, "lift up their hands to praise love," whereas naked power is in the saddle. He pictures "the young Jew writhing on the doomed hill in the earthquake," sacrificing himself out of love for the people, for this religious obsession is actually a sickness. Where, then, is peace to be found, what is the solution? The people demand a blood-sacrifice, a crucifixion, before they are ready to believe; they know not that the promise of peace awaits them at the end, when they will sink into oceanic unconsciousness, be merged with the heart of Nature, become one with stone and dust, storm and mist and the tides of the sea. They have experienced a brief, flashing moment of consciousness before returning, as they must, to the primordial fountain.

What Jeffers, one of the tormented prophets of our age, urgently counsels is detachment. To become involved in the contemporary madhouse, to be consumed with pity for the suffering masses, to join in the saturnalia of blood-letting—that is the way of destruction. Beholding man caught fast in the trap of illusion, Jeffers preaches a gospel of Inhumanism. Suffering at least serves the purpose of reducing the ferocity of the will to live and finally makes possible the renunciation of life. Combating the disease of introspection, the malady of self-love, Jeffers points to consciousness as the sickness that drives man to destruction, and self-love as the mark of a declining civilization. Lonely and frightened in the starry spaces, the people in their distress turn pitifully to saviors, prepared to believe in anything.

Rejecting the Calvinistic belief in the innate depravity of man, Jeffers cannot believe in either salvation or damnation in a life after death. No hope of immortality sustains any of his characters. Though stricken with guilt, his principal characters have no expectation that they will be punished in an afterlife; but the awareness of their guilt remains, and they crave to be cleansed. That is why they suffer so excruciatingly: because there is no hell, no redemptive justice. In *Dear Judas,* Christ chooses crucifixion as a means to power. In this poem Jeffers says of Christ:

His personal anguish and insane solution
Have stained an age; nearly two thousand years are one vast poem drunk
  with the wine of his blood.

When Jeffers bids man turn from himself and love God, he is not referring to the Christian God but to the God of Nature that provides an escape from the trap of life. Since man cannot become God, let him suffer and learn to die. That is the sense, according to Jeffers' philosophy, in which one must love God rather than humanity. Though Jeffers harps on the insignificance of man, he would not, like the religious Existentialists, recommend the transcendence of the life of reason. He is rooted in the earth, in nature. Unlike Eliot who upholds Christianity as the creed and institution which can save civilization, Jeffers clings to a kind of rationalism which is perfectly compatible with a scientific view of life.

Jeffers, though a major poet, has never received the recognition he deserves, and the reason for this is perfectly plain: the religious humanists among the literary critics cannot stomach his scientific pessimism. It is strange to find critics venting their spleen against the scientific outlook and its assimilation by the poetic sensibility. It is strange indeed. To reject poetry on the ground that the philosophy it embodies is mistaken is as illogical and unfair as to reject poetry because it is Thomistic or Marxist in content. It is the poetry, not the philosophy or the creed, that counts. To maintain that poetry is the locus of meaning and value, and then to belabor—as Hyatt Howe Waggoner does in *The Heel of Elohim*—a number of poets (MacLeish, Hart Crane, E. A. Robinson, and Robinson Jeffers, among others) for subordinating their genius to the scientific outlook, does not make much sense. Shall poets be consigned to the lower circles of Dante's hell for not holding the proper religious beliefs?

The greatness of literature is not measured by the philosophy of life or religious faith it shadows forth. What critic worth his salt would dismiss Dante because he did not agree with his Thomistic philosophy? The most we can ask of a poet is that he should be "sincere" (a treacherously difficult quality to define) and that he should believe deeply in what he writes. Fundamentally, what some literary critics are fighting about, when they inveigh against the dangers of science, is how the nature and destiny of man should be interpreted. Is man a part of Nature or is he a special creation? If he is but a member of the animal kingdom, then he can possess no tragic dignity or stature. He is deprived of the very possibility of religious faith. A purely scientific philosophy negates all that religious-minded people believe and know to be true. Waggoner, writing his book as a "Christian realist and rationalist," condemns the poetry of Robinson Jeffers because it is steeped in the strictly scientific point of view. Waggoner makes the attempt to dispose of science as a "myth" that is guilty of the flagrant offense of eliminating value from the universe of discourse. Under its auspices we have reached a point where there are no longer any fixed points of reference, no absolutes. The Einsteinean world has succeeded in driving out spirit, and modern man, alienated in the universe, is plunged into a world of mathematical equations. In the present crisis, the fulminations against the hegemony of science and the rage for orthodoxy have increased.

This is a mistaken view of the matter. Actually the faith that animates the scientist is not opposed to the religious vision. Martin Johnson, in *Time and Universe for the Scientific Conscience,* maintains that there is no hostility—and there need be none— between scientific experience and religious experience. Each man experiences his own unique religious moments. The scientist is bound to respect these experiences, though he need not go so far as to offer assent to special creeds and dogmas. He is steadily aware of the insuperable limitations placed on the never-ending quest for knowledge; he is aware, too, of the mystery that cradles human life; he is responsive to the beauty and grandeur of the cosmos. In short, he perceives the enigmas of existence, the "miracle" inherent in the extraordinary history of man who, though small in size and feeble in strength, has been the Promethean creator of ideals. The scientist takes cognizance of the fact that man in the course of his pilgrimage through time has given birth to philosophy, religion, and art, as well as science.

The twentieth-century scientist beholds a universe that is intractably abstract, compounded of the "unreal" stuff of thought. The unknowable still remains unknowable. Science sheds light on only a small portion of total reality. Moreover, the scientist is compelled to recognize that there is an imperious reaching out for beauty as well as an irresistible passion for truth, and where do these impulses come from? They exist because man believes in them and creates them. Science indeed could not function if it were finally assumed that life is utterly purposeless. George Sarton, a historian of science, in his introduction to *Science, Religion and Reality,* declares:

If there were no freedom, if all the vicissitudes of life, the pains and pleasures, the beauty as well as the ugliness were due only to accidents, if everything were as meaningless as a game of poker, if our ideas were simply jokes, bad jokes, and our spiritual life were nothing but stupidity and hypocrisy, then I would prefer to die, to call the joke off as far as I was concerned, and to die at once.

This is a "religious" utterance; it represents a religious commitment to meaning, an expression of what Paul Tillich calls "the courage to be," an affirmation that transcends the metaphysics of futility and despair. Though science has bred pessimism as it disclosed the inexorable limits set to man's quest for knowledge and his seeming helplessness to control the world he lives in, it has enabled man to understand at last that he is a part of the world he is observing. It is foolish and irresponsible talk to arraign science as being nihilistic. As J. Bronowski points out in *The Common Sense of Science,* the sense of doom that is alive today springs not from a fear of science, the false Messiah, but from a fear of war. In our time, the loss of faith in life, apart from the loss of faith in God, is staggering, but the distress this has caused may help to usher in the birth of a new age of faith. The prophets who appear, whether in literature or religion or philosophy, will have the courage to proclaim their faith in life. In the framing of this new faith, science will play a mighty role. Why should it not be so? For if God made man, as Lancelot Law Whyte declares in *Accent on Form,* he also made science. "A living science may be more divine than a dead religion." When that consummation takes place, the creative paralysis of our time will be brought to an end, and drama and fiction as well as poetry will take a new lease on life.

PART THREE

THE WORLD OF THE DRAMA

X

THE MODERN PLAYWRIGHT
AND THE ABSOLUTE

NOTHING, as we have pointed out, is more paralyzing to the creative spirit than the loss of faith in life. The failure on the part of many contemporary writers to believe that the life of mankind is essentially meaningful has seriously affected the quality and content of their work. Infected with the deadly suspicion that the ferment of biological activity on earth is not only futile but absurd, alone in a universe that is alien and forever incomprehensible, they are incapable of uttering any heartening affirmation. To speak out boldly in praise of life—that is beyond their powers. Even to write is a manifestation of the cosmic absurdity that gnaws like a worm at the heart of existence. For what conceivable purpose should one create, to what end?

Yet even this nihilistic glimpse into the desolateness of reality could become charged with "religious" values if the writer pushed his inquiry far enough and arrived at the ultimate of despair: the tragic vision of life. For then he would either have to abandon life as an affront not to be borne, an ontological ignominy that is insufferable, or else, if the will to live is stronger than the protesting voice of reason, he would have to transform his negation into a vital acceptance of life. If he is going to live, he must in some way live meaningfully. Hence he must set his spiritual house in order, make it his home, and embrace the positive values that will integrate his life and quicken his work with the pulse of meaning. The riddle of existence remains insoluble. Nevertheless, the playwrights —like the poets and novelists—of our time are unable to rest content with a tolerant and amused skepticism. They must, through their art, affirm the meaning, or lack of meaning, of life, and their preponderant message, especially during the past two decades, has been one of fairly consistent negation.

In its beginnings, the drama was closely related to the communal worship of the gods, the religious attitude of a people. But today the playwright is compelled to come to grips with ultimate issues at a time when traditional religion has fallen apart and can no longer command instantaneous and universal assent. In an age of rampant disbelief, an age of anxiety and unreason, he looks out on life which has lost both its spontaneity and its certitude, not to speak of its supernatural affiliation. His metaphysical distress, his spiritual alienation, his divided state of being—these are the symptoms of a "disease" afflicting his whole generation. All writers today are, in varying degrees, involved in this collective neurosis of the spirit, which expresses itself as a painful sense of not belonging in the universe. Thus many writers are driven frantically to face the question of their existence, the problem of their destiny. What meaning, if any, can they derive from a life that is overshadowed by the cruel finality of death or from a Nature that is completely indifferent to their aspirations?

Those who contemplate the starry spaces that frightened Pascal seek at first to reaffirm the enduring goodness of life, its glory and beauty, the miracle as well as the mystery of being alive. Unfortunately they cannot long sustain this "innocent" ecstasy of perception, just as they cannot, in the language of Jacques Maritain in *Art and Scholasticism,* contemplate "the myriad landscapes bearing God's signature at every revolution of light." The mythical but symbolically alive serpent crawls into their Garden of Eden and destroys their happiness with the knowledge that life is ugly and evil. William Saroyan, for example, composes plays that are vibrantly lyrical, dramatic hymns that celebrate the beauty and wonder of life; but since life, the subject of his dramatic song, is manifestly neither good nor beautiful he is trapped in a contradiction that makes his dithyrambic affirmation border closely on the sentimental. Maxwell Anderson has struggled to compose plays that rise to the height of authentic tragedy, but his affirmations, too, are lacking in dynamic power, the creative *élan* that springs from assured faith. Surely most typical of our age are those playwrights who have gazed deep into the eyes of Medusa and are concerned to reveal their petrifying vision of the naked horror of life. Though they endeavor to disclose a pattern of redemptive meaning, they are usually foiled in their quest. Beholding only the specter of nihilistic futility, they dwell sadly on man's inescapable need for living in a compensatory world of illusions. That is why there are today few truly tragic poets in the theater.

The tragic rhythm, as Susanne K. Langer points out in *Feeling and Form,* is based fundamentally on the deathward progression of the individual, and the form of tragedy reflects this inexorable cycle. The spectator confronts his own destiny, viewed as a whole, depicted on the stage. The failure of the modern hero to rise to tragic heights springs from his own realization that he cannot possibly fulfil his potentialities; he is doomed, and he knows it, before he plunges into battle or even understands the nature of the struggle he must wage. Stricken with the palsy of doubt, he cannot confidently pursue his destiny, for he peceives that it is compounded of frustration and despair. Though the dramatist does not set out to elaborate a system of philosophical beliefs, he cannot altogether keep his spiritual perturbations out of the picture. Hence he represents man as struggling to achieve a salvation that is bound to elude him; he cannot escape from the disaster that is imminent and inevitable. In his efforts to portray the evil and emptiness of existence, he falls short of the tragic, for his protagonist, as is true of Willy Loman in *Death of a Salesman,* does not comprehend what is happening to him, or why. Destruction finally overtakes the modern "tragic hero," but he never gains the grace of insight and understanding. This is in keeping with Karl Jaspers' revealing remark in *Tragedy Is Not Enough* that "Tragedy shows man as he is transformed at the edge of doom." In the pseudo-tragedy of our day, this transformation never takes place. The modern agonistic "hero" falters and draws back before the edge of doom. He cannot affirm the greatness of the human spirit because he believes neither in himself nor in life. He lacks the strength and the courage to break the bonds that tie him to existence. There is nothing grandiose or inspiring about the spectacle of life that such playwrights as Chekhov or Eugene O'Neill or Sartre exhibit.

Confronted by an enigmatic, forever unknowable, and contingent universe, the Existentialist of our time perceives only the terrible irrationality and absurdity of life. He knows all the haunting questions asked by the Sphinx, but he can furnish no answers. Absurdity is rendered absolute. What reason, what justification, is there for man's existence on earth? None at all. Man is an utter stranger on this planet, without a vocation, without a genuine excuse for being. Alone and useless in infinite space, he engages in activities and spawns religious and teleological systems which are but extravagant and vain methods of blinding himself to the knowledge of his abandonment. Out of this sense of estrangement the playwright creates his febrile dramas of despair. Existentialism, accepting the metaphysics of despair, bids man embrace his miserable fate. The human personality, recognizing the precariousness of its position, is aware of itself, in the words of Emmanuel Mounier, as "a frail existent in the bitter ocean of infinity; I am the weak and lonely god without whom this spontaneous creation of myself by myself is liable at any moment to sink in the depths of nothingness."

The language used here—and it is employed by a religious thinker—is profoundly revealing. It is this motif of nothingness which is the source of perpetual anguish and which negates the condition that makes for tragedy. The anguish arises from the fact of the human predicament in a problematical world. It is born of the knowledge that man marches ineluctably toward death. It is the expression of cosmic homelessness and absolute despair. Life today is characterized by this very state of incompleteness, uncertainty, unspeakable dread. Since man is driven relentlessly toward death, no one can ever hope to become master of his fate. He lives for the sole purpose of dying. But if that is so, then life is unutterably absurd. However, to present characters who live in constant, demoralized expectation of death—that is the antithesis of the tragic outlook. Death cannot lend any exalted meaning—or any kind of meaning—to life. It is absurd for man to be born; it is equally absurd to die. Both are accidental and meaningless. The modern "tragic hero" (who can name him?) is thus reduced to the intolerable condition of striving for freedom in the face of death, of seeking to affirm the nothingness that infects existence.

Strindberg, the modern of the moderns, pictures in *The Dream Play* a queer surrealistic world, an insane world, full of contradictions, in which judgment is confounded and justice perverted. Life often seems a purposeless routine, a meaningless bore, people asking the same questions until death finally comes to release them from their senseless torture. In the last scene, the Daughter of Indra declares that the earth is unclean and life evil. Victims of time, creatures of dust, men live as they can, but why must life be so full of suffering? The Daughter of Indra knows at last the lot of man: he is a split creature, burdened with impossible desires and irreconcilable conflicts. *The Spook Sonata* voices the despairing cry: "A curse lies on the whole creation and on life." Though Strindberg's expressionistic plays are informed with a profound pessimistic strain, they are at least not devoid of compassion.

In Chekhov's plays, too, the characters, wasting their years in apathy and indecision, are tormented by the question of what they shall do with their life. They feel the necessity of resting in illusion, for this is better than nothing. In *Uncle Vanya,* Voitski cries out that his life has been a failure, and he does not know what to do with the years that lie ahead of him. All that is left is the peace to be found in the eternity of the grave. But at least the Chekhovian characters endure to the end, however bitter and frustrate their existence may be. They are not "outsiders" or nihilists; they are simply embodiments of despair. In *The Lower Depths,* Gorki presents a number of derelicts who philosophize broodingly about the world that has treated them so cruelly, but the most wretched and degraded of these creatures has a soul, a secret aspiration, a private dream, a longing to redeem himself by reaching out after goodness. Though the total impression left by this naturalistic play is one of sordidness, it is relieved by the light of compassion. For Luka, the pilgrim, all men, whatever their status, are alike. The deeper man sinks, the higher his aspiration soars. When he is asked by one of the lodgers whether God exists, he replies: "If you believe in Him, there is a God; believe not and none exists.... What you believe in ... exists."

Like Gorki, Arthur Schnitzler is saved from the doctrinaire extremes of naturalism by his tender compassion, his melancholy perception of the loneliness of the human situation, his awareness of the failure and frustrations that overtake the noblest souls. He knows the feverish longings that consume the heart, the dreams men seek achingly to fulfil, the defeat that inevitably overtakes them in their quest. Just as death annuls the brightness of love, so defeat ends the hopes of mankind. Despite the note he strikes of gentle and genuine compassion, Schnitzler, like Chekhov a doctor by profession, has no scheme of salvation to offer. He proposes no solution and even suggests that there is no ultimate meaning. Buoyed up by illusions, men cannot withstand the traumatic shock of reality; they need illusions to nourish them as the bread of life, illusions which will conceal from them the shattering truth of the destiny toward which they are being dragged irresistibly. And who is to say what is illusion and what is reality? Men cling to their dreams even in the face of the most crushing truth. What else shall men do who are under sentence of death, condemned to the oblivion of the grave? Obsessed by this knowledge, they snatch at experience as it passes, in the hope of enjoying a fugitive pleasure, a transient taste of happiness. *The Lonely Way* gives us Schnitzler's ironic but humane commentary on life. There are no categorical imperatives, no assurances of happiness on earth. Life is a precarious hazard, and there is, alas, no measure of correspondence between effort and achievement. Each one walks in darkness, and walks alone. In a world of flux and illusion that is the only abiding value: to be true to the self, not to sin against our innermost being. But it is clear that Schnitzler, despite all his skepticism, still believes in life and still values the truth.

So long as the playwright voices compassion, he is still attached to life, he still labors to project a meaning, even if it is only the meaning to be salvaged from a solidarity born of suffering. Throughout the history of civilization, the creative spirit has had to face the tragic truth of life. Each writer faced it in his own way, but invariably with a measure of fortitude. Whatever else might be denied, life was not negated, humanity was not relegated to the ash-heap, death did not become an all-devouring obsession. Today we have come a long way from the mood of compassion that informs the work of Strindberg, Gorki, and Schnitzler. Today we have even lost the rationalistic faith that sustained the optimistic liberalism of George Bernard Shaw. Though in *Heartbreak House* he poured out all his wrath of disenchantment and sounded his prophetic warning of the catastrophe that would befall not only England but all of Europe, he at least believed firmly in a number of values that transcend the mechanistic approach of science. Heartbreak House, which symbolizes the England of his time, was mesmerized by the materialism of science. It is indicted on the ground of indifference, cynicism, heartlessness, and unconscionable cruelty. When World War I came, practically everybody went mad. The war tore off the masks of science, art, and religion and revealed the barbarism of our civilization. But even in this epidemic of destructive madness, Shaw was convinced that the theater—and therefore civilization—would survive.

Although Shaw presents an unforgettable picture of Europe headed for destruction, he did not altogether despair, for he was certain that while Nature would make us pay the price for our catastrophic folly by invoking the sentence of extinction, she would then try another daring experiment in the evolution of life. One character declares: "I tell you, one of two things must happen.

Either out of that darkness some new creation will come to supplant us as we have supplanted the animals, or the heavens will fall in thunder and destroy us." What is terribly wrong with the inhabitants of Heartbreak House is that they have lost the capacity to love and are without a controlling sense of purpose. All this, declares Captain Shotover in the play, is highly immoral. Drifting should be a crime. Man should take charge of his destiny. When Hector asks: "And this ship that we are all in? This soul's prison we call England?" Captain Shotover replies like a modern Jeremiah: "The captain is in his bunk, drinking bottled ditch-water; and the crew is gambling in the forecastle. She will strike and sink and split. Do you think the laws of God will be suspended in favor of England because you were born in it? The English must learn the art of living or perish miserably."

What is of considerable interest in this bit of dialogue is the language used. The appeal is to universal moral law, a categorical sense of duty, the laws of God. Life is an art whose fundamental demands must be respected. What Shaw darkly prophesied has come to pass, but in a nihilistic sense he could not possibly have foreseen. Captain Shotover's reference to the laws of God is no mere literary metaphor, no rhetorical locution. Shaw, for all his rationalist fulminations against the church, was essentially a "religious" man. All his life long he was dedicated to a high purpose, and his faith in mankind emerges not only in *Man and Superman* but in *Back to Methuselah*. Shaw sought to transform the theater into a holy place, a true church. In his early dramatic criticism, he maintained that the theater was as important as the church was in the Middle Ages. The prime duty of the New Church, he contended, was to take itself seriously as a prompter of thought, "a prompter of conscience, an elucidator of social conduct, an armoury against despair and dullness, and a temple of the Ascent of Man." That is the spirit which animated him when he composed his own plays. He refused to believe that the church is the house of God and the theater the dwelling place of the Devil. "The theatre is identical with a church service as a combination of artistic ritual, profession of faith, and sermon. Wherever the theatre is alive, there the church is alive also..." He listed plays like *Brand* and *Parsifal* as exemplifying the unity of church and theater. In fact, the Wagnerian drama was "nothing less than the Communion presented in theatrical instead of ecclesiastical form."

But Shaw never interpreted God in traditional theological terms. For him God manifests himself as the Life Force, forever creating something new. Shaw pursued the spiritual quest outside the fold of the church. Many different roads lead to the perception of the numinous in existence; a writer like Shaw, alienated from formal Christianity, frequently voices insights and intuitions that are profoundly religious in character. How different in temper and outlook is Shaw from contemporary man, who is alone in the universe, committed to no humanistic or transcendent ideal, wedded to a soul-destroying nihilism. The problem for the modern writer has become what it was for Nietzsche in moments of agonizing despair: How can one live while believing in nothing? How can he resign himself to a world that is, as far as his spiritual needs are concerned, lawless? How can he affirm his destiny in a world given over to undeclared wars, political purges, totalitarianism, unabashed tyranny, concentration camps, crematoria, menticide and genocide?

It is Existentialism, as we have demonstrated, that shrilly expresses the anxiety neurosis of our age, its haunting fear of life. The Sartrean "hero" perpetually questions the meaning of existence; life is incomprehensible, fortuitous, absurd. Everything on earth is without reason, without justification. Existence is simply gratuitous, not necessary. One is born and lives and dies without meaning. Reality dissolves and discloses the nothingness of death that waits for all men. Nature has trapped man in this ridiculous and degrading predicament. Sartre's plays and novels repeat a single theme: man is superfluous. The world will go on without him, and "the free man" is fully aware that this is so.

The heart of Existentialist doctrine is shadowed forth in *The Flies,* by Sartre, which celebrates the death of the gods. Orestes, tired of his rootlessness, his lack of fixed purpose, his unchartered freedom, combats the old religious consciousness, the superstitious abasement of man before the gods. Henceforth he will take orders from no one, neither man nor god. The veil has fallen, the reign of the gods has ended. Orestes is a liberator of mankind, a savior, because he is no longer under the domination of Zeus. His eyes are opened to the liberating truth that justice is man-made. He has found himself. In his final debate with Zeus, Orestes affirms his newly-won freedom. Why should he atone for an act of murder that he does not regard as a crime? He defies Zeus to do his worst, fully aware that Zeus can have no power over him. He declares: "I *am* my freedom. No sooner had you created me than I ceased to be young." Man comes of age when he arrives at the knowledge that he is entirely alone in the universe. "I am doomed to have no other law but mine," Orestes says. Zeus finally admits that "each of us is alone." But why, asks Zeus, should he open people's eyes and make them see that their lives are meaningless and futile? Orestes, a puissant Existentialist dialectician, maintains that there is no reason why men should be denied the precious gift of despair. "They're free; and human life begins on the far side of despair." Alone in the universe and with no superior power to help him, man must accept his limited destiny and live his life in the light of truth.

In *The Flies,* the antireligious emphasis of Sartre makes itself strongly felt. The gods are slain and man is urged to triumph over despair. Sartre asks man to become god. Not all contemporary playwrights, by any manner of means, have surrendered to this metaphysical plague of meaninglessness. Some are struggling to break through the wall of darkness, to transcend the horror of existence in an act of creative affirmation. In *Camino Real,* Tennessee Williams tries to communicate his interpretation of the hopelessness men feel in this time of trouble. Though the theme is never explicitly stated, he is obviously making the attempt to portray, by means of a series of dramatically viable symbols, the reality of our wasteland culture. Humanity has gone dry, its roots have been severed, its fountain is without a flow of living water. Humanity has suffered a grievous loss not only of vitality but also of faith in life. People are lonely and fearful and lost. But why? In a brilliant and moving dramatization of the history of mankind, Tennessee Williams labors to work out the answer. Before us he holds up the staggering defeats suffered by the human race, its demoralization of spirit, its inertia and drugged despair, but he also reveals its determination to go forward and fight the evil forces that impede its progress.

The characters that march through this play are chiefly archetypes of fundamental attitudes that the author singles out as expressive of his age of disaster. *Camino Real* possesses the timeless, universal dimensions of myth designed to reveal expressionistically the condition of life in the modern world. Strange things happen in Camino Real, the place where the spring of humanity has run dry. Kilroy arrives on the scene and hears the voice of the Gypsy proclaiming over the loudspeaker:

Do you feel yourself to be spiritually unprepared for the age of exploding atoms? ... Have you arrived at a point on the Camino Real where the walls converge not in the distance but right in front of your nose? Does further progress appear impossible to you? Are you afraid of anything at all? Afraid of your heartbeat?

Here is the ghastly fear, born of the awakening to the cruelty and heartlessness of life, that constricts the souls of men. Always in back of them the people of Camino Real hear the piping of the Streetcleaners, the undertakers of society, the hirelings of Death, trundling their white barrels, giggling inanely, pointing at their victims, and waiting for the appointed time when they will cart the corpse away.

Kilroy makes a number of startling discoveries in Camino Real. Life is decadent. Nothing seems real. Men are not allowed to communicate freely with each other; a total state of terror prevails, especially the fear of the unknown, the terror induced by the imminence of death. Man looks into his own heart and asks if this can be all. Neither wealth nor power can distract the work of the Streetcleaners. The best one can do is to pretend to ignore them, though sooner or later everyone must deal with them. That is the

fate which all men frenziedly struggle to escape. In their loneliness
and fear people distrust each other, not realizing that love is their
only defense against betrayal, their only means of salvation. Mar-
guerite, an archetypal figure, asks:

What are we sure of? Not even of our existence.... And whom can
we ask the questions that torment us? "What is this place?" "Where are
we?" ... What else are we offered? The never-broken procession of
little events that assure us that we and strangers about us are still going
on! Where? Why? and the perch that we hold is unstable! We're
threatened with eviction, for this is a port of entry and departure,
there are no permanent guests! And where else have we to go when
we leave here? ... We're lonely.... We hear the Streetcleaners' piping
not far away.

In this speech, as in many of the symbolic scenes in the play,
we hear the modern cry of alienation. Is the battle of life lost before
it is fought? Williams tries to end his fantasia on a note of hope.
Though Kilroy, who stands for Everyman, is doomed, he is moved
by pity before the end comes—pity for himself, for the world, and
for the God who made it. Though his number is up, he does not
cringe and deny his humanity. There is nothing that man is not
courageous enough to face. But when one tries to go beyond this and
formulate what it is the play affirms, one gets lost; the only certainty is death. It is a negative diagnosis of the malady of modern
man, brilliantly presented.

Something has happened to the playwright during the past fifty
years which has progressively robbed him of his illusions and compelled him to adopt a new attitude of disenchantment toward the
absolute. In confronting the reality of death, he is inevitably led
to seek reasons why he should go on living, and he can generally
find none that is convincing. His fundamental desire is to achieve a
more authentic life, but how is this possible when he is ravaged by a
moral nihilism that rejects God and insists on the absurdity of the
universe? This is the spiritual crisis that Albert Camus sums up in
The Rebel. If one is void of belief, then nothing makes sense, and
everything is permissible. It is exactly the problem that haunted

Dostoevski in the nineteenth century. In one of his letters he raises this ultimate issue: "Why am I to live decently and do good if I die irrevocably here below? If there is no immortality I need but live out my appointed time and let the rest go hang.... For I shall die, and all the rest will die and utterly vanish."

How is the modern writer to affirm life, to believe in man, when the universe appears to him in the image of a nihilistic nightmare? If the members of the lonely crowd no longer believe in the slain God and his resurrection, then they become terrorized at the thought of death. And what is the writer to tell them? How shall he interpret the contemporary scene? Alienated, aware of the absurdity of existence, without the support of the absolute, he must learn to accept his human limitations and function creatively within a world of relative values. Whatever gods he rejects, he realizes that as an artist he cannot afford to deny his relationship and responsibility to mankind. If his art is to survive, he must work in behalf of life. In all humility, he must reconcile himself to the inherent limitations of human nature. If he can somehow make his peace with existence, he will struggle as far as possible against the arbitrary emergence of evil, though nevertheless aware that life is always accompanied by suffering. And his art will be a perpetual protest against the injustice and suffering that life entails. Albert Camus made the pregnant remark that "the secret of Europe is that it no longer loves life." It is true. A spirit of weariness has overtaken contemporary man. The writer, by resisting the temptation to play the role of god, will have to make the difficult adjustment to the fact of death and affirm realistically his condition as a man. Though he is confronted with a superhuman challenge, he must decide on those values which enhance life and make it more truly productive.

XI

THE RELIGIOUS PROBLEM
AND THE DRAMA

IN THE DRAMA as in poetry, the effects the author produces are part of his artistic intention and design, though, of course, much may come through that he never consciously put in. The drama as art does not, however, serve as a gloss on moral or religious themes; it is not a disguised allegory on the workings of Karma or a vindication of the ways of God. The religious, like the moral, element is not the central, energizing principle of art; for all literature, whatever its particular genre, triumphs by virtue of its form. The religious theme, when the dramatist chooses to deal with it, must be subordinated to the illusion of reality the work struggles to create and must become integrated within the pattern of realized experience the artist expresses. Thus religious exaltation, the quest for God, the expiation of sin, the passage through the dark night of the soul, do not constitute the heart of the drama; they are but rough source material to be explored and transmuted, subjects to be developed and given flesh and blood. In the drama as in poetry, art is always concerned with individualized form; it therefore abhors both generalizations and preachment. It communicates the mysterious, infinitely various, fascinating, and ever changing sense of life.

If we look upon the drama as essentially an art form, not a propagandistic tract or evangelical sermon, we cease to make demands upon it that it cannot legitimately hope to satisfy. Though it is obviously free to deal as it pleases with moral and religious issues, it is not primarily an instrument of either reform or redemption. Those who turn to it for that kind of magic, sacred or profane, are doomed to be disappointed. The playwright is fundamentally a poet who gives expression, in controlled dramatic form, to the realities—and hence the mysteries—of existence, its deep-cutting and perennial crises. His concern is invariably with the human soul and its fate on earth. The so-called "spiritual element" which is to be found in the modern drama exists by virtue of the fact that it deals with life in all its far-reaching complexities. It cannot function properly as a means of conversion. True, some dramatists, notably Tolstoy, have employed their work for the express purpose of diffusing "the light" that shines in darkness. Since a man can only write out of the depths of what he is and hopes to become, and since what he is is of necessity *colored* by his beliefs, religious convictions do enter into the fabric of literature—but only indirectly, only after they have been "distanced" and transformed into the material of artistic expression, and never as overt doctrine.

There is thus no reason why the religious experience, like every other type of experience, cannot be treated in dramatic literature, but how? That is the crucial question. To analyze the "religious" element in modern drama, one must first determine how the key term "religious" is to be used. Is it to be defined as creed and ceremonial, prescribed orthodoxy and traditional ritual, dogma and denomination, or as the search and illumination, however fitful, of the spirit, even if the spirit in its confrontation of the ontological mystery is led into heresy? Somerset Maugham, in *The Unknown,* voices the philosophy of agnosticism. In *Outward Bound,* Sutton Vane concerns himself with the theme of death and what lies beyond. But the authentically Christian writer is not satisfied, as we shall note in the case of T. S. Eliot's poetic plays, with merely dwelling on the religious problem. The aesthetic attitude is not enough and must be transcended. Beholding the multiple dangers besetting mankind—the temptations of worldly pride, the sin of secularism, the growth of technological power, the absorption in material things of men who are not restrained by a sense of their human limitations, the ascendancy of the scientific temper that has no concern for the spiritual needs of mankind, the alarming spread of evil in the world —the Christian writers frequently demand conformity; they call for repentance, a radical change of heart, a renewal of faith in God. But it is impossible in our age to attain credal conformity. While the return to Christianity on the part of a number of writers represents a significant movement in our time, they still constitute a minority, and their obsession with the dogma of original sin, their urgent call for the renunciation of the temporal order, will not gain many converts. The spiritual integration of the Western world, if it is ever to be achieved, will not, despite the evangelical appeals of a historian like Toynbee, take place under the auspices of a single church.

For even the modern religious believer suffers from the virus of doubt. He cannot simply purge himself of the effects of skepticism and his knowledge of science. The re-emergence of the theological debate points eloquently to a changed spiritual condition. Some writers have turned to God because they cannot go on living a life that is without ultimate meaning or purpose. For them, that is the only way out of the void of indifference and despair. The question of "sincerity" does not enter in at this point, for the profane writer and the Christian literatus are both in earnest; but whereas the former is secular in his outlook and defends a system of ideological pluralism, presenting the actual body of the world in his work without seeking to preach, the latter believes that mankind can be saved only by a return to Christianity, and that this "return" is contingent upon an awareness of sin and a craving for spiritual unification. Since he cannot breathe in a universe that is dedicated to Nothingness, he has come to believe in the miracle of the divine birth.

Yet it is clearly evident that many of these conversions are products of the will. The demand for orthodoxy is bound to be self-defeating, especially in the theater, which is not committed to dogma and is not meant to serve as a pulpit. If the dramatist must choose between a theology that is God-centered and a *Weltanschauung* that is man-centered, he is not being offered a real choice. The stage is inevitably the scene of the adventures of man on this earth, his trials and adversities, his temptations by the Devil and his triumph or fall. No playwright of our time can, by losing himself in a myth, throw off the burden of complexity, the heritage of intellectual doubt, the compulsion to question the ambiguous meaning of existence. He cannot escape the pressures of his age. It is enormously significant that for Martin Heidegger the ground-question of metaphysics is born out of the womb of Nothing: "Why is there any Being at all—why not far rather Nothing?" Once the drama broke away from its theological or religious moorings, it created an autonomous world of values that reflected the existential crises and contradictions of modernity.

Unquestionably this involves a sacrifice of a sort for the artist, who must give up whatever stake he once had, or thought he had, in an immortal destiny. Harold W. Watts, an English literary critic with a pronounced religious conviction, declares in *Hound and Quarry* that "the artist must accept the limitations of being without *as an artist* an immortal destiny. Art has only a mortal destiny; art brought into the actual presence of the absolute, of the timeless, sinks to nothingness...." That is it exactly. When art seeks to grapple with the absolute, that is formless and ineffable, it falls into impotence, it sinks to nothingness. It must confine itself to the terrible miseries and occasional grandeur of human life, the limitations of existence which the finite creature that is man on earth cannot overstep.

Despite his awareness of the inexorable limitations of finite existence and therefore of art, Harold W. Watts clings to his religious commitment, which shapes his appraisal of modern literature and his prescription of the remedy that is called for. The artist, he insists, must include within the compass of his vision intuitions about reality that lie beyond the reach of empirical proof. Hence the need for mystical insight, for glimpses of the salvation that is the proper concern of theology. In brief, the circle of eternity must be brought within the purview of art, though he fails to show how this can be done. At bottom he is quarreling with the conception of reality basic to the work of the modern writers who, having been cut off from their relations to the eternal, operate on the assumption that they have included everything "real," everything that exists, within the framework of their vision. As a result they are compelled to accept "substitutes" for the old absolute values, whereas the older writers steadily confronted the truth of their own nothingness and the possibility of attaining salvation beyond the brief and precarious tenure of human life. That is the sum and substance of the indictment Watts draws up. On the secular, naturalistic terms he has chosen, the modern writer is unable to speak for humanity on its pilgrimage to the frontiers of eternity. According to this Christian critic, then, art must comprise terms that are both human and theological, and thus face the tragic ambiguities and tensions of the human condition.

What are the aesthetic implications, for the drama, of such concepts as God and eternity? The Christian apologist, his gaze fixed on eternity, argues that man is not enough. But the drama, like all art, is plunged of necessity in the river of time and the context of history; it cannot, without destroying itself, ever transcend this limitation. For how can the contact of man with eternity be communicated in dramatic terms? What kind of meaning can the writer find, and render convincing, in a realm beyond history? In the sphere of the drama, all conflicts, all truths, all meanings are human; all morality must be judged by relative—that is, human—standards. If the dramatist ventures to present God, or faith in God, as the solution for all the ills that afflict his characters, he finds himself caught on the horns of a dilemma. A resolution engineered by the grace of God is not dramatically viable. The dramatist must believe —that is the premise conditioning his work—that man has been freed from bondage to God's will.

Thus, even the writer who is a practicing Christian may find it difficult to sustain faith without falling into heresy. The creative imagination functions according to its own independent and incommensurable laws. As Rayner Heppenstall expresses it aptly in *The Double Image:* "There is a sense in which the creative imagination is repugnant to Christianity and to any fixed and embodied myth." Differently put: the creative personality is by nature heretical in its outlook and therefore unable for long to rest at peace in any dogma; it must have no intermediaries, neither prophets nor doctrines, between its vision and the ever-mysterious world of experience. Consequently, even if the writer retains the pattern of Christianity, he is bound to discover that only through heresy and paradox can his imagination be quickened and find release.

The work of the French Catholic writer, Paul Claudel, is a case in point. His play, *The Tidings Brought to Mary,* is an excursion into abnormal psychology. The author treats with complete seriousness the miracles brought about by the power of faith. Whereas George Bernard Shaw was brought up on the rationalism of his age, Claudel had undergone an experience of religious conversion in his youth and thus escaped from the cult of scientific materialism that dominated the nineteenth-century mind. Throughout an active life he kept his religious faith unimpaired and consequently never ceased to oppose a naturalism that concerned itself, as he felt, exclusively with the animal side of man. Nor could he give his allegiance to any form of art that was not instinct with faith in the evidence of things unseen. *The Tidings Brought to Mary* requires for its full appreciation that the members of the audience free themselves from the skeptical, naturalistic temper of their age and transport themselves to the Middle Ages when people possessed absolute faith and accepted miracles as perfectly natural and convincing. Though a beautiful and tender poetic apostrophe to faith and the glory of God, *The Tidings Brought to Mary* is not a powerfully moving and effective play. It is, rather, a religious spectacle. The use of miracles as a means of resolving conflicts represents a negation of the art of the drama.

For more or less similar reasons, *Hotel Universe,* by Philip Barry, is a failure. Though the playwright tries earnestly enough to state his vision of life and what man must do in order to be saved, the play fails to come alive. The author is toying with metaphysical questions that get beyond his control and turn into confused and empty abstractions. The mystic seances of these frustrated characters, their broodings on eternity, their talk about suicide and salvation, all this is thin and lifeless in substance. Barry has composed a pseudo-religious play in which everyone, as one character remarks, is "looking for the answer when there isn't any." These characters cannot find a way out; they do not know whether to embrace psychoanalysis or the church. They seek to articulate a mystical vision for which there are no words.

Dramatists may, if they wish, come to grips with intrinsically "theological" themes and religious problems, but they must treat them in ways that are "untheological." For the drama is committed to ultimate values; the dramatist presents some conception of human destiny on earth. That is why, in tragedy, the protagonist cannot be represented as a hapless victim of mechanical forces or as a creature of clay subject to the absolute and inscrutable will of God. The naturalistic drama introduced characters who were essentially victims, trapped by life, doomed to the ignoble martyrdom of insignificance, unendowed with any saving grace of free will, unsustained by faith in life's ultimate meaning. It has therefore been argued that tragedy is not possible in an age that is dominated by the scientific synthesis. Modern drama portrays for the most part the conflicts of little people who lead drab, constricted, monotonous, spiritually unawakened lives. What is wrong with modern man, according to the thesis propounded by Joseph Wood Krutch in *The Modern Temper,* is that God is dead; the universe is alien and indifferent, if not hostile, to human desires and aspirations. There is no providence that shapes our ends. How can the modern dramatist interpret the universe as being in the least concerned about the fate of man? The profound religious faith out of which tragedy originally sprang has perished. For tragedy, according to Krutch, is "a profession of faith, and a sort of religion; a way of looking at life by virtue of which it is robbed of its pain." Or, as he phrases it more arrestingly: "A tragic writer does not have to believe in God, but he must believe in man."

Since he did not believe in man, Eugene O'Neill struggled unavailingly to discover a faith that would render both his life and his work meaningful. The dramatist, he felt, must probe to the roots of the sickness that has spread throughout the world—the death of the old God and the failure of science and materialism to give any new one "for the surviving primitive religious instinct to find a meaning for life and to comfort its fears of death with." Even his manner of stating the predicament of the modern dramatist is shot through with doubt. Yet he is convinced that this is the major theme which must inform the drama.

In *The Iceman Cometh,* O'Neill is exploring unimaginably dark depths of the human soul never lit up by a gleam of hope or faith. His work projects the ultima Thule of despair, the contemporary hell from which there is no exit except through death. The scene opens in the summer of 1912, in the back room of the bar of Harry Hope's saloon where the jetsam and flotsam of society foregather, men who have lost their reason for living, each battered soul weighed down by his private sense of futility. So hopeless and so lost do they feel that the drama of suffering they enact can never rise to the plane of tragedy. They lack the energy, the strength of will, to become aware of their degraded condition and to make the effort necessary to save themselves. The best they can do is to indulge in pipe dreams, to cling forlornly to their empty, alcoholic illusions. Larry Slade, himself an unregenerate drunkard, declares that "a pipe dream is what gives life to the whole misbegotten lot of us, drunk or sober." All he looks forward to is death. He abandoned his anarchism after he found out that men had no wish to be saved from themselves. Now he does not care if the world perishes and all things go to ruin. Finding refuge in Hope's saloon, which is the last harbor, the cesspool beyond tragedy, these wrecks that once were men can sink no lower, even though they still pretend they can go back and rehabilitate themselves or that the future will some-how make them different. Larry Slade, who now believes in nothing, has no answer to any of the pathetic questions men continue to ask, except to say that death is better than sleep and that it is best of all never to be born.

What O'Neill is saying is that these derelicts—and we are all, the whole misbegotten lot of us, derelicts and wastrels—cannot face the truth about themselves. The perception of reality, the revelation of the truth, would crush them. They must, like the rest of us, have their pipe dreams. One character lashes out with this piercing cry: "All I know is I'm sick of life! I'm through! I've forgotten myself! I'm drowned and contented on the bottom of a bottle. Honor or dishonor, faith or treachery are nothing to me but the opposites of the same stupidity which is ruler and king of life, and in the end they rot into dust in the same grave." These men know—it is the stock joke of the play—that the Iceman of Death is coming soon. They prefer the consolation of the lie to the cruel disclosure of the truth. They cannot live without the opiate of illusion.

No philosopher or doctrinaire preacher, O'Neill ends his work on a note of absolute negation. Values are meaningless; the grave annuls all meaning. Maxwell Anderson, like O'Neill, has been deeply influenced by the skeptical thought of his time. Though he is a naturalist, he cannot rid himself of the contradictions spawned by the twentieth century. Though his major characters are moved by godlike longings, they cannot get themselves to believe in God with unquestioning faith. And it is this lack of absolute faith which prevents the creation of tragedy in our time; for how can the dramatist invest a protagonist with tragic significance if man is but the blind victim of mechanical forces, an electron tossed about capriciously in the universal flux of energy? Doomed from the start, the modern "hero" stands alone and dismayed in a cruelly uncaring and deterministic universe, and is eventually dragged down to ignominious defeat.

If man perceives no ultimate purpose in living, his individual life lacks a central unifying principle. Everything he does seems senseless and futile. Hence the metaphysics of absurdity that a number of writers despairingly espouse. Their bitter indictment of the universe simply represents an unconscious will to die. The efforts of the Existentialists to choose their freedom are nothing more than feeble, suicidal gestures. While man believes that his life is ruled by pure contingency, he cannot affirm the meaning of his existence. What is more, he loses faith in his own reality. His precious boon of existential freedom amounts to little more than a miserable awareness of the Nothingness that hems him in on all sides. Out of this perception of the meaninglessness of existence springs the nihilistic insight, which makes for "freedom," that man must embrace his mortal fate and learn to live with the bride of Nothingness. Once he has made this final commitment, he is no longer blinded by vital fictions, the pipe dreams to which O'Neill's doomed creatures cling, but recognizes stoically that he is alone and powerless in the universe.

It is evident that the most vital contemporary plays that come to grips with the spiritual problem are being written by men who are unregenerately secular in their outlook. Since they discern no sign of God or good in the universe, they cannot affirm the old values with any degree of conviction or imaginative faith. The vision of the supernatural, as far as they are concerned, is dead. But if the writer seeks to return to the past in the hope of renewing his lost creative energies, he runs a serious danger. He counterbalances the relativism and rootlessness of his age by surrendering to the Absolute, but he does so by rejecting much in life that he knows to be precious and valid. He cannot hope to solve the problems that plague the modern soul by simply fixing his gaze on eternity. The theology of crisis, as it finds expression in literature, represents a flight from life, a denial of "reality," rather than a genuine act of transcendence. Freud has, for good or evil, been a more potent influence on the drama than St. Thomas Aquinas, and Freud did not believe that human destiny conformed to any principle of justice or that an omniscient supernatural power existed who rewarded man for his self-denying virtues.

The dramatist who seeks to propound a religious doctrine in his play is as mistaken in his intention and method as the dramatist who seeks to use the theater for frankly propagandist purposes. In fact, the former is actually a propagandist. His attempt is certain to back-fire; the modern audience is singularly resistant to preachment on the stage. Direct statement proves highly ineffectual, in the drama as well as in poetry, because it cannot take the place of the inte-grated series of actions and awareness, the objective correlatives, which produce a moving aesthetic effect. The theater-goer seeks an intensification and illumination of experience in all its baffling com-plexity and contradictions. The outcome of the action is always unpredictable, even if in the end it is seen as having been inevitable from the very start. The suspense inheres in the element of the human will, the effort of the protagonist to escape the fate which he has himself, knowingly or unknowingly, prepared. The presen-tation of orthodoxies or even miracles offers a foregone conclusion. The end is in the beginning, but not in an organic sense, but as something dogmatically imposed or supernaturally contrived.

This does not mean, as we have said, that the religious theme is excluded from the spacious domain of the drama. Nothing of the kind. Dramatic literature is free to deal with any and all of life's inexplicable dilemmas, only what it deals with, essentially, is the experience of struggle and suffering, the search and the doubt, the pressure of need and despair, the conflict between illusion and reality. Man in quest of God, man finally subordinating himself to or defiantly rejecting the divine will, man passing through the dark night of the soul—all that is unmistakably the stuff of literature. But the conclusion is unavoidable that a drama which employs the machinery of the supernatural, as Eliot does in *The Cocktail Party,* to resolve the central conflict, will not produce a truly tragic effect. Whether we like it or not, the modern intelligence has ceased to believe that God governs human affairs. A naturalist by convic-tion, the secular dramatist of our time discovers the source of his values in the struggle of the finite, natural self, whereas the religious dramatist invokes the aid of the supernatural as a means of transcend-ing the limitations of the human. The secular dramatist has no inter-est in going beyond the facts of terrestrial experience and is not tempted to "leap" into the mystical realm of revelation. He portrays characters fighting against the forces of evil and adversity in a world that furnishes no hint of a providential dispensation. As a working dramatic device, the beliefs of formal religion are alien to the drama, especially to the spirit of tragedy. For if the protagonist must depend on God to lift him out of his tragic suffering, then he is no longer responsible for shaping and controlling his own destiny. If everything rests ultimately in the hands of God, then the struggle is indeed in vain, and the hero must turn to God for the strength and the courage that he cannot find in himself.

Many critics agree with Krutch that tragedy cannot be produced in our time. The tragic writer is limited by the recalcitrance of his material, his circumscribed vision of reality; he cannot, as a naturalist, portray the greatness of the human spirit in its efforts to achieve transcendence. Though his protagonists are plunged in suffering, they never reach a point where they comprehend the meaning of their suffering. They suffer cruelly but meaninglessly in a universe that reveals no pattern of moral justification. Yet even naturalistic nihilism, as it confronts the mystery of existence, struggles to achieve some synthesis of values. For even the nihilist finally arrives at the "religious" intuition that the world, which eludes understanding, is not to be comprehended within some finite conceptual system. The human situation remains intractably mysterious as well as precarious. Like the paradox which is established at the heart of the religious consciousness, the drama envisages the existential dichotomies of life and death, the awareness of the void. That is the only "affirmation" the leading dramatists of our age seem to be able to utter.

XII

THE SPIRITUAL QUEST
IN ELIOT'S PLAYS

IT IS TIME to put to the test these critical reflections on the relationship between literature and religion. Let us examine concretely how the most gifted poet of our age, who happens to be an extremely influential critic as well, treats the religious problem in his poetic dramas.

From the start of his career, Eliot was concerned with the exploration of reality in all its complexity, its spiritual as well as social dimensions. In *The Waste Land,* the hero symbolizes the alienation of modern man, perishing of thirst in the desert, and the hideously ugly, dehumanized civilization in which he is forced to live. On the one hand, we behold those who are spiritually unawakened, people who lead aimless, senseless lives, the sleepwalkers in a nightmare, sordid and vulgar, of material reality. These are the living dead; they give in to animal sensuality but do not know the meaning of love. As he muses on death, the eponymous hero of the modern waste land hears only the sound of horns and motors, which shall bring "Sweeney to Mrs. Porter in the spring." In *The Hollow Men,* we catch glimpses of "the Shadow," which falls on every conception and every act, and we hear, too, of death's essential kingdom.

Here we get intimations of the contrapuntal motif that crops up again and again in Eliot's poetry and plays—though it appears, too, if in impersonal terms, in his literary criticism. Few writers of our time have voiced more poignantly their awareness of the horror of a life that is without meaning or purpose, the horror that reveals itself when there is a crack in the polished surface of life and the abyss opens up beneath. Eliot brilliantly analyzes the condition of modern man: the specter of ghastly futility that materializes in the darkness of night, the recurrent visions of metaphysical despair, the pressure of time, the burden of the irretrievable yet active past, the present that is so fugitive and the future that cannot be conceived and yet is already fated, and finally the persistent sense of sin and guilt, the furies that tear at the flesh of the mind.

Throughout the ages creative man has given expression to the myth that is at the heart of all tragic art: man's realization of the emptiness of life as it is spelled out within the sphere of the finite and the mundane. That is the haunting cry one hears in tragedy, in Pascal's confessions, in the writings of Kierkegaard and the latter-day Existentialists. Something happens that leads to this crucial and often traumatic experience of spiritual awakening. The hero undergoes a series of struggles that shake him to the very depths and he sets out on the journey from which he will return spiritually reborn. Dante describes how in the middle of the life journey man discovers that he is lost in a dark wood and he must seek anew to find his way. Cut off from all men, surrounded on all sides by danger, he must keep searching until at the moment of highest suffering he beholds the light. He is saved.

In his literary essays as well as his plays, Eliot deals with this experience of spiritual liberation. Baudelaire, he declares, was a great poet because he was fundamentally concerned with the age-old problems of good and evil, the basic issue of Sin and Redemption. Paradoxically Eliot argues that damnation itself is an immediate form of salvation because, opposing as it does the ennui of modern life, "it at last gives some significance to living." Eliot's religious emphasis comes out challengingly in his statement: "So far as we are human, what we do must be either evil or good; so far as we do evil or good, we are human; and it is better, in a paradoxical way, to do evil than to do nothing: at least we exist. It is true to say that the glory of man is his capacity for damnation." Here is a diagnosis that would certainly receive the enthusiastic endorsement of Graham Greene, whose religious novels are devoted to the elaboration of the thesis that "the glory of man is his capacity for damnation."

Thus Eliot concludes that Christianity is essential to civilization. The true nature of man emerges in his ability to recognize and accept supernatural realities. He does not invent. Either man is an animal or he is made in the image of God. Eliot declares: "There is no avoiding that dilemma: you must be either a naturalist or a supernaturalist. If you remove from the word 'human' all that the belief in the supernatural has given to man, you can view him finally as no more than an extremely clever, adaptable, and mischievous little animal."

These are the themes that Eliot grapples with in his plays. The higher reality makes itself felt not when people merely conform to custom or act out of habit but when they are faced with a profound moral or spiritual choice. Eliot endeavors to re-establish a sharp dichotomy between good and evil. The reality of evil must be reaffirmed. Since morality rests inevitably upon religious sanctions, Christendom must be united. Temporal values can be judged only in the light of eternal values. It is therefore incumbent on every Catholic to aim at the conversion of the whole world.

In experimenting with the drama, Eliot relies from the beginning on the element of the supernatural. *The Rock,* a pageant, contrasts the religious sphere with the temporal order of society. In his plays, Eliot concentrates on a special moment of crisis: the spiritual conflict that confronts the protagonist. The "hero" must choose between the temporal realm and the eternal life: a choice, literally, between life and death. *Murder in the Cathedral,* based on a theme drawn from a remote historical epoch, illuminates the condition of the modern world. By the time Eliot made his contribution to the theater, he had become converted to a new vision of life and therefore turned to religious themes for dramatic development. Reviving the original ritualistic function of the drama, he attempts to communicate overtones of the spiritual reality that is beyond the compass of rational language. As the result of his suffering, the protagonist is made the bearer of supernatural grace, the agent who aids in the working out of a divine plan.

Murder in the Cathedral celebrates the spiritual triumph of a martyr of the church. As soon as Thomas arrives on the scene, he sets the mood of the play, which is in keeping with his mystical insight "that acting is suffering/And suffering is action." Throughout, Thomas speaks in the pregnant paradoxes that constitute the language of the mystic whose vision soars beyond the confines of the practical world. Thomas resists all the solicitations of the Tempter, for he believes that there can be no worldly order not controlled by God. The invitation to ease and plenty, the promise of power in the present and holiness in the hereafter, the glory of sainthood, martyrdom as the road to heavenly grandeur—he spurns all these temptations, conquering his own desires, his sinful pride, his soul's sickness. When he preaches in the Cathedral on Christmas morning, he stresses the idea that the true martyr is the one who subordinates his will completely to God.

In Part II, the hour of martyrdom approaches, and the Chorus points to the horror that covers the sky. They are giving voice to the obscene corruption of Nature, the death in flowers, the worm in the soil, the birds of prey, the fact of putrefaction. Thomas tells them of the moment of illumination when they shall come to understand God's purpose. Humankind, he declares, "cannot bear very much reality." When the Priests announce that his murderers are coming, he replies that they have been coming all his life. It is then, when he is convinced that all things are proceeding, as ordained, to a joyful consummation, that the Chorus cries out:

The agents of hell disappear, the human, they shrink and dissolve
Into dust on the wind, forgotten, unmemorable; only is here
The white flat face of death, God's silent servant,
And behind the face of Death the Judgement
And behind the Judgement the Void, more horrid than active shapes
    of hell;

Emptiness, absence, separation from God;
The horror of the effortless journey, to the empty land
Which is no land, only emptiness, absence, the Void,
Where those who were men can no longer turn the mind
To distraction, delusion, escape into dream, pretence,
Where the soul is no longer deceived, for there are no objects, no tones,
No colours, no forms to distract, to divert the soul
From seeing itself, foully united forever, nothing with nothing,
Not what we call death, but what beyond death is not death,
We fear, we fear.

Here are the negative symbols that reduce the mind of contemporary man to abject terror: Death, the Judgment, the Void,
emptiness, separation from God, the ultimate union of nothing
with nothing. This is the fear of death that torments the masses,
but Thomas meets his end bravely, like a martyr. His decision is one
not made in time. He has given his life to the law of God that
is exalted infinitely above the law of man. When the murder is
committed, it is the Chorus that points to the collective guilt of
mankind, the world that is wholly foul. Then, ironically, the
Knights come forward out of history to justify their deed and
defend the ethics of violence.

In *The Family Reunion,* as in *Murder in the Cathedral,* Eliot
develops a "religious" theme. Though the tone of the dialogue
in *The Family Reunion* is that of upper-middle-class life in
contemporary England, the spiritual struggle the characters pass
through is timeless, classless, universal. The play elaborates the
universal theme of evil and its expiation, the evil that dwells
in every human heart. Eliot presents a hero who portrays modern
man's desperate struggle for salvation. The drama of redemption
is worked out in the conscience of Harry. There is no concrete
proof that he murdered his wife; he is guilty of the evil wish to
kill her, in the same way that his father had dreamed and schemed
to get rid of Amy. That is why he must struggle with himself and
fight off the furies that pursue him.

T. S. Eliot has caught a vision of horror which has shaped not
only his work but also the direction his life has taken. This "numi-

nous" experience, as embodied in his plays, divides itself, roughly, into two parts. First comes the perception of the massive indifference of Nature, with its alien skies, imperturbable stars, and frightening infinite spaces. Each man, a finite particle, is hurtled dizzily through time to the doom of death from which there is no returning. Under such a dispensation, life seems meaningless, singularly empty and futile, a tale told by an idiot, full of sound and fury, signifying nothing. While the poet beholds this sight of the horror that lies beyond this relativistic, secular, depressingly banal world, the people proceed with their practical concerns, the round of getting and spending, eating and enjoying, pursuing the pleasures of the flesh and the feverish distractions of the moment, indifferent to questions of sin or guilt, content to fritter their life away without faith in God or a redemptive vision of eternity.

The second part comes as a reaction against the first. It represents an effort to release the soul from bondage to time and prepare it for redemption: an experience of transcendence, of wordless communion with the unitive ground of being. Eliot's early poetry is filled with symbols revelatory of this spiritual crisis: this inner dying and the anguish it calls forth. Eliot's one experiment in the dramatic genre at this stage was *Sweeney Agonistes,* a fragment which is introduced by a quotation from *Choephoroi:* "You don't see them—but I see them: they are hunting me down, I must move on." Then came Eliot's conversion, when he found refuge under the sheltering wings of the Traditional Church. Yet the memory of "the horror," once experienced, never entirely leaves the one who is redeemed. Everything Eliot writes is instinct with his own spiritual conflicts, and it is these lyrical elements, not his theological principle of salvation, that save his plays from utter failure.

In *The Family Reunion,* all the characters pass through some "numinous" experience. The play is full of symbolism: light and darkness, curtains and windows, the Furies. At the opening of the play, Amy has come to see that what she once took for granted—

the Sun, the Light—when she was young, has taken on new fearful meanings now that she is old. But the others, with the exception of Harry, who arrives later, are still unawakened, and the vacuousness of their life serves to intensify the horror. Agatha, who is the mouthpiece of the higher truths, the voice of the horror transcended, says:

When the loop in time comes—and it does not come for everybody—
The hidden is revealed, and the spectres show themselves.

It is Agatha who sees the pattern that is working itself out in all these preparations to instal Harry at Wishwood and all the plans to insure his happiness.

Harry's first words reveal his disturbed state of mind. He feels that he is being stared at by eyes through a window, and he cries out (it is the voice of Eliot calling out to his lost generation):

Can't you see them? *You* don't see them, but I see them,
And they see me.

The Eumenides represent the furies born of a stricken conscience, the infernal torment of those not yet redeemed by the vision of God. But the others in the family, the unawakened, keep on talking as if nothing has happened. How can he make them understand the unimportance of events? He declares:

                                         You have gone through life in sleep,
Never woken to the nightmare. I tell you, life would be unendurable
If you were wide awake.

Though he realizes beforehand they cannot and will not understand, he tries to draw a picture of the horror of life when people live without direction and a sense of purpose.

          The partial anesthesia of suffering without feeling
          And partial observation of one's own automatism
          While the slow stain sinks deeper through the skin
          Tainting the flesh and discolouring the bone —
          This is what matters, but it is unspeakable....

This is indeed the heart of the matter. There is no escape from this unspeakable horror. Wherever one flees, one is still alone. That is why Harry feels he pushed his wife overboard; he was trying to reverse the senseless automatism of his life. The others remain fixed in the delusion that somehow they will be immune, exceptions to the universal fate. The worldly are also aware of the horror, the noises in the cellar, the presences at the window, the shadows gathering ominously in the darkness, but they make every effort to hide the truth, not to open the door or draw the curtain aside, for then they would become unsure of what is real or unreal. They must insist that the world is what they imagine it to be.

The complications of the plot in *The Family Reunion* are relatively unimportant. What is important is its religious meaning. Harry feels that he is lost, that he has reached the end of his strength and cannot move forward another step. He has joined the legion of the hopeless, the damned. Though all that haunts him may be a dream, the dream itself is real. Harry knows that he will find no redemption at home. The Furies are forever after him; they are inside of him too, "in the nightly panic/Of dreaming dissolution." How can others comprehend what he has gone through? They must see for themselves; otherwise they cannot enter that other world. Harry knows that he must face the Furies and fight them alone. Suffering has made him aware of deeper and higher dimensions of consciousness. What the members of his family call the normal is merely the unreal and unimportant. It is not his own life that lies in shattered ruins; he is but part of some monstrous aberration of all men throughout the world. Purged by suffering, Harry knows at last that the Eumenides are not simply outside.

His business is not to run away but to seek. All men are fugitives and those who take the opposite direction—toward their true haven, the home of spiritual fulfilment—will seem to be running away. But where does one go from a world of insanity? The answer is: "Somewhere on the other side of despair." This is the second stage of the journey all men must take: toward redemption through sacrifice. This is the destiny he has always sought. He has crossed the frontier and been reborn. How can man safeguard himself against God? Agatha, in the last speech, points out the way toward salvation. If the crooked is to be made straight and the curse lifted, it must be through the intercession of those who set forth on the journey to redemption.

The Cocktail Party is a further statement of Eliot's new vision of salvation, but it includes at the same time a scathing criticism of the hollowness of modern life. The psychoanalyst in this play, who represents the all-seeing eye and mind of God, reveals the most uncomfortable truths about the self. Patiently he analyzes the marital conflict between Edward and Lavinia. Edward has lost touch with the person he thought he was and has suddenly been reduced to the status of an object. Like the other members of society, he has become depersonalized, an automaton in an air-conditioned nightmare. He possesses a body but lacks a sense of identity. Edward has to set out on a quest for his real being. This is another aspect of the quest that Eliot deals with: the search for personal identity, the attempt to define the essence of the self as it flows through time, changeable in structure and yet basically the same. The one thing the self must resist, if it is to retain its integrity, is the fate of becoming mechanized, an object among objects.

But Edward insists that he must find out what Lavinia is before he can discover who he is. Must he always remain lost in the dark? The psychoanalyst replies that the sole purpose of remaining in the dark is to dispel the illusion that one was ever in the light. The other characters are also concerned with the nature of reality. Celia, with whom Edward has had an affair, finds that she was not real for him because he lacked reality himself. Not knowing his own mind, he is incapable of loving. Edward is passing through the painful crisis of discovering that no man can run away from himself. It is the psychoanalyst who points out that people die to each other daily. The self is forever changing in relation to other selves in the continuum of time. All this is designed to drive home the point that many a husband and wife are only pretending that they are not strangers to each other—a theme that is further explored in *The Confidential Clerk*. Both Lavinia and Edward have made some shattering discoveries about themselves. Edward declares:

> Why could I not walk out of my prison?
> What is hell? Hell is oneself,
> Hell is alone, the other figures in it
> Merely projections. There is nothing to escape from
> And nothing to escape to. One is always alone.

Here is a conception of hell altogether different from Sartre's interpretation, in *No Exit,* of hell as being other people.

Edward confesses to Reilly what it is that troubles him so acutely: he has ceased to believe in his own personality. Edward cries out: "I am obsessed by the thought of my own insignificance." In trying to get to the root of his malady, Edward discovers that there is a form of suffering which exceeds the worst pain the body is made to endure. It is not the death of the body but the death of the spirit that he finds so terrifying. He wishes to be sent to the sanatorium, but people like Edward, who are eternally self-deceived, cannot enter the sanatorium. The analyst tells Edward that most people must make the best of a bad job. The only exceptions are the saints and it is they who go to the sanatorium. Lavinia and Edward cannot break away from the world of illusion.

Then Celia comes to the psychoanalyst for help. She feels perfectly well, as far as her responses are concerned, but her sense of reality is irreparably damaged; she is lost in a dark wood and cannot find her way out. She has nothing to work for or live for. The world around her seems "all a delusion." In fact, she would prefer to believe that there is something wrong with her rather than with the world itself. For she can be restored to "normality." It is then that the analyst raises the question of what constitutes "normality." Celia has suddenly and overwhelmingly become aware that she has always been alone, "that one always is alone." Another symptom she suffers from is a sense of sin, though not sin in the conventional sense. What she feels is an inner emptiness, and now she is driven by the need to atone.

The psychoanalyst declares that she can be cured but she must choose the form of treatment. He can lead her to make the adjustment to the common human condition. Many return to the past situation, which they call being "normal," living unregenerately in time, taking all things for granted, avoiding excessive expectations and becoming tolerant of themselves and of others. In a world ruled by greed, stupidity, violence, and madness, that is a good life, but it is not the best life. The second way of life is the mystical life of renunciation and self-transcendence. One must finally choose between these two paths.

> The second is unknown, and so requires faith —
> The kind of faith that issues from despair.
> The destination cannot be described;
> You will know very little until you get there;
> You will journey blind.

This is how Eliot attempts to incorporate his "message" within the body of the play.

Celia decides to go to the sanatorium. She is willing to suffer in order to transcend the human condition. In the last scene, at the cocktail party, we learn what has happened to Celia. She joined an austere order and was sent to Kinkanja, where she was crucified near an anthill. Her suffering, though ghastly, is part of the design. To suffer a violent death is a triumphant affirmation of her destiny. Each one must accept the past and, by acceptance, change its meaning. The psychoanalyst sums up the theme of the play by quoting these lines from Shelley:

> For know there are two worlds of life and death:
> One that which thou beholdest; but the other
> Is underneath the grave, where do inhabit
> The shadows of all forms that think and live
> Till death unite them and they part no more.

Even in *The Confidential Clerk,* Eliot's most secular and "realistic" play, the same symbolic motifs of "the quest" are sounded. The old dramatic convention of the foundling in search of his father and mother is used as a springboard for the exploration of the high mysteries of the self. The so-called real world of experience, the universe of events, is contrasted with the world of the spirit. Which is more real? What is the real self, and how is one to reach the heart of the mystery that is the other person? The fundamental theme of this play is based on the search of people to recover their lost integrity. Colby Simpkins, the new confidential clerk, frequently doubts the reality of the outer world. He is alone; his two worlds are unrelated, and therefore both are unreal. It is Colby, too, who asks: "Does one ever come to understand anyone?" There is no end to this struggle to understand another person, for the other is forever changing. He is eager to find out what a person is, not who he is. People often play a part in order to satisfy the conception others have of them. When Colby learns the truth about his father, he is content to assume his humble destiny as a second-rate organist.

Honestly and fearlessly Eliot faces the horror of existence. He reveals the intense conflict that goes on within the self, its struggle to achieve unification; he portrays, too, the shadow which observes everything and judges everything. What is this shadow? It symbolizes the knowledge of the futility that encompasses so much of modern life, the nothingness which waits for man at the end of the road, unless he chooses the way of salvation. Modern man is afraid of his shadow, of discovering his identity, of coming to grips with ultimate spiritual reality.

Whereas the Existentialists maintain the tension of faith by clinging to their skepticism, fighting constantly to affirm the reality of a God they can never prove or know, Eliot does not believe that mystical certitude is beyond human reach. The Existentialists remain outside the church; Eliot has entered it in all humility. The Existentialists reject ritual and tradition, dogma and authoritative, inspired truth; Eliot accepts them. Eliot pictures dramatically the self-defeating absurdity and anguish of the lonely, disintegrated individual trying to find fulfilment in a life that is mechanical and meaningless. Only those who go beyond the finite and the relative are saved. Whether or not one accepts Eliot's religious solution, one cannot deny the creative force with which, in his plays, he uses symbolism and myth to dramatize the desperate plight of modern man: his spiritual alienation, his loss of a sense of purpose, his quest for salvation through faith. Eliot highlights the drought and sterility of the waste land of modern life, but he also holds up a shining vision of the journey that must be taken if one is to emerge at the end spiritually saved. His "message" comes through with unmistakable force of conviction, but his poetic dramas cannot by any stretch of the imagination be called tragedies. To introduce the dimensions of the afterlife, the horizons of eternity—all this implies a negation of the tragic vision. Religion alone cannot save a civilization that is dying. Christianity, despite the evangelical efforts of T. S. Eliot and the warnings of Toynbee, cannot be revived as a practical measure of salvation.

XIII

TRAGEDY AND RELIGION

THE RELIGIOUS CRITIC who ana-
lyzes literature in order to discover the leading symptoms of the
spiritual sickness of our time must reconcile himself to the observ-
able fact that much of contemporary writing is not only secular
in content but divorced from the main stream of Christian thought.
There is, to be sure, a body of literature which, though secular in
its orientation, betrays unmistakably, by the way it comes to grips
with the problems of this age, the central and persistent influence
of the Christian tradition. For example, Joyce, by the very violence
with which he repudiated the Catholic faith, revealed how deeply
it had left its impress upon his sensitive mind. It is particularly the
Protestant heritage, hospitable to experiment and innovation, that
welcomes newness of vision, revaluation, creative rebirth; it takes
its stand on personal revelation rather than authority. Emerson,
in the nineteenth century, admirably illustrates this nonconformist
strain, this demand for direct communion, if possible, with the
source of all being. Living as he did wholly from within, why
should he be compelled to pay tribute to the sacredness of tradition?
And if someone should suggest that this revolt might be prompted
by impulses from below, then Emerson had his reply ready: "They
do not seem to me to be such; but if I am the Devil's child, I will
live then from the Devil"—a conclusion that shocked many con-

servative thinkers of his day. This was entirely consistent with Emerson's conviction that man in the bush may meet with God.

The forces that make for secularization have gathered vast strength since the time when Emerson spoke out. Not that the work produced by the champions of the secular outlook in the nineteenth and twentieth centuries is completely cut off from the Christian tradition. We can trace the idealistic ferment in the writings of such iconoclasts as Nietzsche, Sartre, Karl Marx, and Camus. Those writers also serve who do not formally align themselves with one of the institutional religions of the West. Heresy, too, as viewed through the perspective of liberal Protestantism, may possess profound spiritual import. In this respect, writers as dissimilar and blasphemous as Baudelaire and Joyce are giving utterance to the Christian element, even though their quest for salvation takes place outside the church. Many roads lead to the perception of the numinous in existence, and many a writer who is outwardly alienated from Christianity may nevertheless give voice to vitally important religious intuition. That is the approach which characterizes a seminal book like Amos Wilder's *Modern Poetry and the Christian Tradition,* in which the author says: "The fateful issues of the Christian faith are often wrestled with more profoundly outside the church than within."

Professor Wilder recognizes, however, that the church has lost much of its influence, its position of leadership, so that the literary prophets of our day operate largely within a secular framework. Increasingly the belief has gained ground that the teachings of the church are sadly out of touch with the complexities of modern experience. But if the spirit can shed its grace on the hearts and minds of men outside the church as well as within, then much of contemporary literature, despite its nihilistic cast, is fundamentally "religious" in its striving. Though the ideological foundations of Christianity have been undermined in the past two centuries, there have been few ages in which men of vision have wrestled so earnestly, though in the main negatively, with ultimate existential issues as they do today. Just as the writer cannot throw off the burdens of the past, so he cannot escape the crises and confusion, the strains and schisms, of his age. Though many contemporary writers who are nonreligious or irreligious have been drawn to "religious" themes, they have treated them in challengingly unorthodox ways.

So long as reality remains mysterious, it will be susceptible of different interpretations; no two eyes will view it from the same perspective. The writer cannot afford to omit any facet of experience from his work, even though he is unable to explain it. The ambiguity of existence persists, the uncertainty, the element that cannot be analyzed in terms of reason. Hence no single interpretation of reality is completely satisfactory, free of contradictions. In giving his interpretation of reality, in drama or poetry or fiction, the writer cannot hope to achieve either perfection or completeness; he must rest content with incompleteness, no matter what worldview he affirms. Yet though the world is full of a rich diversity of religious beliefs, there are some critics who are convinced that the Christian system offers a unifying as well as true perspective for the writer. Had not Eliot argued that the purpose of every Catholic is to aim at the conversion of the world? But why is the Christian outlook inherently superior to others in its creative potential? Is it because Christianity brings the writer in fruitful relation to eternity? But Buddhism shadows forth a radically different conception of time in its ideal of Nirvana. The one argument consistently presented for the creative value of Christianity is that it enables the writer to work with established traditional beliefs; he is spared the agonizing labor of having to create them anew. Yet that is precisely what the writer, regardless of his commitment, is impelled to do: to test his beliefs, to revise them periodically, to cast off what is false, to discover and hold on to those values of the spirit that are viable and enduring. The truth of faith is strengthened and renewed every time it is questioned and survives the test of doubt.

The problem comes to a head when we attempt to deal with the controversial question whether a play that resolves its basic conflict in terms of Christian orthodoxy can be a tragedy. Is not a Christian tragedy, in which the protagonist is assured of immortality and can transcend not only the power of evil but even the finality of death, a contradiction in terms? The hero may die but his death, as in *The Cocktail Party,* is a willed martyrdom, a deliberatetly sought triumph. Faith in immortality militates against the tragic sense of life, which cannot blind itself to the precariousness of human existence, the helplessness of man as he faces extinction, his awareness of the lack of ultimate meaning to justify his stay on earth, the contingency and perhaps utter uselessness of all human projects. That is the point of view, more or less, advanced by Karl Jaspers in *Tragedy Is Not Enough* and by Herbert Weisinger in *Tragedy and the Paradox of the Fortunate Fall.* It is this doctrine that is anathema to the religious-minded critic. In *Studies in Literature and Belief,* Martin Jarrett-Kerr argues that this point of view is based on a misconception. It is a misreading of Christian doctrine, he argues, to say that the idea of immortality eliminates the possibility of tragedy.

Briefly: only in a world where real tragedy is possible is redemption also possible. Perhaps the reverse is also true: only in a world where redemption—and therefore damnation—is possible, is tragedy also possible. Thus it is not true that there can be no genuine Christian tragic drama within and compatible with a Christian metaphysic; on the contrary, all genuine tragic drama is material for Christian understanding.

Though he presents his case with admirable succinctness, on what grounds can Jarrett-Kerr defend his position? Though tragic dramas have been written by men who were Christian, their trage-dies hardly conform to Christian metaphysical assumptions, for if they did where would the conflict come from? If in the end there is promise of salvation and everlasting life, why should death, the ultimate catastrophe, be resisted so strenuously? If redemption is the basis of tragedy, then what is the meaning of the tragic experi-ence? The tragedy derives its central and sustaining power from the fear, ever present, that faith in the life after death is mistaken. And if that is so, then what shall men live for? Wealth? Success? Power?

It was George Orwell who declared that the old religious faith cannot be restored. Suffering will always go on, suffering that cannot be justified by reliance on some eschatological hope. Christianity, he declared, despite the verbal professions of faith men make, is defunct. His reasons for thinking so throw a light on the problem of tragedy in relation to a Christian metaphysic. Everyone today acts (and that is what counts, Orwell insisted, behavior, not verbal beliefs) as if he knows that death is the end and that this is the only world he will ever enjoy.

But if tragedy cannot be written under the Christian dispensation, the attempt to construct it on naturalistic or nihilistic lines is beset with difficulties that are extremely hard to overcome. Implicit in every conception of tragedy is a *Weltanschauung,* accepted by both the dramatist and the audience, in the light of which the fate of the hero is interpreted. Out of suffering and adversity is born an extremity of despair which is finally transcended so that the tragedy becomes meaningful. But how? Under what auspices? If man is only a machine, then the possibilities of tragedy are sharply curtailed, if not annulled. On what naturalistic basis can a morality of justification be worked out? How account for the triumph of unreason, the demoniac upsurge of evil, the malevolence of destiny?

The heart of tragedy lies in this very weakness of the hero, his failure to bear his share of moral responsibility for his action. But how is the modern dramatist to affirm the worth of the individual and his faith in the moral structure of the universe? It is the struggle to make this affirmation in the face of suffering and evil and shipwreck that provides the tensions and ambiguities of the tragic dilemma. For this faith, though beset with sorry contradictions and essential doubt, must nevertheless be affirmed, or else all is darkness and futility. Man is the battleground, or stage, on which this battle is fought between instinct and reason, chaos and order,

passion and moral control, ultimate meaning and meaninglessness.
The hero tries to escape from the fell clutch of circumstance and
the compulsion of the instinctual life, but even in his noblest aspirations and struggles he cannot drive out the devil of doubt. That
is the reason why tragedy in the twentieth century has progressively
weaned itself away from the Christian metaphysic. Christianity
cannot provide the soil in which tragedy will flourish. Essentially
antitragic in outlook, it exalts the principle of renunciation, it rec-
ommends the sacrificial acceptance of death as the means of
delivery into eternal life, whereas tragedy must cherish the bitter
anguish of doubt, the perennial sense of dread, even as it endeavors
to transcend them.

It is in this sense that the theater may be looked upon as the
secular temple designed to celebrate the mystery of life in all its
strange and multifarious manifestations. On the stage is re-enacted
the struggle of man against fate, his grandeur and misery, his
splendid aspirations and wretched failures, his minuscule triumphs
and eventual defeat by time and death. In shaping this inchoate,
refractory material, the dramatist must of necessity confront the
contradictions of life that make for despair, the darkness that
blots out the light of the sun; but today, regardless of the
religious views he may hold, he cannot resolve them in the light
of religious orthodoxy. Neither doctrinaire in method nor didactic
in purpose, he seeks to reveal the truth of life, as much of it as he
can encompass in his vision. His treatment will, of course, depend
on how he defines the nature of man, how he interprets the character of reality. If he is a naturalist, like Chekhov or O'Neill, he will
portray man as a biological organism, no different from the plants
and animals, a victim of forces beyond his control, doomed despite
all his scientific knowledge and technological mastery to suffer
the oblivion of death.

For the theater is not a church nor the stage a pulpit. Whereas
the Christian humanist must interpret the universe in the light of
God's wisdom, the dramatist, as artist, must represent the human
condition in all its snarled complexity and ambiguity. Hence he

concentrates not on the gaining of the Holy Grail but on the quest itself; he can, in the world of the drama, offer no assurance of divine forgiveness or providential redemption, only the forlorn struggle. In the imaginative universe he creates the light is forever pitted against darkness. He projects the torment in the heart of man striving to achieve the faith which his rational mind rejects as an impossibility. Far from presenting a coherent theological doctrine, the dramatist is seeking to communicate the elusive quality of human experience, the untidy and intractable stuff of life. That is why he focuses attention on the inner debate, the spiritual travail, the lonely journey.

But how can an age that looks upon man as insignificant as an ephemerid and on human life as a useless passion produce a literature that exhibits the tragic sense of life? For if the human experiment is of no account in the unfoldment of history, if all that man aspires to and struggles so fiercely to achieve is meaningless, an illusion born of illusion, a dream within a mechanical dream, then the creative act itself becomes a vain endeavor, a species of absurdity, just as the writer who is too preoccupied with the promise of heaven will cease to be interested in the life of art. Whatever frustrated religiosity the nihilistic attitude voices, it has seriously weakened the attitude the modern writer has toward his work.

Let us see how Eugene O'Neill, a thoroughgoing naturalist, in contrast to T. S. Eliot, deals with the theme of the modern struggle for faith. A tragically split personality, Eugene O'Neill recorded in many of his plays the spiritual conflicts from which he suffered all his life long, his strenuous but unavailing search for a faith by which he might govern his life. In *Days Without End,* the hero at the end recaptures his faith, but the resolution is not dramatically embodied; it is a resolution born of frayed nerves and neurasthenic desperation. O'Neill never found the way, and his later plays—witness *The Iceman Cometh*—are a confession of his failure. Though weakly constructed, *Days Without End* reveals the nature of the spiritual struggle O'Neill waged, the confusion that plagued him, the madness of denial that seized hold of him

and would not let him go. For the author stands unmistakably
delineated, guilt-stricken, anguished, driven to embrace God and
yet incapable of combating the ugly suspicion that there is nothing
beyond this earth. A divided personality like his begetter, the
central character is both seeker and sinner, saint and blasphemer.
John has passed through a painful struggle to find some reason
for living, while his alter ego, Loving, is a scornful mocker, whose
eyes stare out blankly from behind the mask he wears. He is the
dark evil self, the sneerer and incurable cynic, uttering aloud
the secret evil thoughts of John: there is nothing either to hope
for or fear, nothing to live for, nothing at all. There are neither
devils nor gods.

In the past John used to fulminate against capitalism and
denounce the hypocrisy of religion. Hating Christianity, he once
sought as a militant atheist to prove that Christ was a myth.
But he had discarded his atheism, his socialism, his anarchism, his
faith in communism, when they failed him in his quest. He had
turned to oriental mysticism, to Buddhism, and finally had embraced
the creed of evolutionary scientism. Having thus come full circle he
had declared himself to be a mechanist, and perversely played the
role of Antichrist. Some evil power had taken possession of his soul.
He thought of suicide, but, as Loving remarks, he was still afraid to
die, too superstitious to believe the truth of life: "that death is the
final release, the warm, dark peace of annihilation." Even during
his worst periods of atheism, his spirit was not at peace. "There
always remained something in him that felt itself damned by life,
damned with distrust, cursed with the inability ever to reach a
lasting belief in any faith, damned by a fear of the lie hiding behind
the mask of truth." Loving, his other self, pronounces harsh judgment upon him: pursuing one illusion after another, John never
had the courage to face the bitter but redemptive lesson "that there
is no truth for men, that human life is unimportant and meaningless." All of John's spiritual turmoil, his craving for freedom and
peace, his search for a faith that would justify his existence, is
cruelly mocked by Loving, who declares: "We know we are all

the slaves of meaningless chance—electricity or something, which
whirls us on—on to Hercules!" But John, the restless pilgrim, will
not abandon the hopeless quest. Perhaps, if man faces the truth
without evasion, he will be able to create new goals, "ends for our
days." Perhaps a new discipline will spring up, a new will to live,
a vision of life as somehow noble even though it is spun out
briefly in time and space. He cries out: "A new savior must be
born who will reveal to us how we can be saved from ourselves,
so that we can be free of the past and inherit the future and not
perish by it!"

Not fooled by this brave splash of rhetoric, the vigilant Loving
announces that there can be no going back: man has passed beyond
the need of God. Suffering from a bad conscience, John is simply
toying with the discarded fancies of his childhood, seeking a supernatural guarantee of life after death. In vain does John dream
of conquering the Devil by kneeling at the foot of the cross, for
the rationalist self in him will not yield to this infantile weakness.
The stubborn reason laughs at these fantasies of salvation. Loving
curses God, though with the pointed ironic reminder that there is
really no need to curse a God that does not exist. John despondently
comes to realize "he can never believe in his lost faith again."

O'Neill provides a "happy" but dramatically unconvincing
ending for *Days Without End:* John kneels before the cross and
reaffirms his faith while his devilish alter ego perishes. What does
it mean, Loving had taunted John, to say that man must go on,
despite all his misery? Why? For life's sake, when there is only
nothingness? Why should man be ruled by the blind, stupid, irrational compulsion of life when death waits for him at the end
of the road? Why not make an end of it all? Why fear death?
Loving tempts John with this desolate knowledge: "Death is not
the dying. Dying is life, its last revenge upon itself. But death
is what the dead know, the warm, dark womb of Nothingness..."
The ending, when John mystically experiences the blessed miracle
of faith, represents O'Neill's sole attempt to portray "the leap"
of affirmation, the mystery of the faith that is recaptured after the

heart surrenders its perverse pride and the mind gives up its Promethean defiance. Making his last stand, Loving, his back to the cross, rages that prayer is useless. First one must believe, but belief is impossible. "There is no God! There is only death!" Loving dies hating and cursing God, while John, his eyes fixed on the Crucified One, cries out: "Thou art the Way—the Truth—the Resurrection and the Life, and he that believeth in Thy love, his love shall never die!"

Though decidedly inferior as a play, *Days Without End* is of considerable importance as a subjective confession indicating the struggle O'Neill waged. For O'Neill was both John and Loving, the two in one, with this exception: it was John who perished and Loving who lived on and triumphed. In the world of O'Neill, no one is held responsible for the tragedy that overtakes him; his characters possess no measure of free will. Victims of fate, they go down fighting against the forces that push them back into the dark womb of Nothingness. Life is a hideous mess for which no one is individually accountable. As a determinist, O'Neill is led to portray men and women—the Hairy Ape, Nina Leeds, Eben Cabot—who are not aware of any higher power or purpose in the universe.

But if man is thus denied the power of free will, if he is inevitably the victim of biological and socio-economic forces acting upon him, then his stature is diminished, his significance in the cosmos dwindles to zero. Tragedies constructed rigorously on deterministic principles are, like those that depend on miracles of faith, a contradiction in terms. In a world ruled absolutely by scientific laws, the role of the human being is reduced to nullity and life is a strange dark interlude. When O'Neill first conceived the idea of a story in the modern manner based on the old Electra theme, he jotted down some notes which reveal the difficulties faced by a naturalistic playwright: "Is it possible to get modern psychological approximation of Greek sense of fate into such a play, which an intelligent audience of today, possessed by no belief in gods or supernatural retribution, could accept and be moved by?"

O'Neill knew that the intellectual audience of his time had, like himself, no belief in God. That is the assumption he had to work with. If the Greek Fates are to be dismissed, then what powers shape the character and destiny of man? Falling back on the philosophy of determinism, O'Neill in *Mourning Becomes Electra* shows that the behavior of the Mannon family is caused not by God but by its past history, the psychological web of the past, the social and physical forces that drove them on.

If O'Neill produced no tragedy, if tragedy is an anomaly in our time, the reasons are to be sought not in the nature of man but in the conception he has of himself. Tragedy is a universal experience, not limited to the Greeks or the Elizabethans. But why, if the tragic experience is universal, has it flourished only briefly and in a few epochs? Out of the perception that man is doomed to die springs the tragic vision, for this perception contradicts not only all that he desires but all he has lived for. But if death is the source of the tragic sense of life, then tragedy is not intended—far from it—to justify the ways of God to man. Tragedy is not a vindication of the divine order; it deals with the paradoxical and terrible aspects of human experience, the ultimate meaning of man's fate. Fundamentally serious in outlook, it struggles with these existential implications as if they were mysteries not to be solved. That is why tragedies do not dispense poetic justice or preach universal goodness and love.

If this interpretation is correct, then it logically follows that the possibility of creating *religious* tragedy must be excluded. God cannot legitimately take a providential hand in the vicissitudes of the tragic characters. If he does so, then the element of freedom of will has been removed and there is no tragic conflict. If God is conceived as blind and mechanical, controlled, like Hardy's "It," by forces beyond its ken, then we get a determinism that again rules out the possibility of tragedy.

Can a theory of tragedy be formulated that fits in with a humanistic rather than religious view of life? The answer is to be found, eloquently stated, in H. J. Muller's *The Spirit of Tragedy.* Tragedy, which is more or less pessimistic in tone, springs from man's revolt against his degraded condition, his bondage to death. Hence it cannot be confined within a specifically religious framework, for it cannot keep out the element of irony and paradox from its interpretation of the workings of providence. The tragic writers may point out and even affirm the presence of a moral law in the world, but they are not convinced that this law is a beneficent one. Were there a providence that ruled man's fate, were evil but an illusion, then there would be no need for tragedy. It requires no great study to perceive that poetic justice is not meted out on earth; there is often little correspondence between the crime committed and the punishment inflicted. The good man may be struck down, the innocent may be chosen as a victim of the angry gods. Hence the tragic vision is not only pessimistic but complex, instinct with existential irony. It centers on the destiny of man, the disproportion between his strivings and his achievement, his expectations and ideals and the fate that finally befalls him. As Muller points out, the tragic spirit would not arise if men were wholly convinced that the meaning of life is summed up in serving God. Essentially tragedy, as it seeks to determine the nature of the powers that rule the universe, confronts the ultimate question of justice. The "tragic hero," having passed through a severe ordeal of suffering, merited or unmerited, emerges a "better" man at the end, for he now comprehends the meaning of his fate—of man's fate—and is capable of accepting it. His death represents an affirmation of the human spirit in its capacity to endure, with brave dignity and without the assurance of a life to come, the worst blows that adversity can deliver.

Here are the reasons, philosophical as well as aesthetic, why tragedy does not conform to any religious principle of justification. Transcending the conventional notions of good and evil, salvation and damnation, the tragic hero confronts his destiny and accepts the consequences that spring from his decision. He is what he is; he may behave absurdly, he may defy God, violate a number of social taboos, but his spirit, even in the hour of defeat, remains unconquerable. These are the stubborn paradoxes that tragedy abundantly exhibits: man acts against his best interests, in defiance of biological caution, the wisdom of the body, or the mandates of society. Refractory, full of contradictions, the tragic hero remains a terrible mystery.

The great tragic writers faced the puzzling meaning of destiny without blinking or softening the truth of their vision. Whereas man is prompted by the all-too-human need to believe in an afterlife and in a transcendental system of rewards for virtue, the tragic poets make it clear that obedience to morality offers no exemption from the cruel sway of death. Even the gods are subject to necessity which knows no mercy and indeed no sense of justice. Necessity is not only inscrutable but inexorable. The injunction to worship God and follow his commandments arouses ambivalent, if not hostile, feelings. Since the yoke of God is too heavy to bear, some men in their conduct betray the fact that they secretly hate as well as fear God. Out of these mixed motives and complex feelings emerges the tragic sense of life. All religious beliefs bear witness to this ineradicable contradiction: nothing is certain; faith is vitiated by doubt, hope neutralized by the acids of despair, heaven opposed by the power of hell, God matched by his infernal Adversary, the Devil. Who can be sure which one will emerge the victor in this contest of wills? The only certainty is the universality of tragedy in an existence that is incomprehensible.

Though Elizabethan tragedy inherited much of the medieval theology, it made many drastic changes in it. For one thing, the Elizabethan tragic writers questioned many of its absolutes. Not that the medieval mind was free from extremes of tension, polarities of the spirit, deep-cutting conflicts of belief. Though it believed in immortality, it was terrified by the thought of death; it was a death-haunted and death-obsessed age. The Renaissance inherited other sources of discord. For Christianity, in its pure form, frowns upon any debates on the ways of providence. How can man presume God to scan? God in his infinite wisdom commits no mistakes. The believer must therefore close his mind to all the contradictions caught by the eye of reason. Hence the Middle Ages, which countenanced no revolt against God, created no tragedies and no tragic hero. The Age of Faith, as Muller reveals in his book, is deficient in ambiguity, incapable of perceiving the basic incongruities of life; it lacks the dramatic imagination. It can compose dramas of salvation, but these are not tragic in either structure or content. The Passion plays, constructed to demonstrate the theme of Resurrection, are free of the dialectic of doubt, the countervailing thrust of skeptical questioning. "In general," Muller says, "the Christian ritual pattern has no tragic potentialities until some element of uncertainty or doubt enters—some sense of actual *mystery* in the mysteries." That is the theme we have been driving home in this study. It is the rebellious or at least the profoundly questioning spirit that truly represents the heart of the tragic vision. If the dramatist sets out to affirm the Christian mythos as the ultimate of the historical process, then he cuts himself off from the world of tragedy.

The Renaissance man, taking pride in his human potentialities and his endowment of natural instincts, was proportionately less concerned with the problem of original sin. Though he still clung to Christianity, he could not deny that it was torn by multiple schisms. Though the prospect of death filled him with terror, he accepted death because he could thus more richly affirm and complete his life. It was in this age of exuberant energy that the tragic hero was born, the Promethean man capable of suffering on a grand scale, the incarnation of will, defiant of limitations, struggling to achieve the impossible. Out of the realization that man cannot possibly fulfil his titanic ambitions arose the tragic conflict. Marlowe, who wrote tragedies based on this theme, offers no hope of salvation.

In Shakespeare's plays, tragedy is concerned with the troubled events that lead up to the death of the hero, but the death must be meaningful, not the result of accident or chance, if it is to be authentically tragic; the protagonist must initiate and be responsible, in part or in whole, for the actions that recoil upon his own head. It is not surprising to find that Shakespeare gives no categorical answer to the riddle of life. He pictures the reality of the tragic struggle without attempting to make a particular system of faith prevail or to vindicate a fixed principle of poetic justice at work in the universe. Though Shakespeare was faithful to his vision of life and exhibited the powerlessness of man in the cruel clutch of circumstance, he also indicates in his tragedies that man is the responsible cause of his undoing, since he does possess a measure of free will. He is not simply the victim of arbitrary destiny, of a determinism that approaches fatalism. If the hero is responsible for the tragic consequences that ensue, then justice, in one sense, stands vindicated; but there is no moral calculus whereby happiness and misery are apportioned according to the merits and defects of character. It is not a question of imposing absolute categories of right and wrong. Shakespeare offers no solution for the mystery of existence and presents no indictment of the gods. The mystery remains. The Shakespearean heroes go to their death without voicing any hope of immortality. They do not formulate a specifically Christian outlook.

It is in the modern age that we come up against the crucial problem of tragedy. Can it possibly exist in this disintegrative climate of thought, in an age that is skeptical, relativistic, irreligious? How make a tragic hero of modern man who leads a routinized, meaningless, mechanical life, without the support of faith in the supernatural? Bewildered by the technological energy he has unleashed, he has lost touch with the eternal verities and has come to a shattering awareness of his own impotence. Can tragedy be based on naturalistic premises, or is the modern tragic dramatist doomed to sterility? There is really no reason why the spread of new knowledge about the universe and the nature of man should arrest the creative impulse. Why must uniformity of belief be imposed before tragedy can arise? For good or evil, the modern temper is characterized by flux, skepticism, a pluralistic variety of values. Indeed, as Muller declares, the decline of faith in the supernatural would help to heighten the importance of man. Why must he be tainted and damned with original sin, be condemned as a fallen creature?

Modern drama in its highest reaches is resolved to tell the truth, however unpleasant it may be, even if it involves the recognition that God does not establish a balance of forces in the universe. This is the whole moral duty of the writer in our time—to tell the truth about life, without offering any opiates or optimistic panaceas. Only by facing the truth about themselves and about life can men become free. This raises a number of difficult, complicated issues in the aesthetics of tragedy. If the dramatist carries naturalism to extremes, how can he present a truly tragic hero, since man is then shown to be victimized by external forces and is denied freedom of will? Yet the insights of naturalism contributed strongly to this impulse to tell the truth at all costs. The modern dramatist, acknowledging the ultimate futility of life, perceives the distance that separates dream from reality, aspiration from accomplishment, and he perceives it through the perspective of irony. He loves life too much to force it within the procrustean bed of a single philosophical or religious point of view. Though he rejects the idea of a divine providence governing human affairs, he nevertheless believes in man and genuinely cherishes human values. Chekhov, Schnitzler, Camus, Anouilh, have abandoned religious dogma and embrace no final certainty, but they portray with sensitive compassion the way men strive—alas, ineffectually—for a richer fulfilment. At the same time, like Samuel Beckett in *Waiting for Godot,* they concentrate on the tragic emotion of our time: the sense of the purposelessness of life on earth. There is the pathetic, often desperate, human search, but there is no solution.

Muller is one of the few critics who root the tragic spirit in the humanistic faith of the West—a spirit that does not abase itself before God but faces the truth of life courageously. Affirming the potential greatness of man, the tragic sense at least makes clear that no single outlook possesses a monopoly of the truth. Humbly aware of the ignorance that circumscribes man, it enables him to face suffering with dignity and death with fortitude. The humanist faith stresses faith in individual effort without reliance on God; it affirms the inherent value of life this side of the grave. Most people in the West are not committed to the belief that the promise of life everlasting in Kingdom Come is the central motivating force of history or that it provides the basic meaning and justification of life. For those who cannot live in the light of eternity, for those who take it for granted that there is nothing beyond life on this earth, the tragic spirit may help to restore order in a badly fragmented world. As H. J. Muller declares,

The tragic spirit can promote a saving irony, in the perception of the naive or absurd aspects of this belief; a spirit of compassion, through the knowledge of irremediable evils and insoluble dilemmas; and a spirit of reverence, for the idealism that keeps seeking truth, goodness, and beauty even though human ideals are not everlasting.

PART FOUR

THE WORLD OF FICTION

XIV

FICTION, PHILOSOPHY, AND FAITH

THE DIFFICULTY of giving expression in fiction to the tragic sense of life, whether it be spiritual nothingness or the redemptive principle of the Absolute that cannot be justified by reason, is compounded by the resistance of the medium to preachment or overt statement. Yet whatever method of narration a novelist uses, he is bound to incorporate a world view in his body of fiction. No matter how objective and detached he remains, refusing to pass judgment on his characters and the actions, however reprehensible, they commit, he cannot refrain from implicitly suggesting some view of life, some philosophical interpretation of existence as a whole. The impressionistic hedonism of *Marius the Epicurean*, the Nietzschean nihilism of Artzibashef in *Sanine*, the cult of art for art's sake that George Moore coupled with a realism derived from French sources, the militant naturalism of Emile Zola, the diabolism of Huysmans, Marcel Proust's attempt to recapture the flavor of the past and suggest the nature of time, the humanism of Thomas Mann, the primitivism of Hemingway in *The Sun Also Rises* and *A Farewell to Arms* — all these represent, in different ways, the distilled outlook on life of a writer, an outlook that shapes his selection of material, his interpretation of character, his dramatic insights and emphases. But there is all the difference in the world between philosophy or a religious view that derives from the action and impact of the novel as a whole, the self-realization of the various characters based on the experiences they pass through, and philosophy or religious beliefs that the author introduces forthrightly into the body of the text. One emerges organically but by implication, as in the plays of Shakespeare; the other represents an alien intrusion. The first is aesthetically consonant with the work of art; the other embodies a spurious effort at preachment or propaganda.

The object of the writer of fiction is to communicate all he knows and feels about life, to reveal the truth about every aspect that falls within his framework. Nothing human is alien to his vision. As a novelist he knows no more shame or stirrings of conscience, as he reports imaginatively the often surprising and tragic vicissitudes of fate, than does the laboratory worker examining a piece of cancerous tissue on a slide. Whatever is is "right," in the sense that it is a part of the flux and phantasmagoria of life. His ruling passion is to tell the uncensored truth about all he beholds, all that man has experienced or can experience, concealing nothing. He will not be deterred by socially imposed taboos or the interdiction of the church. He holds nothing back because, in art as in life, he believes that truth is anterior to morality. Out of his burdens, his conflicts, his temptations, his "evil" infections, he fashions the means of his catharsis and cure. Once the secret is told, once the "poison" is out of his system, he is free. Hence he strips the mask of hypocrisy from the face of society and strives to include all of reality within his scope. He explores the unconscious, the ugly, the evil, the abnormal, the absolute, the craving for God.

Every novelist starts, of course, with some controlling philosophy of life, even if he does not take the trouble to formulate it. Hardy struggled to reconcile the scientific outlook with the spiritual. As a disciple of Schopenhauer, he was impressed by the element of automatism or blind impulsion in human affairs. As a novelist he felt that the art of fiction called for some distortion so that the distinctive features of reality might emerge. Though he was a realist, he consistently maintained that a slice of life was not enough. If a story is to be told, it should be exceptional enough to warrant the telling. As he pointed out in *Jude the Obscure,* life demonstrates a universal contradiction between the ideal and social reality. The one philosophical conviction to which he clung stubbornly, both as a poet and as a novelist, was that the First Cause is either unknowing or immitigably cruel. But he sought to avoid the dangerous entanglements of metaphysics, the temptation of mapping out a comprehensive and logically cohesive philosophical system. Since the history of philosophy was so full of solecisms and contradictions, he finally came to the conclusion: *"Let every man make a philosophy for himself out of his own experiences."* He could not conceive of a morality, benign or malevolent, associated with Nature, not even one of which the human mind has no awareness. No theory of morality, however consolatory in aim, can annul the omnipresent fact of pain or transform it into pleasure. Yet Hardy warns those who turn to fiction for edification that a novelist seeks to portray honestly and completely the people who inhabit his imaginative world. It does not matter what philosophy the characters in his novel happen to embrace. The universal is implicit in and emerges out of the particular case.

Chekhov's philosophy of fiction also stresses the need to achieve untrammeled objectivity. It is not the duty of the novelist to pass judgment on people, to picture them as good or bad, to work out an ethical system, or to justify the ways of God to man. Like a surgeon, he must be impersonal, disinterested, picturing people as they are, without distorting their individuality. He must get as close as he can to the truth of life. But if he is scrupulously objective, it does not mean that he must approach his subject matter with repellent coldness. All that Chekhov warns against is the temptation to propose solutions to problems which lie beyond the ken and competence of the novelist. It is not the writer's function to expound a thesis or a comforting faith. In 1888, Chekhov wrote to a correspondent:

It seems to me that the writer of fiction should not try to solve such questions as those of God, pessimism, etc. His business is but to describe those who have been speaking or thinking about God and pessimism, how, and under what circumstances. The artist should be, not the judge of his characters, and their conversations, but only an unbiased witness.

Let the characters speak their own thoughts in their own language, while the novelist confines himself to selecting what is significant and important. He may raise questions, but it is not his task to provide answers. For there is a profound distinction between stating a problem correctly in fiction and attempting to solve it.

A writer of a radically different outlook and temperament, Marcel Proust distrusted manifestoes and proclamations of theory; the true work of art, he believed, was produced organically in silence. The quality of the language used in fiction is more important than the theory it is supposed to illustrate. The subject is in itself a minor consideration; it is what the writer does with it that counts. Logical reasoning and preachment lessen the value of a literary work. All art worthy of the name communicates an essence that is in part subjective and incommunicable. That is why, Proust contends, the art of fiction cannot be patriotic or optimistic or democratic or religious. In short, the basic value of a work of literature is not to be measured by criteria derived from morality or metaphysics or theology, for it is not to be judged intellectually.

Another writer who agreed with the gentle Chekhov and in part with Proust is Joseph Conrad, who was a humanistic nihilist, one who felt compassion for benighted, suffering mankind on its journey to the end of night but who held up no ideal of redemption. Though he knew that the end of the human story is always and inescapably tragic, he realized also that man-made ideals of honor and courage, of faith and fortitude, are all we can cling to before the ship goes down with all on board. He is not bitter or cynical, or even pessimistic; he is rigorously truthful, imaginatively honest, a conscientious literary artist who strove to formulate and abide by the high standards which would guide him in his work. In his art, he endeavored to render the truth that underlies all the protean and bafflingly complex manifestations of the visible universe. The artist is thus in quest of the truth, but when he is confronted by the spectacle of a universe that is enigmatic and inscrutable, he is compelled to seek understanding within himself. Ideas change, theories vanish, political movements and metaphysical and theological systems are forgotten, but the work of art endures. Conrad always struggled to remain faithful to the truth of his sensations, to make unfamiliar things credible. He never allowed himself to be dominated by general philosophical principles, and to love or hate life, to say Yea or Nay to the universe, according to these principles. Like Hardy, he could not get himself to believe in the ethical or religious view of the universe, for it involved one in too many gross and fantastic contradictions. As an artist, he preferred to believe that the object of the universe is purely spectacular.

The writer continues to be plagued by the spiritual problem of meaninglessness, but if he takes himself seriously as an artist he is wary of importing metaphysical or religious ideas bodily into his fiction. He cannot prevent himself from asking questions of the universe, but he must not allow his metaphysical prepossessions to dominate his work. Franz Kafka, for example, took his spiritual dilemmas with the utmost seriousness, and these crept into his fiction and gave it its peculiar dreamlike cast. The one question that stood uppermost in his mind was why men live. What is the purpose of life? How can one go on living without discovering the answer to this painful riddle? Hence Kafka, in his despair, fashions a weird world of the imagination, portraying characters who wrestle unavailingly with phantom adversaries in the dark, wandering alone on a journey the end of which they do not know. What Kafka communicates is not only a sense of dread, but also a feeling of existential incertitude and insecurity. Exploring the depths of the irrational and the inexplicable, Kafka represents life as a dream within a dream.

With how much greater understanding does Tolstoy, in *War and Peace,* present an amazingly varied gallery of characters and the spiritual problems they must face. Those who are familiar with the personal development of the Russian novelist will recognize those scenes and passages in which his two favorite characters, Andrew and Pierre, individually or together discuss God, fate, free will, death, and the meaning of life. But the material is integrated within the dynamic, structured plot; it is an essential part of the action. After wounding Dolokhov and parting from his wife, Pierre, deeply agitated, engaged in painful reflections, is eager to solve the problem of existence. What, he asks himself in perplexity, is good, what is bad? "What should one love and what hate? What does one live for? And what am I? What is life, and what is death? What power governs all?" And the only reply he can make is that death will come and end everything. Then one will know all or cease asking foolish and futile questions. Here are metaphysical "burdens," adapted to the needs of this profound psychological novel, which precipitated Tolstoy's own spiritual crisis and led him to write his *Confession.*

In a different way, Theodore Dreiser throughout his troubled life sought to discover a clue to the meaning of the universe, a formula that would explain the inscrutable welter of life. Life was beautiful, a magnificent display of energy, but it was not meaningful. Though Dreiser's writings, like his mind, were full of patent contradictions, he made no pretense to being a formal philosopher; he was not constructing a philosophical system but giving voice to his own interpretation of the universe. If life is nothing more than a series of physico-chemical reactions, then ethics obviously plays no role, and man is but an insignificant pawn in the cosmic process. Dreiser thus came to the conclusion that the universe is neutral, indifferent to the fate of mankind. Hence there are no final truths, no sustaining purpose, no principle of justice in Nature. This deterministic outlook was part of his plan for describing life as it is, not as it might be or ought to be. That is why, like Hardy, he arrived finally at pessimistic conclusions. He saw that the individual has no particular importance in the scheme of things. Though he turned to science as the method best calculated to provide him with an understanding of life, it did not give him the answer he sought as to the why of creation. The individual, Dreiser felt, is but an infinitesimal cog in a greater machine; therefore he as a novelist could make no meaningful affirmation about life. If he made any assertion at all, it was to accept the mechanistic outlook, at least in his early period.

But if Dreiser had been consistent in his belief that life is essentially meaningless, he would have had to abandon his career as a novelist. Here is the very problem that Camus grapples with in *The Myth of Sisyphus* as he tries to transcend the contradiction and justify an aesthetic of absurdity. But if no meaningful comment can be passed on life, then art is useless. Ignoring the hobgoblins of consistency, Dreiser persisted in his creative quest and produced characters like Sister Carrie, Eugene Witla, Jennie Gerhardt, and Clyde Griffiths, who are authentically alive. From the viewpoint of the relativist, however, all attitudes are equally untenable and absurd. That is the fictional perspective Aldous Huxley used in *Antic Hay* and *Point Counter Point*.

The metaphysical novel sprang up as a protest against the limitations of naturalism in fiction. Though it did not disdain the use of factual material, the influence of social, biological, and environmental forces, it refused to accept the validity of a deterministic philosophy which regards man as the victim of socio-economic compulsions and freedom of will as an illusion. It gave us introspections, imaginary monologues and dialogues, visions, dreams, fantasies, philosophical excursions. It questioned the truth of the empirical, documented reality the naturalistic novelist painstakingly portrayed. Finding that human nature was far more refractory and complex than scientific determinism makes it out to be, the metaphysical novelist included in his work such "impure" ingredients as dreams, subjective fancies, moral volitions, symbols, and myths, and thus achieved a multidimensional reality. There is not only the external world to be considered; there is also the internal world of imagination, feeling, and ideals, and these are decisive in their influence on human character and fate. As Henry Adams well knew, man is deeply troubled by the need to discover meaning in the Heraclitean flux; he must arrive at unity in the midst of multiplicity. Behind the maelstrom of economic competition and political conflict, the metaphysical novelist discerned the underlying dynamism of fear and desire, aspiration and spiritual hunger. Men and women, death-haunted and death-doomed, struggle feverishly to understand the meaning of their days and nights and to fulfil themselves before the inevitable overtakes them. Like Tolstoy's Pierre, they seek some myth or symbol, some ideal or power that will liberate them from bondage to the tyrant, Time.

This type of fiction was bound to come into its own sooner or later. For want of a better term it is called "metaphysical," though it is not concerned primarily with philosophy. It delineates characters from all walks of life passionately engaged in seeking to discover a pattern in the carpet, a master purpose which would give direction and meaning and continuity to their brief stay on earth. Such fiction, in seeking to impose order on the multiplicity of events, extracts their essential significance, their spiritual essence. Reality is but a symbolical clue to a more fundamental state of existence; the key to the mystery is at least provided. Unlike what happens in Walter de la Mare's poem, "The Listeners," the knock on the door is answered, even if ambiguously and in a strange tongue. Someone is there. Someone must be there. Face to face with the infinite, surrounded by enigmas which defy naturalistic explanations, the central characters in metaphysical fiction try to formulate a *Weltanschauung;* as in *The Brothers Karamazov* or *The Possessed* or Jakob Wassermann's *The World's Illusion,* they battle the congregated powers of evil and darkness and death. Hans Castorp, Myshkin, Ivan Karamazov, August Esch in *The Sleepwalkers* by Hermann Broch—each of these, like Galahad, Parsifal, Faust, Hamlet, Manfred, is a crusader of the spirit, determined to wrest an answer, if not a blessing, from the angel with whom he wrestles in the night.

But the answer they receive is not always an affirmative one. Like *War and Peace,* Céline's *Journey to the End of the Night* is not a novel in the strict sense of the term, but a confession of the intolerable torment of living. It is as far a cry from realism as the dream is from reality. Indeed, the novel projects the quality of a continuous nightmare, horribly cruel, obscene, hideously grotesque, unceasingly tragic. Céline's "journey"—the twentieth-century Inferno—symbolizes the horror that rides the modern world: the absence of ultimate meaning. The author is pursued by the Furies of an obsession that will not let him go. All the avenues of escape, he warns us, are forever closed. Life is a madhouse, but when everyone is mad it is considered the worst treason to remain stubbornly sane. How, asks Céline, can one find strength enough

to go on doing what one has been doing the day before, and for so much too long before that—strength for the whole mad business, for a thousand and one vain projects: attempts to escape crushing necessity; attempts which are always stillborn; and all just to convince oneself once more that Destiny is insurmountable, that one must fall back each evening to the bottom of the wall, under the burden of the next day, each time more precarious and sordid.

This is the characteristic "metaphysical" motif sounded in a world without God, the obsession with the lack of meaning of man's pilgrimage to the end of night. On all sides he is threatened with annihilation. "And where can one go, I ask you, when one is no longer sufficiently mad? Truth is a pain which will not stop. And the truth of the world is to die. You must choose: either dying or lying." That is the burden of the central theme, the secret content of Céline's madness. Life is sordid, selfish, dirty, cruel: a sac of abscessed hate. The main character cannot cure his desire to run away from everything in search of he knows not what. He believes in nothing, and yet he is moved by the longing "to learn about Life beyond all this blackness."

Céline, the crippled giant, suffers to the point of madness from the absence of God. It is possible, of course, for a writer to be a passionate, even "religious," man without diluting or distorting the substance of his art. The example of D. H. Lawrence immediately comes to mind. In his foreword to *Fantasia of the Unconscious,* Lawrence characteristically insisted that art is utterly dependent on a philosophy or metaphysic. "The metaphysic or philosophy may not be anywhere very accurately stated, and may be quite uncon-

scious, in the artist, yet it is a metaphysic that governs men at the
time, and is by all men more or less comprehended and lived." Every
novelist, in short, is animated by a profound purpose, by a deep-
cutting philosophy of life. But in his study of Thomas Hardy, Lawrence stresses that this metaphysic "must always subserve the artistic
purpose beyond the artist's conscious aim. Otherwise the novel
becomes a treatise." That is the point exactly. Though every novel
has a social content and a metaphysic, this can never become dominant to the point where the author seeks to impose his theory on the
world and make the world conform absolutely to his theory. By
doing so, he narrows the compass of his vision and impoverishes
his art.

Somerset Maugham, like Lawrence, had also arrived at the perception that there is no absolute good, no absolute truth. Accepting
the teachings of science without question, he produced fiction that
was naturalistic in its orientation; but he was too gifted a craftsman
and too skeptical at heart ever to indulge in philosophical preachment. If, like Dreiser, he believes that the universe is but a vast
machine and the earth nothing more than a speck of mud whirling
round a sun that is cooling off, he takes good care—in *Of Human
Bondage*, for example—to translate his beliefs into terms organically appropriate to fiction. Nevertheless, his metaphysical assumptions enter constitutively into the warp and woof of his novelistic
fabric. A thread of ideological consistency runs through Maugham's
writings, but without impairing the vitality and authenticity of his
work. He has continued to believe, as he reports in *The Summing Up,*
"that we were wretched puppets at the mercy of a ruthless fate; and
that, bound by the inexorable laws of nature, we were doomed to
take part in the ceaseless struggle for existence with nothing to look
forward to but inevitable defeat."

The novelist thus builds a microcosm which reflects, with cosmic
or tragic overtones, the fate of the characters presented on the stage
of fiction. It does not matter what philosophy or religion the author
espouses. What counts is what he does with his material. Ideals, doctrines, and beliefs are only the by-products of literature. What

makes a work of fiction live is the degree to which its material is integrated and coherent—the degree, that is, to which its view of the world is presented in aesthetically satisfying terms. Yet a number of prophets, especially in the United States, have arisen to cry woe upon the present generation of false and decadent writers. What they have done, it seems, is to portray human nature in its worst light—fallen, brutal, depraved, evil, without hope of redemption. Instead of battling against the epidemic of demoralized pessimism that has swept the land, they yield to it supinely, looking upon mankind as a species of inferior ants slated inevitably for extinction. A pathetic victim of circumstance, man is shown to possess no freedom of will, no power of spiritual transcendence. His biological instincts or his "complexes" rule him.

It is on these grounds that the present generation of "lost" writers is condemned: for their total inability to affirm positive values, for their lack of faith in life, for their implied contempt for the human race, for their uncompromising nihilism. Yet what good would it do if the novelist repented of his past sins and abandoned his pernicious errors, his abysmally false values? Once he began to write, the old heresies, which he inwardly accepts as truth, would unfailingly crop up. For he is not concerned with metaphysics or ideology or religion. Van Wyck Brooks is one of those liberal critics who raise the cry of alarm as they view the literary temper of the time. The remedy he suggests in *The Writer in America* is to rehumanize literature, "to celebrate the grandeur of humanity and rejoice in its nature," yet the remedy prescribed cannot possibly succeed. Adjurations of this kind, however well-meaning and inspirational in tone, prove utterly futile when the writer sets out to apply them in his work. For he "betrays" himself in everything he writes. He cannot write optimistically or "religiously" to order, simply because the fate of civilization hangs in the balance. Convinced that he lives at present in the worst of all possible times, he is concerned, in this period of crisis and catastrophe, to tell the truth without equivocation or evasion, the whole truth as he sees it, and that truth comprehends a vision of nothingness which he beholds with anguish. He cannot recapture his lost faith. If an evil spirit has overcome him and he is "possessed," then he must succumb to it and write out that compelling vision of evil. As Emerson replied to those who suggested that his impulses might come from below, not from above: "But if I am the Devil's child, I will live then from the Devil."

Van Wyck Brooks is wrong in his condemnation. Unlike the writers of the first quarter of the twentieth century who could somehow make their peace with naturalistic nihilism, the writers of our time, stricken with the metaphysical plague, are actively striving to affirm life and, in various ways, to discover the hidden God of life.

XV

THE GOD OF FICTION

To-day it is not so much what the modern predicament is, as what the creative writer thinks it is or says it is. So that even if there is no predicament, if the anxiety of the age ... turns out eventually, in the larger perspective of history, to have been imaginary, the fact that such a predicament has obsessed the writers of the age and has produced creative works of a high order is in itself a real thing, and will give its color to the age.

        —J. ISAACS, *An Assessment of Twentieth-Century Literature*

THERE IS no mistaking the *Angst* that is dominating the consciousness of this age; and the novel, the literary form that most clearly reflects the malaise of our time, offers a revealing clue to the metaphysical bedevilments and neurotic dilemmas of contemporary sensibility. In fiction, as in poetry and drama, we get a poignant and imaginatively true picture of the chaos that is threatening to swallow up our culture, the sickness that gnaws at the conscience of mankind. Everywhere there are signs of disintegration, not the least important of which, diagnostically, is the belief that mankind has reached the end of the road, that civilization is about to suffer an apocalyptic smashup. Widespread and unresisted is the oppressive, nightmarish feeling that the race is doomed.

If one is to judge by some of the titles published during the past three decades or so, the spokesmen of the West hold a despairing view of the future. *Catastrophe, decline, twilight, death* — these por-

tentous key words recur too frequently in the books they write to be
without clinical significance. Spengler's *The Decline of the West*,
Nicholas Berdyaev's *The End of Our Time*, Leslie Paul's *The Annihilation of Man*, Ralph T. Flewelling's *The Survival of Western
Culture*, Franz Alexander's *The Age of Unreason*, W. H. Auden's
The Age of Anxiety, Aldous Huxley's *Time Must Have a Stop:* such
books indicate two things. First there is the belief that this is a
desperately sick, anxiety-ridden, neurotically driven age. Coupled
with this is the conviction that Western civilization is inevitably
doomed. Denied the spiritual solace and support of religion, modern
man is at the mercy of irrational, demonic forces of evil beyond
his powers of comprehension or control. The victim of a naturalistic
universe that seems hostile as well as alien, he suffers from a host of
"plagues."

Obviously, this nihilistic convulsion in the arts, this inner certainty that man is doomed, did not start three decades ago but
has its historical roots and antecedents in the past. The point is
that the writers of today are members of a sick as well as a lost generation; a race of spiritual hypochondriacs, obsessed with thoughts
of nothingness, destruction, and death, they teeter nervously on the
edge of a nervous breakdown. Modern novelists, engaged in tracing
the physiognomy of their culture, find themselves increasingly
concerned with themes of abnormality, maladjustment, frustration,
sadism, alienation, guilt, cruelty, metaphysical homelessness, loss
of faith. The contemporary novel vividly reflects the complex of
beliefs and unbeliefs and sentiments characteristic of our culture,
the values which even negatively help to hold its fabric together
in some kind of uneasy but unified pattern—a *Weltanschauung*.
Novels by such men as Alex Comfort, Paul Bowles, Camus, Aldous
Huxley, and Sartre give us a frightening portrait of our age.

While Céline in *Journey to the End of the Night* sounded a note
of destructive nihilism, embracing the nothingness of death which
must come to all, the novelists of the forties were more concerned
with the crises and contradictions of the moral life, the loss of ultimate meaning. Existentialism reaffirmed the central importance of

subjectivity and explored the demons of irrationality that govern so much of modern life. Sartre and his disciples faced the age-old problem of man: Does God exist, and in what sense? What is the nature of being? Does freedom of will exist? Can justice be objectively vindicated, without seeking to invoke a religious justification? Is there any compelling reason why men should follow good rather than evil?

A powerful novel that has a direct bearing on the "plague" of our time is *On This Side Nothing,* by Alex Comfort, a profound indictment of the barbarism of our culture. Unmercifully Comfort castigates a society that sanctions and encourages wholesale killing, a civilization bathed in an atmosphere of fear and hatred and repression. The implications are unmistakable and fit in consistently with the views the author stated in *The Novel and Our Time* and *Art and Social Responsibility:* the realization that all of us are involved in the corporate guilt and damnation of modern society. Unlike Céline, Comfort feels a deep sense of responsibility for the fate of human beings. Unlike Camus, he does not hesitate to pass judgment and indulge in prophecy. The protagonist is a Jew who has come to understand the character of the age he lives in, its hellish potential of destructiveness, and what civilization does to obliterate humane values and to eliminate the precious quality of humanness. Whereas in the past the hero wondered when he would be able to return to a normal cycle of living, now he speculates uneasily whether he will go on living at all, whether he will survive tomorrow. On all sides Comfort detects a foul conspiracy against those who wish to live, a wicked plot to instal a reign of death. Repeatedly he sounds the warning that civilization is about to die.

Paul Bowles's *The Sheltering Sky* is not only a condemnation of our intolerable civilization but a searing revelation of the conflicts that contemporary intellectuals must face. Both Port and Kit, the principal characters in the novel, are lost; they are lost and doomed, the way the world is today. What adds grimness to their tragedy is that they know it. They wait for the hour of horror to strike, the doom to fall, living in a void, without roots, without connections, though they are still painfully searching for a meaning that they are inwardly convinced they will never find. Port, at least, is certain that life, despite all its freakish vicissitudes of fortune, adds up to zero. No matter where one stands, in the end the equation equals zero. In short, he has ceased to believe in anything, in any truth, though he persists wearily in his quest, as if eager to prove himself wrong, wandering restlessly in the Orient from one disease-infested town in the desert to another, punishing his body and torturing his rebellious spirit. Feeling that life has no value and needs no justification, Port refuses to participate in this farce, to accept any responsibility for the conduct of his life, preferring to drift, to flee from the curse of civilization. "For in order to avoid having to deal with relative values, he had long since come to deny all purpose to the phenomena of existence—it was more expedient and comforting." Immured in his own isolated self, incapable of the surrender that love demands, thoroughly disillusioned, Port does not and cannot believe there is any system of justice in life. The final sum of zero is inevitable, no matter what kind of mathematics one uses. For Paul Bowles life is nightmarish precisely because it is meaningless. In *Let It Come Down,* he portrays the moral disintegration of Westerners who are sustained by no purpose in life and who perceive no meaning in their existence.

This is the impasse at which the contemporary artist has arrived: Nothingness has supplanted God and the Absurd has taken the place of the Absolute. Since he cannot depend upon a common background of religious values, the artist must remain spiritually uncommitted to any hard-and-fast dogma, despite the discomforts and downright dangers that such a position entails. The death of God that Nietzsche triumphantly proclaimed has meant, especially in literature, not only a radical break with the traditional assumptions of the past but also a fundamental reconsideration of the spiritual bases of the writer's vision, his universe of values. The modern novelist has often been compelled to operate in a kind of spiritual vacuum, to wander in a desert where he is not only lost but doomed to suffer unquenchable thirst and ultimate defeat. Hence he searches desperately for a principle of meaning, a light that will shine through the darkness. His quest for salvation is, however, a bitter and desolate one, not only because it takes place under secular auspices but also because at heart he does not believe that salvation is possible for man.

The alienated, Godless, or God-seeking novelist of our time thus faces a staggeringly difficult challenge. He dwells in a climate of thought which has done away with the trappings of the supernatural. Once the Christian mythos loses its efficacy as an object of absolute faith, the supernatural becomes merely a literary property, a fruitful symbol, but no more than that, for imaginative elaboration. How can the writer who has been exposed to the work of Vico, Darwin, Nietzsche, Freud, Karl Marx, Dewey, Einstein, and Bertrand Russell hope to recapture the old purity and passion of faith in the supernatural? He has lost his reliance on the Absolute. If skepticism, according to Santayana, is a form of belief, then even skepticism has ceased to be affirmative and creative. Even the cataclysm of war and the prospects of global disaster, the apocalyptic agonies of our time, cannot restore the certitudes of the religious synthesis of the past. Whatever functional relationship may obtain between literature and belief (and it poses a tremendously complex problem in literary criticism), it is obvious that the writers of our day have been profoundly affected by this ideological revolution. The earnest attempts of Christian apologists to revive the faith and make it impregnate the current body of literature have not borne much fruit.

Certainly there is no correspondence, in the realm of fiction any more than in that of poetry, between "correctness" of belief and literary greatness. How would Camus or Sartre or Dreiser fare if they were judged by such standards? Some religious-minded critics, however, insist that the writer's attitude toward life, the beliefs that control his thought and behavior, are bound to flow into his imaginative activities, his vision, his use of language. That, in brief, is the thesis that Martin Jarrett-Kerr defends in *Studies in Literature and Belief*. But if that is the case, then we are fairly certain to discover that the concept of God, embodied as an object of belief,

has suffered a thoroughgoing transformation. As mirrored in
the fiction of the present, man has usurped the throne of God.
Therefore, whatever religious values penetrate this man-centered
vision of life as it is lived today are bound to be critical of
traditional religion.

We are forced to assume that this transformation of consciousness, this drastic revision in the interpretation that writers give of
their world and of life as a whole, constitutes a "religious" reorien-
tation basically different from the religious consciousness which prevailed in the past. For the writer has not given up his dependence
on the divine Absolute without a struggle; the abandonment,
as we have seen, has caused him intense agony: it has left him with
what William James calls a "sick soul." Now that faith is fled,
man suffers on earth without meaning or purpose. In a universe
stripped of meaning and a sense of ordered unity, the writer is
afflicted with fear and trembling, consumed by a metaphysical
melancholy which, in its extreme form, turns to positive anguish.
The world, lacking a foundation of meaning, becomes alien,
uncanny, hostile, unbearable. God is not in his heaven and all is
wrong with the world.

Dostoevski's main characters, rebels seeking a solution to the
riddle of existence, stand accusingly before the bar of life. Either/or!
Life is a phantasmagoria of illusion or God and the Kingdom of
Eternity are real. Dostoevski presents this dilemma in passionate,
concretely human, and imaginative terms. If life is indeed absurd, if
God is only a pathetic pipe dream, then why not commit logical
suicide as an act of revenge? That is what animates Kirillov in
The Possessed: he takes his life because he is obsessed by an idea.
If God does not exist, then he is god. But God does not exist; it is
all a lie; therefore, he must demonstrate this redemptive meaning
by killing himself. That is Kirillov's madness in a universe without
God, and yet he is not mad. His freedom lies in asserting his
independence and refusing to serve any divine being. He kills
himself in order to liberate man from the thraldom of hope.
Paradoxically enough, it is out of love for mankind that he takes his

life; he will point out the way—the goal of death that leads to nothingness.

Kirillov is, in a sense, the first Existentialist hero. He is dead, but he has unknowingly fathered many children who today carry on his crusade. Dostoevski, of course, shows that his satanic characters, his rebels against God, are defeated. An existential novelist, Dostoevski embraces Christian mysticism, but the dramatic tension present in his work arises from this very conflict over the existence of God. As a great imaginative artist, Dostoevski sympathized strongly with the blasphemers, the diabolists, the nihilists—a point that Irving Howe develops in his book, *Politics and the Novel*. Indeed, Dostoevski's main characters suffer from this metaphysical torment of doubt, the compulsion to negate the absolute, the contradiction that is at the heart of life. At the end he offers a Christian solution, a stake in the future life, but even as he roots himself fervently in the soil of faith he cannot rid himself of the sacrilegious doubt. If Satan is the real hero of *Paradise Lost*, the Devil is never absent from the fictional world that Dostoevski creates.

Dostoevski believed in the reality of the divine, but what kind of religious vision can the modern novelist call forth when he lacks the conviction to believe in the destiny of man? He cannot believe and he cannot even affirm that in which he does not believe. Once God, the anthropomorphic deity who took heed of the fall of every sparrow, is acknowledged to be dead, then man can no longer live in the light of eternity. Henceforth, caught in the trap of time, he remains a dweller in the realm of history, which is secular, brief, and precarious. He is thrust into an existence that he cannot, try as he will, endow with meaning; though given freedom to choose, he is nevertheless doomed to die. Consequently, as we have already pointed out, he can discover no sound reason why he should commit himself to any established system of morality. André Gide and Aldous Huxley portray characters who kill without compunction because for them there is nothing sacred in life. The death of God has given rise to the metaphysics of absurdity that is so bizarre and disheartening a manifestation of the failure of faith.

Though there are some signs of a spiritual revival in contemporary letters, the religious consciousness, at least in its traditional form, seems to have largely disappeared. Whereas the medieval order believed in reason as the foundation of faith, the present age, as portrayed by some of its leading literary spokesmen, is utterly without faith, but its deification of reason has also been badly shaken. Few intellectuals now cherish a faith in salvation to be achieved exclusively through the instrumentality of reason and the scientific method. Fewer still venture to speak of a "science of man." But this recession, this disenchantment with the utopian dream of perfection through Marxist or scientific or technological auspices, does not mean a precipitate return to religious orthodoxy. Few writers today give traditional religious answers to the riddle that none of the sciences can solve.

If the minds of men are busy formulating a cosmology that is naturalistic and secular and relativistic in orientation, then the novelist, if he is to give a faithful report of the groundswell of opinion and belief in his time, must take cognizance of this rise of secularism and reflect it, whether or not he agrees with it, in his work. Even if, like Graham Greene, he is rooted in Catholicism, he must of necessity reveal the feverish spread of irreligious thought. In his early astringent satiric novels, Aldous Huxley gives voice to the skepticism and even cynicism of a generation in revolt against Victorian moral absolutes. But Huxley for one was soon spiritually dissatisfied with playing the role of ironic relativist.

Eyeless in Gaza marks a transition in Huxley's philosophy of life. The chief character in this novel is in the end converted to a form of Buddhist discipline. Huxley has at last hit upon a theme that calls forth his deepest aesthetic response: his awareness of the brevity of time, the precariousness of life, the ultimacy of death. He has arrived at the final stage of his mystical journey, and now preaches earnestly that before one can gain the liberating knowledge of God, he must throw off the bondage of selfhood. The way to achieve oneness with God is to repudiate this preoccupation with the private and possessive ego. Unfortunately, Huxley goes so far in his rejection of purely human values as to end by abolishing them completely; for in the light of eternity and the unitive knowledge of God, of what importance are the frantic struggles of mankind, the agonistic conflicts of history? In short, Huxley has become a seeker after religious unity, though, as is evident in *The Perennial Philosophy,* he does not embrace a single creed but eclectically selects the best that mysticism, of all ages and races, has to offer. It is his repudiation of history, of human concerns, and of the dimension of time —it is this very vision of an abstract God and of eternity as Nirvana which led one critic, D. S. Savage, to condemn Huxley's mysticism as fundamentally atheistic. Huxley seems to believe that God is completely present only when what we call our humanity is completely absent. In *Time Must Have a Stop,* the same thesis is stressed: self-will must be sacrificed to make room for the supernal knowledge of God. One must rise above the expedients of nation, class, party, culture, and even art. The paradoxical upshot of this obsession with the unitive knowledge of the divine Ground is that the mystic loses all interest in and all desire for art. Huxley as a novelist has thus become a "religious" propagandist, and his fiction is intellectual rather than dramatic in structure. He has ceased, in fact, to be a novelist who delights in sensuous observation, beauty of form, the vigorous exercise of his sensibility and imagination. A novelist who sets out to annihilate the personality destroys the very source of his creative power. If life is a cheat and the self a snare, and human activities a sorry illusion, then what earthly justification is there for the production of art?

Huxley illustrates the supreme difficulty faced by the novelist who, having turned mystic, seeks to communicate the incommunicable; but he is not in the main tradition of contemporary literary thought. It is striking that both Huxley and Camus finally arrive, though from different routes and for different reasons, at the same dead-end question: why engage in art? But whereas Camus affirms the necessity of the creative project as a protest against the outrageous absurdity of life, Huxley, according to his lights, has no underlying motive for writing except to preach, and this he does.

The novelist who is a "rebel" can capitalize on the tensions and contradictions that his rejection of God entails, whereas a Catholic novelist must use doubt and heresy to add complexity to his fabric of fiction. The Existentialist writers, however, seek to break away entirely from the pursuing Hound of Heaven. Richard Wright, for example, a Negro novelist, is heavily indebted in *The Outsider* to the work of Sartre and Camus. In this novel he sharply poses the question that Camus sets forth so challengingly in *The Rebel:* What is to become of the uncontrollable will to power if man seriously strives to become God? Such a usurpation inevitably culminates in moral nihilism, in an absolutist worship of power. Nihilism ushers in a nightmare of inhumanity. Wright's Existentialist "hero," obsessed with anxiety, feels insulted at being alive, intimidated by the condition of existence. He asserts his freedom—a familiar Existentialist strain—in a world that is no longer supported by supernatural sanctions, accepting full responsibility for all his decisions. What is man? Endeavoring to answer in new terms this puzzling and perennial question, he comes to suspect that the "nausea" man experiences today is born of the perception that man "is nothing in particular."

Thus we are introduced to a criminal who, in rejecting moral and divine law, recognizes the insignificance of man. He has become the source of his own values, his own god. Whereas in the past primitive man projected his myths so as to reconstruct the world around him in the image of desire and thereby overcome his abysmal fears of the menacing darkness and the unknown, so even today twentieth-century man seeks to disguise the unbearable truth of reality and hide behind the consolatory myths of religion. Man, in short, craves the solace of the absolute lie. As Wright's protagonist points out: "We twentieth-century Westerners have outlived the faith of our fathers; our minds have grown so skeptical that we cannot accept the old schemes of moral precepts which once guided man's life." Here we have brought into the open the irreconcilable conflict between reason and faith, atheism and the inexpugnable need for belief in God. The consequences of atheism must be realistically faced. Living their lives on the assumption that there is no God, the atheists discover that the implications of such a *Weltanschauung* are nothing less than catastrophic. "It means that God no longer really concerns us as a reality beyond life, but simply as something projected compulsively from men's minds in answer to their chronic need to be rid of fear, something to meet the obscure needs of daily lives lived amidst strange and threatening facts." Though the religious compulsion is still powerful and affects practically every human activity, men can no longer confidently define the goal toward which they are striving. For if man no longer places his trust in God, then, as Wright's "hero" points out with unflinching logic, man can do very much as he pleases on earth. All higher laws, all moral restraints, are rendered invalid. Here is a character, then, an outsider, who has cast off the bonds of marriage and children and love and friendship, a man without culture or tradition or myth or faith, incurably skeptical and defiant, nourished on the work of Nietzsche, Heidegger, Husserl, Kierkegaard, and Dostoevski. Cross Damon, in *The Outsider,* is the tragic little man of the twentieth century who, rejecting the teachings of Christianity, turns into a wanton killer.

The unique achievement of *The Outsider* is that the "hero" is a Negro not obsessed by the race problem. He is a thinking man, self-conscious and introspective to the point of nihilistic alienation, bowed down by the metaphysical burdens of existence. If Wright fails to master his theme, it is because he has not imaginatively assimilated the philosophy of Existentialism and managed to create a living character.

XVI

LITERARY EXISTENTIALISM

EXISTENTIALIST FICTION is essentially a literature based upon a philosophy. At the heart of the Existentialist philosophy is the belief that man makes himself and that in this consists his fundamental freedom. Nothing is finished and final. In Christian as in atheistic Existentialism there is a consistent emphasis on living rather than cognition. If the Existentialists stress the doom that awaits man, it is in order to make clear the nature of the crucial choice that lies before him. Every moment, a point of intersection between two eternities, is a leap in the dark, emblematic of the paradox of all existence. In the theology of crisis, the polarity of consciousness leads to the abandonment of natural reason and the transcendence to the sphere of the miraculous. First comes the decisive act of choice and then the faith crystallizes. Just when man despairs and is about to give up the struggle, that is his moment of spiritual victory. As Kierkegaard declares in *Either/Or:* "It is impossible to live artistically before one has made up one's mind to abandon hope; for hope precludes self-limitation." Trapped in anxiety, Kierkegaard writes: "I have the courage, I believe, to doubt everything. . . ." And what extraordinary dialectical variations he can play, in *The Concept of Dread,* on the term "nothing" on which the eye is hypnotically fixed!

The modern Existentialist writer, however, in portraying the disintegration of his sense of values, his inner demoralization, is expressing what is common to the men of his time. The hero in *Nausea*, by Sartre, makes the terrifying discovery that he can no longer do what he wills; he is atrophied, immobilized. There we have the Existentialist thesis, applied to fiction, that life is without meaning or purpose. The universe of matter is not interested in the fate of man, his aspirations or ideals, his sufferings and sacrifices and heroic dreams. Man is alone in the space-time continuum, and there is no one to whom he can turn for help. Man is his own God, dependent on his own volition. Sartre makes much of these ideas in his book, *What Is Literature?* The most revealing part of *What Is Literature?* is the section concerned with the art of fiction as practiced in accordance with the Existentialist philosophy.

Sartre, significantly enough, rejects the determinism of the naturalistic novel on the ground that it interprets life as a dead mechanism. The men of this age of anxiety and terror are faced with the task of creating "a literature which unites and reconciles the metaphysical absolute and the relativity of the historical fact. . . ." The urgent questions that the modern writer faces are these: What is his place in the historical process? How can he synthesize his unique consciousness and his sense of relativity? "Since we were *situated,*" Sartre declares, "the only novels we could dream of were novels of *situation,* without internal narrators or all-knowing witnesses. In short, if we wished to give an account of our age, we had to make the technique of the novel shift from Newtonian mechanics to generalized relativity . . ." Newtonian mechanics thus gives way to Einsteinean relativity. The confused, vertiginous events of our day are essentially incomprehensible, since they can be viewed from a bewildering multiplicity of perspectives. Historical relativism, by stressing the factor of subjectivity, makes the present come alive. The technical problem in fiction is to present the relativity of subjective states, simultaneously, from multiple points of view, or, as Sartre phrases it, "to find an orchestration of consciousness which may permit us to render the multidimensionality of the event."

The importance of the Existentialist innovation in fiction, however, lies not in its experiments in form and technique but in its attempt to question the very basis of existence: What justification is there for human life? What right have we to exist? The modern anti-hero, unlike the good solid bourgeois of nineteenth-century fiction, has no duties, no responsibilities, no loyalties; everything is problematical, cankered with doubt. He is not sure of his relation to the objects around him or of the connection of the present with the past and the future. We swallow the dominant illusions and fictions of our age and invest the world with a simulacrum of significance, but behind the booming, buzzing confusion of appearance there is nothing. Each major character Sartre presents asks himself the recurrent Existentialist question: What am I? And yet, one *is* somehow responsible for the continuation of his thoughts, the mental perturbations which confirm that one exists. It is impossible to annul this sense of existence.

The introspection in which the Existentialist protagonist indulges, the *cogito ergo sum,* the burden of the unique and ubiquitous self, all this comes out with poignant vividness in Sartre's fiction, but the consciousness of existence is generally accompanied by an obsessive feeling of purposelessness. Whatever one does, in the end it does not matter. The hero of *Nausea* broods:

My thought is *me;* that's why I can't stop, I exist because I think...
and I can't stop from thinking. At this very moment—it's frightful—
if I exist, it is because I am horrified at existing. *I am the one* who
pulls myself from the nothingness to which I aspire: the hatred, the
disgust of existence, there are as many ways to *make* myself exist,
to thrust myself into existence.

Such a soliloquy can go on interminably. Every statement is also a question; every provisional affirmation is countered by its negation. Nothing is certain. These characters are somnambulists in a Surrealist nightmare of nothingness. Even as the hero runs, fleeing from his madness, he is aware of his impulse to flight and of the questions concerning the impulse, and of the question bearing on the question, ad infinitum. Now he knows what "nausea" is. Thus he has discovered the key to Existence, the secret of his own life, its fundamental absurdity.

But how suggest this experience of absurdity, which, like the mystical vision of the Wholly Other, is ineffable? The objects we behold sensuously are not to be grasped conceptually, through the instrumentality of reason or logic. This experience in perception is a kind of horrible ecstasy, not a transfiguration but an annihilation. It is the meaning of Nausea. Existence is marked by contingency, not necessity. "To exist is simply *to be there....*" No one can explain the mystery of existence. Everything is free and contingent and absurd. But that is precisely the knowledge most people flee from: the knowledge that no one has any rights, that each one is alone and entirely free. "Every existing thing is born without reason, prolongs itself out of weakness and dies by chance." Existentialism simply proclaims the truth of the absurd, the gratuitous gift of freedom, the absolute of nothingness. All this culminates in the conviction that there is no good reason for living. At the age of thirty-one, the hero of *Nausea* declares that he is free, but then he goes on to say: "There is absolutely no more reason for living, all the ones I have tried have given way and I can't imagine any more of them."

When *The Age of Reason* is read in the light of this Existentialist doctrine it takes on added meaning. Sartre seeks to picture the dilemma of the French intellectual endeavoring to assert his freedom, to gain control over his life, not to become the helpless victim of circumstance. The protagonist of *The Age of Reason* is Mathieu, a teacher of philosophy, who has been undone by his mania for self-analysis, since he can no longer act spontaneously. He is literally mad on the subject, forever watching himself in a mirror, reducing himself to nothingness. Introspection and self-analysis, a form of moral masochism, are his chief vice. Yet he cannot believe in himself or his metaphysical formulations; and he cannot act decisively, with his whole being. He lives in a mental void, without bourgeois convictions or proletarian attachments, adrift on a sea of abstractions, "a man who is not there." Mathieu knows what ails him: "I've finally lost all sense of reality; nothing now seems to be altogether true." Even suffering is not real. There he is, trapped in his own self, unable to get out, hemmed in by his life, by the past and the future and the meaningless present. Mathieu, nevertheless, says to himself: "Whatever happens, it is *by my agency* that everything must happen." He must choose his own hell, his own type of damnation.

In *The Reprieve,* Mathieu reappears, still suffering from his old "disease": he cannot commit himself. Each of the characters in this novel is wrapped up in his own misery but also brought face to face with an intractable contradiction. If man is what he chooses, how shall he reckon with the cataclysmic outbreak of war? What of the intrusion of accident, chance, luck, external forces beyond his control? Sartre tries to get out of this metaphysical impasse by insisting that we are all responsible for everything that happens, that everything we have done has brought the war into being. But of what avail is it to assume responsibility for one's decisions and one's actions when one is caught in the centripetal pull of destructive forces that are beyond human control? There is poignancy but little logic in Mathieu's reflection that history is also the diary of individuals. The war had swooped down and crushed his future to nothing. And what was this self, this identity, to which he had clung so jealously through all the years of the past? He felt he had lost his soul, but there was at least the eternity of this moment. Then we get this brief but illuminating passage of Existentialist awareness:

There had been, and forever would be, that cold glare upon those stones under the black sky; the absolute, forever; the absolute, without cause or sense or purpose, without past or future, save a gratuitous, fortuitous, splendid permanence. "I am free," he said suddenly. And his joy changed, on the spot, to a crushing sense of anguish.

Finally he comes to see that the liberty he had sought so long was in fact himself. "I am my own freedom." But this brought only desolation and anguish. "I am nothing; I possess nothing.... Outside the world, outside the past, outside myself: freedom is exile, and I am condemned to be free." He is alone in the world, and he is free for nothing.

Troubled Sleep, the third novel in the trilogy, opens on June 15, 1940, and describes the demoralization of soldiers and civilians in France after the victories won by the Nazi armies. Mathieu, in this dispersed French army, finds existence incredibly absurd. He is still intensely preoccupied with the problem of time and freedom and the realization that each time he decided not to choose, he had already chosen. In deciding to fight the Germans and thus delay their advance, Mathieu confronts this enigma: Was he justified, at this crucial hour, in dying for nothing? At last he makes up his mind. "Here and now I have decided that all along death has been the secret of my life, that I have lived for the purpose of dying. I die in order to demonstrate the impossibility of living...."

This utterance might be paraphrased to read: Sartre writes fiction and philosophy in order to demonstrate the impossibility of living. Sartre is, of course, far from consistent in building up his house of values. Though Existentialism presents a decidedly "decadent" and pessimistic philosophy of life, Sartre in *Existentialism* insists that Existentialism for the first time makes life possible. Christian thinkers have fulminated against Sartrean Existentialism on the ground that it rejects God and makes the individual the sole arbiter of value and the architect of destiny. There is some truth in the latter charge. Sartre himself in *Existentialism* declares: "It states that if God does not exist, there is at least one being in whom existence precedes essence, a being who exists before he can be defined by any concept, and that this being is man...."

But whatever the Existentialist philosophy may assert in formal propositions, in fiction it portrays man as carried along helplessly on the current of time, incapable of taking on himself the responsibility for his existence. What is disturbingly new about the Existentialist fiction that Sartre composes is the monomaniac intensity with which it stresses the theme of man's alienation, his nothingness as viewed against the background of the universe, his unavailing search for an absolute. But despite its anguished perception of nothingness, its blinding knowledge of the doom of death, it intensifies the drama of existence, which it interprets dialectically as a perpetually renewed crisis. Existentialism breaks up the mind into discontinuous psychological states; it denies the possibility of arriving at a truth that is true for everybody. Every case is unique and exceptional. It is this which makes it possible for Sartre to disintegrate the plot, to dwell so minutely on the fugitiveness and contradictory flux of psychic events, to experiment with simultaneity of impressions, to probe the philosophy of time and the enigma of personal identity, and to present characters who, even in love or in war, are eternally alone, each one his own relentless psychoanalyst and dialectician of death.

The novels of Sartre, like those of Camus, are instinct with the passionate subjectivity which is the basis of existence; they strive to give imaginative embodiment to Existentialist mysteries and ambiguities, paradox and irony, darkness and nothingness. In fiction the absence of systematization is a virtue, but the reiterated affirmation of the mysterious complexity and uniqueness and insignificance of man remains, when all is said, doctrinaire and unsatisfactory; it is not integrated into the texture of the action. At the heart of the Existentialist outlook there is a pervasive pessimism that filters through all the fiction we have examined, a conviction that man is predestined, for all his brave struggles, to suffer defeat at the hands of life.

The formidable problem the contemporary novelist faces is how to shape his life and work in a universe that is no longer seen (seeing is believing) as created and controlled by God. Obviously human existence on such terms, without religious commitments, without an ultimate aim justified by God and his promised kingdom of eternity, becomes for many people meaningless. In the name of what purpose shall the writer dedicate himself to art? Thus we come back to the problem that obsesses the mind of the contemporary writer. If he is genuinely convinced of the absurdity of existence, for the individual as well as the race, then what incentive can he summon forth to sustain him during the trying ordeal of creation? If life is judged as inherently absurd, then it follows that art, too, is an absurdity. Is an absurd work of art possible? These are the questions that Camus tries to answer on aesthetic grounds by arguing that the godless man is not concerned to explain, to solve mysteries, but to experience all things given. The novelist reveals life, he does not justify the universe.

XVII

THE LITERATURE OF ABSURDITY

THE SENSE of absurdity was born when man ceased to believe in the existence of God. Once the sea of faith was at the full and lay, according to Matthew Arnold, like the folds of a bright girdle furled round earth's shore; but even during the age of universal faith many believers must have suffered from the torments of doubt, though they tried to combat the doubt as if it were the work of the Devil. But today faith, when it is still vital and articulate, is in itself a species of absurdity. In order to believe one must transcend the negative arguments presented by logic, reason, and empiricism—and even then the doubt often paradoxically persists, for how can twentieth-century man know for certain that the belief is genuine? In his *Journals,* Kierkegaard, that radical skeptic and also ecstatic dialectician of faith, makes clear what gulfs of incomprehension separate man from God. "A second belief," he writes, "is needed in relation to belief—the belief that one believes. Yes, one surely needs an extraordinary dose of belief to believe that he believes." Such a reduction of motives, which admirably captures the modern accent of disintegrative doubt, can go on ad infinitum, as in Sartre's fictional characters, belief generating doubt which is then annihilated by a counteraffirmation of faith, which is shattered once more by fresh intrusions of diabolical doubt.

200

That is why, as we have seen, Kierkegaard appeals so strongly to the literary mind of our time; he dramatizes poignantly the struggle of modern man to overcome the spiritual paralysis, the intellectual despair, induced by a sense of the purposelessness of existence. Heightened awareness of the meaninglessness of the human situation in a meaningless cosmos has driven modern man into a state of extreme despair, for he cannot live permanently in the void; he must, if he is to go on living, formulate some philosophy of courage, even if it is only the courage of despair. This is, as we have shown, the crucial problem of the "hero" in much of contemporary fiction and drama: the man who cannot affirm with conviction, the man who cannot commit himself, the metaphysical "shadow" who has no sure grasp of reality and no capacity for positive feeling, only a haunting vision of the essential absurdity of his condition.

This is the crisis of absurdity the contemporary "hero" faces. Because he cannot escape the realization that everything in the universe culminates in this bankruptcy of values, this apocalypse of absurdity (it is the one conviction he embraces in anguish), he has reached a spiritual dead end. Since life has become infected with the disease of absurdity, he is reduced to silence. Periodically, though, he will continue to raise disturbingly negative questions: Why does he feel like a stranger on earth, completely superfluous? Why should there be anything in the world, why not nothing? A victim of forces beyond his control, all he knows is that he suffers without justification and that he cannot escape from this horror of nothingness. And once he postulates, and begins to believe in, the reality of Nothingness, he falls, like Heidegger, into nihilism, and all of life is henceforth beyond hope of redemption.

This is the ontological malady which has given a new, morbid twist to the tragic sense of life, for how can the absurd be rendered in tragic terms? If the ultimate essence of reality is equal to Nothingness, then we are plunged not only into the uncanny but also into the absurd. Heidegger employs the category of Nothing as if it were an active force, an embodied being. Here is the Nemesis of Nothingness, always present, which drives home to men their own insignificance. And because death exists, death the source of every project, the mother of time, then life is incurably absurd. Thus modern man arrives at the crushing metaphysical knowledge that there is no reason for the world's or his own existence. This is the spiritual dereliction from which a number of writers suffer. They have caught a glimpse of the inherent absurdity of existence, and their insight can no longer be transcended by the resources of irony. It is too late to transform the tragic into the comic perspective, to go beyond death, to the freedom that explodes in the catharsis of laughter. Thus emerges what we have called the dialectics of nothingness, the discovery that everything is inexplicable—and absurd. The Devil who has now supplanted God walks the earth, sowing the seeds of confusion and whispering his message of nothingness into the hearts and minds of men. Committed to the absolute of nothingness, man now lives solely in the temporal realm. Since there is no possibility of appeal to the supernatural, how can man create out of absurdity a meaning by which he can shape his life?

This is the cul-de-sac in which contemporary literary nihilists are caught and from which they can find no way out. Life in a universe without meaning is inexpressibly absurd. Yet the contradiction remains: man is condemned to choose his freedom in a world that is invested with absurdity. But what kind of life can he lead in such a world? Literary Existentialism, for all its atheistic bravado, gives expression to the anguish modern man feels when he is cut off from God. The "nausea" that Antoine Roquentin experiences in Sartre's novel demonstrates symbolically the crisis of the spirit through which modern man is passing. The crisis involves more than the repudiation of religious absolutes; it focuses attention on the inescapable absurdity of existence.

A more gifted defender of the philosophy of the absurd is Albert Camus, whose *The Myth of Sisyphus* offers a lucid and vigorously reasoned presentation of his views. In *The Stranger* he introduces a hero who represents the "absurd man" who has faced the naked, unrelieved truth about life: its unresolved contradictions, the contingency of all human existence. Camus is not propounding a thesis in this novel, for art, like life, is contingent. And if life is absurd, then art is also tainted with absurdity. In discussing this novel, Sartre tries to make us believe that Camus wrote *The Stranger* as a magnificently sterile act. Yet we cannot help but pass critical judgment on the "meaning" the novel seeks to convey. Life may seem absurd, but art—the effort in this case to compose an organically unified work of fiction—is never absurd. In depicting a lonely pilgrim dedicated to "the religion" of the absurd, Camus is defining a movement in history, even as he arrives at the conclusion that no ultimate meaning is to be derived from the universe. Here is a fictional world which, as Sartre indeed points out, has been stripped of causality. In a world that is instinct with absurdity, everything is equally meaningful—or equally meaningless. Sartre utters this verdict, which is really meant as high praise: *The Stranger* is "a classical work, an orderly work, composed about the absurd and against the absurd."

What Camus poses is the age-old religious question: Why strive? Why suffer? Why live? For what end? A stranger in a world that is indifferent to his needs and utterly incomprehensible, deprived of all supernatural aid, modern man comes to the dismaying realization that his life—indeed, all life on earth—is absurd. If that is so, then what is he to do? Is suicide the only logical way out? In any event, he is bound to be profoundly affected by this rooted belief in the absurdity of existence. If he is unflinchingly honest, he will resist the temptation to devote himself to some cause which he feels will fill his life with meaning, for it is the illusion of hope that invariably betrays him. But what does logic reveal when it is followed inexorably to the end? Should one carry logic to the point of death? Is logic the lord of life? The process of reasoning explodes in a climax of absurdity.

Modern man has looked into the heart of darkness and his obsessions are born of the darkness. The absurd man of the twentieth century, having traveled beyond the last outpost of reason, enters the kingdom of the irrational, like one of Kafka's heroes who stand condemned but who can never find out the nature of their guilt. No longer master in his own house, he must resign himself to living with absurdity in a universe that is shot through with the grotesque, the inexplicable, the irrational. His knowledge of the inevitability of death forces him to concentrate on the absurdity of living in a world in which nothing lasts. Since nothing awaits him at the end of his useless journey, life completely fails to make sense. This is the tragedy of modern man.

The sense of the absurd originates in the human mind but it grows out of the world of experience. The two poles—mind and world, consciousness and reality—combine to form the dialectical conflict, a conflict which, as Camus has defined it in *The Myth of Sisyphus,* is entirely devoid of hope. The man involved in this struggle is stricken with restlessness and revolt. "The absurd has meaning," Camus declares, "only in so far as it is not agreed to." There we have it: the Promethean defiance, only this time it is not uttered in the name of humanity; it is not directed against the tyranny of a supreme ruler who would keep his subjects—the world of men—in mindless ignorance; it is proclaimed for its own sake, simply because the human spirit cannot reconcile itself to the condition of existence.

For how can the awakened one go on living on the old terms after beholding this vision of the universality of the absurd? The philosophy of the absurd calls for the abandonment of all hope, and offers no justification for the Pascalian wager or the Kierkegaardian "leap." To cling to the promise of eternity, to believe in the cult of salvation—that is a subtle strategy of escape, a form of narcotic evasion. Even though the absurd man acknowledges the power of the irrational, he cannot, he must not, silence the voice of reason. Camus refuses to resort to the transcendence of the irrational by means of an irrational intuition. Whereas Kierkegaard elevated the absurd to the role of Godhood, incomprehensible and unjust, Camus holds that "The absurd, which is the metaphysical state of the conscious man, does not lead to God."

The absurd man must pursue the truth even if it does not satisfy the prompting of desire. He has learned to live in the midst of contradictions; he is determined to know, even though he is aware of the strict limits imposed on reason. Having discarded the illusion of the divine, he reveals in acute form the spiritual distress of our time. He is "the outsider" who must live out his brief life without the support of God, seeking justification for his existence neither in morality nor in the doctrine of immortality. Man is his own and only end; death obliterates consciousness and the world, and it is death that is the supreme injustice. In short, the absurd man confronts his destiny without invoking the images of heaven or hell.

But if man is doomed to defeat no matter what role he plays, why continue to play the game at all? Camus replies that the absurd man remains faithful to the rules of warfare, but surely this is no answer to the question. Why is there a principle of honor involved in enduring the absurdity of the human condition? Why battle with the absurd? Why, in particular, undertake the adventure of art if creation is no less absurd than acting or conquest? Why use up precious energy in the effort to create? Camus in *The Myth of Sisyphus* offers an explanation that is ingenious and no doubt sincere but scarcely convincing. The absurd man as artist, he maintains, is not concerned to explain, to solve problems, to justify; his object is to experience—and express—all things given. The artist describes sensuously the universe that is both inexhaustible and incomprehensible. Camus does not, of course, shrink from the logical consequences of his philosophy: art, too, is absurd and so, for that matter, is discussion seeking to show that it is absurd to believe in absurdity. Camus contends that while art reflects the sickness we suffer from, it enables us to get outside of ourselves and see our plight clearly. The work of art incarnates all the contradictions of thought involved in the metaphysics of absurdity. But the supreme question to be asked is still this: is an absurd work of art possible?

Camus makes the attempt to answer this question honestly. The work of art, wedded triumphantly to the concrete, succeeds in overcoming the despotism of thought. The work of art—this imaginative embodiment of the concrete—signifies that it is neither faith nor philosophy, neither logic nor morality. The writer knows that his creation alters nothing and therefore does not prize his work. But by emphasizing experience, not reasoning, he puts thought in its place. As Camus puts it: "Expression begins where thought ends." Art thus provides no panaceas. Even the philosophical novelists of our day do not reason or argue but use the sensuous language of imagery. Why? Because no system of thought can serve to explain, whereas sensuous appearances are real.

But Camus is still under the necessity of disclosing how the novelist can forge ahead with his work without the support of faith and the stimulus of hope. Camus writes:

I want to know whether accepting a life *without appeal,* one can also agree to work and create without appeal and what is the way leading to these liberties. I want to liberate my universe of its phantoms and to people it solely with flesh-and-blood truths whose presence I cannot deny. I can perform absurd work, choose the creative attitude rather than another. But an absurd attitude, if it is to remain so, must remain aware of its gratuitousness. So it is with the work of art. If the commandments of the absurd are not respected, if the work does not illustrate divorce and revolt, if it sacrifices no illusions and arouses hope, it ceases to be gratuitous.

Despite the calculated use of the Gidean adjective "gratuitous," this is a far cry from the doctrine of art for art's sake. Concretely, what is the issue Camus is raising, one that would not have occurred to a Pater, a Gautier, or a Baudelaire? What is the point he is making in this manifesto of the absurd? Can the artist work productively without invoking supernatural presences, without relying on transcendental truths ("phantoms") that would shed the light of meaning on his work and his life? Only by casting aside all illusions and denying himself the opiate of hope can he hope to create gratuitously and remain obedient to the mandates of the absurd. His work must, in brief, be composed with uncompromising detachment. The novelist, for example, must resist the temptation to judge. Camus rightly cites *The Possessed* as an example of the fictional absurd.

Camus holds that whatever ultimate meaning the world may possess is beyond the grasp of the human mind. Refusing to blind himself to "flesh-and-blood truths," the absurd man will have the courage to live with what he "knows" and with nothing but that. Indeed, he comes to perceive that life can be lived all the better if it has no meaning. He accepts experience in all its mysterious and fascinating diversity, but he lives it to the full by virtue of keeping the liberating truth of the absurd steadily before his eyes. According to Camus, "Living is keeping the absurd alive." Though fate will crush him, we are told that the absurd man is not resigned to his fate. That is why he refrains from suicide. Suicide represents surrender, and the absurd man depends on his instinct of revolt.

If this conjunction of absurdity and the ethics of revolt seems, to say the least, paradoxical, Camus's reply is that the absurd, though it abolishes the foundations of eternity, restores to man his freedom of action. But on the basis of what principle is the absurd man to be roused to revolt? Camus draws a distinction at this point that, strangely enough, reminds one of nineteenth-century utilitarianism with its rationalistic faith in the quantitative measurement of happiness. If life has no meaning, then it is no longer a question, declares Camus, of fine but quantitative living, for it includes a larger *amount* of experience. Or is this an unconscious echo of the famous conclusion of Pater's *Renaissance?* Pater declared that "Not the fruit of experience, but experience itself, is the end. A certain number of pulses only is given to us of a variegated, dramatic life." But Pater at least believed seriously in the poetic passion, the appeal of beauty, the love of art for its own sake. Camus cannot shake himself loose from the absurdity inherent in the act of embracing the absurd, for why, if all things end in death, deliberately seek out more and more experience?

Enough has been said to illustrate the numerous contradictions that issue from the aesthetics as well as metaphysics of absurdity. For the artist to cling to the absurd, whatever his professed motive

—that is a contradiction not only absurd but fatal to his art. How can he draw nourishment—and of what kind—from the sterile soil of the absurd? Yet that is precisely what Camus contends must be the case. Art is a gratuitous gift, without an excuse for being. This is the curious confession he makes: "To work and create 'for nothing,' to sculpture clay, to know that one's creation has no future, to see one's work destroyed in a day while being aware that this has no more importance than building for centuries—this is the difficult wisdom that absurd thought sanctions." Are we now to believe that the writer can go beyond good and evil, beyond all illusion, and root himself fruitfully in nihilistic negations that represent for him the naked truth of life? Are we to believe that the existential dichotomies inherent in his vocation, the realization that nothing may come of all his sustained efforts, that the most glorious works of the human imagination are, like their begetters, mortal, that all aspirations and achievements are futile when measured against the backdrop of the illimitable time-span of the stars—that all this will not deter him from going ahead with his writing? Have artists in the past ever created under such fatal compulsions? Unswerving in his belief, Camus replies that the artist carries out his project even as he senses that it will fail. Here behold the aesthetics of absurdity reaching a stoical crescendo of metaphysical despair.

For can the writer function creatively without a *Weltanschauung* to sustain him, a purpose to strive for? Without it his work is bound to suffer from an excruciating sense of aimlessness. How can he overcome the cruel and crushing suspicion that his work, too, is a form of make-believe, a meaningless performance? Why should he strive for the perfect realization of an aesthetic ideal that seems, in the face of the infinite absurd, but an empty and foolish gesture? Without faith in the value and even sacredness of life and in the continuity of culture, how can he summon up the energy to create?

Since he must question all over again, if not reject *in toto*, all the values and beliefs which many generations in the past took confidently for granted, the writer faces a creative problem that has been rendered incalculably more difficult. An intrepid Victorian might question the divinely inspired source of the Old Testament, but who would venture to bring life before the bar of judgment? When Darwin's *The Origin of Species* set the world agog, some novelists—Meredith, for example—were able to perceive in this doctrine of evolution confirmation of the design of deity, the hand of the providential architect of the universe. History could now be understood from a radically different perspective—a cosmic one— but such an interpretation did little to shatter the world-picture the intellectuals of that time cherished. The theists retained unshaken faith that a supernatural power, call it what you will, governed the mysterious and miraculous experiment of life. Even a dramatist like Shaw, for all his militant rationalism, was basically "religious" in his orientation, committed to the ideal of progress, never abandoning his faith in the future. Even Hardy, despite his pessimistic outlook, never dreamed of rejecting life itself.

In the twentieth century, the impulse to question life is intensified to such an abnormal degree that some writers arrive at the conclusion—"logical" for them—that life is incurably absurd. How do they manage to resign themselves to such a faith? To say, as Camus does, that the function of the artist is to reveal, not to explain or condemn, is to evade the central issue. Can the writer create a meaningful work of art when the materials he works with, the universe of experience he beholds, have been drained of all meaning? Why, if he is but revealing the absurdity of life and therefore the uselessness of his own project, does he remain faithful to his work, his calling? If he were truly convinced of the absurdity of existence, he would surely abandon all effort. The inexorable logic of a philosophy of absurdity, like that of Dada, points in the direction of suicide. It is obviously futile, however, to judge the implications of the absurd in the cool light of logic. The leaders of the cult of absurdity have no intention of putting an end to their life, and they have reasons. For them suicide is as absurd as the decision to go on living, and of the two types of absurdity they prefer to remain alive and creatively plead their cause. There is a paradox at the heart of Camus's thinking, in both *The Rebel* and *The Myth of Sisyphus:* condemned to live in a universe that is incomprehensible and absurd, why does he revolt, why does he appeal to ethical standards? Even to protest against an absurd universe is absurd.

The aesthetics as well as the ethics of the cult of absurdity springs from an inverted religiosity. Frustrated in his quest of the absolute, the seeker stridently announces that life can have no justification beyond itself. This is, however, by no means the same thing as saying that life is meaningless. Moreover, as we have repeatedly pointed out, Camus fails to make clear why, if life is but a thing of sound and fury signifying nothing, the writer should persist in his creative endeavor. Why does Camus voice his protest against the destiny of death that reduces existence to absurdity? Why does he labor so brilliantly and so earnestly to create a literature of absurdity?

Our contention has been that there is and can be no such thing. Literature, whatever the philosophy a writer may espouse, is never absurd. What the writer produces, even if it is only a hymn to nothingness, an imaginative projection of the city of dreadful night, is never either meaningless or absurd. To perceive and then to express the numinous absurdity of existence, the ineffable mystical experience of "Nausea"—that is already, in one sense, a triumph of transcendence. Others in the past, forsaken of God, may have uttered this dolorous cry, but it constituted only one chord in a richly modulated symphony of affirmation, of unquestioning loyalty to life. The modern absurdist is obsessed by a single motif. Only by an ingenious display of casuistry can he justify his singular devotion to an art that strives to reveal the character of the absurd. His one redeeming trait—and it betrays his ingrained "religious" self—is that he revolts against the comfortable and often complacent illusions of the unauthentic life. He does attempt to wrest some meaning out of the void of the meaningless, but his tragedy is that he fails and that he knows he must fail. As F. H. Heinemann declares in *Existentialism and the Modern Predicament:* "The absurd man needs no refutation, he is his own *reductio ad absurdum.*" Similarly, the literature of absurdity needs no refutation. One of the most talented of French contemporary novelists, Camus produced fiction and critical studies that are the negation of absurdity. The absurdity would have arisen had he sacrificed his creative gifts and his powers of vision on the altars of nothingness. The writer who is still driven to protest against a life that gravitates irresistibly toward death is motivated by a passion that is essentially "religious" in nature.

XVIII
CAMUS'S QUEST FOR GOD

BY A PARADOXICAL inversion of values, God is today more obsessively alive in the consciousness of the modern "rebel" than he was in the past, when everyone took God for granted. He is "present" in a negative sense; he manifests himself in the fever of atheistic denial. God is in some influential quarters declared dead; yet the persistent furore of debate about his demise makes one suspicious, for why continue to argue with such passion and pertinacity about a God who is supposed to be dead? If God is actually null and void, an infantile superstition, a personification of nothingness, then why indulge in these interminable metaphysical wars?

Yet the battle over the existence and meaning of God goes on, the only difference being that theology has been translated into ideology. The question concerning God has somehow become a vital contemporary issue. Camus composed novels as well as philosophical essays in which he discussed the ontological problem with God, as if to ask, "What shall man do now that you are gone forever?" This is no abstract conjuration, no pursuit of a semantic ghost, no trafficking with "phantoms." Even as the "rebel" denies the existence of God, he invokes his presence. God inevitably lurks in the background of the Existentialist declaration of defiance.

The irony of the contemporary situation is heightened, as we have noted, by the fact that many writers, who unfortunately lack the gift of faith, turn to the study of belief as something intensely to be desired. It is the sterility of their skeptical attitude that drives them curiously yet compellingly to engage in the search for transcendent symbols, archetypal myths, the nonexistent God. They crave the promise of a salvation that their scientifically-conditioned intelligence rejects. Since they cannot abandon the spiritual struggle, what happens is that they project symbols and values which are the product of a high-powered critical consciousness. The myths they embrace are intellectual constructions, as-if fictions. The faith they profess—if it finally comes to that point—is born of the will to believe. In short, their approach to religion is psychological or poetic. Many of them conceive of God as an archetypal image, a source of creative renewal.

There is, alas, no spontaneous, deep-rooted faith in this type of literary "theology." These writers in search of a God in whom they do not and cannot believe are profoundly in earnest only about the absolute they have repudiated—the orthodox evangel of Christianity. The truth is, they have no coherent body of religious faith to affirm. They talk incessantly about God but they do not include him in their vision of life. The crisis of belief in our age is basically centered in the problem of unbelief. If historically Nietzsche played the role of the gravedigger of God, then what the modern rebels are attempting to do is to bring about, through intellectual magic, the miracle of the resurrection. They would like to behold a miracle which, by definition, they are convinced can never take place.

Camus was a rebel who faced realistically the tragic consequences that follow from the act of rejecting the religious synthesis. For if redemption is to be postponed until the end of eternity, then it means that the injustices which flourish on earth will be allowed to go on unchecked. Is man justified in choosing the eternal Kingdom of God and resigning himself, in effect, to the existence and perpetuation of evil in this world? These are some of the "theological" contradictions that plague the heart and mind of the rebel. How can God and Caesar be reconciled? To accept as final the verdict of history, which is itself essentially corrupt, is to wind up in nihilism.

Camus refused, however, to work in terms of absolutes; he aspired solely to the relative, to live in a universe of relative values. He believed in the wisdom of establishing human limits and in striving for what is possible. Yet for all that, the spiritual conflict he describes in *The Rebel* is a religious one. In his acceptance of the inherent limitations of human nature, he is reaffirming the traditional Christian virtue of humility, just as he is fundamentally Christian in outlook when he declares that each one must acknowledge his share of guilt in the historic process. His concept of social responsibility is at bottom a reaffirmation of the principle that each man is in a profound spiritual sense his brother's keeper. "I have need," he says in *The Rebel,* "of others who have need of me and of each other."

Even in his contemplation of death the rebel re-enacts the "pathos" of the Christian myth. As he faces the incomprehensible injustice of death, man knows that neither hope nor faith can transcend this tragic condition. But if man is stripped of God and cannot discover the meaning of his existence in the historic context, the river of time, then what is there left for him to do but live for the humiliated and the oppressed? This is the logic of despair which gives birth to a "religion" of ethical responsibility. Like a Simone Weil, Camus insists that all must be saved, without exception. Thus the rebel's dedication to life, not death, to love, not hate, to affirmation, not denial, marks the beginning of a religious reintegration, however paradoxical its formulation turns out to be. If the secret of Europe, according to Camus, is that it no longer loves life, it is largely because modern man has been deprived of God. How can modern man live without faith?

A sensitive, serious-minded writer like Camus cannot simply ignore the crucial issues which have been fought out in the course of centuries of theological conflict, for these issues underlie much of his work, even though he interprets them in secular, relative terms. In *The Myth of Sisyphus* he argued that the absurd "does not lead to God." Indeed, he calls the attitude of the mystical Existentialists a mad attempt, foredoomed to failure, to transform the abstract process of negation into the simulacrum of God. In *The Rebel* he cogently points out that the metaphysical rebel is not an atheist but a blasphemer. "He simply blasphemes, primarily in the name of order, by denouncing God as the origin of death and as the supreme disillusionment." The blasphemer (one thinks of a novelist like Joyce) acknowledges the existence of God even as he curses him.

As we see, God still plays a conspicuous part in this "theology" of negation. Camus defines nihilism as not only despair and negation, "but above all the desire to despair and negate." Whence this compulsive desire to despair and negate? Because God, when he is judged by his creations, does not deserve to exist. In other words, God is denied on "religious" grounds: because he does not satisfy the expectations man sets up in the name of the ideal God. If God is all-knowing and all-powerful, then man has no freedom of choice and God must be held responsible as the author of evil. What kind of freedom, after all, can God confer on man? Fighting in behalf of life, the rebel resorts to blasphemy as a means of expressing his frustrated but ineradicable need for religious roots. Religious paradox as it appears in the novels of Camus reveals the existential contradictions of life and death, the awareness of the void and the quest of the absolute, negation and affirmation. Nirvana and the infinite, nothingness and God.

Camus introduces us to "heroes" who confront the desperateness of their situation in life without the illusions of religion. Strangers in this world, they march lonely, alienated, and always doomed, on this road that leads to death, deprived of moral will and the capacity to feel. When the protagonist in *The Stranger* is thrown into prison and society tries to get him to repent, to believe in God, he is perversely not interested. The problem that continues to torment him is how to kill time. Perhaps the most powerful scene in *The Stranger* is the one in which the priest comes to convert the "anti-hero," but he angrily rejects all that the priest has to offer: the mercy of God or the promise of salvation. After death, he informs the priest, there is nothing; though he has often wished there would be an afterlife, he places no trust in such pathetic wish-fantasies. When the priest persists in his ministrations, the "anti-hero" goes berserk and violently negates the truth that religion holds up. Nothing is of any importance, neither life nor death, neither love nor God. Everyone will one day be condemned to die; no one will escape. Since that is so, nothing matters; death annuls all obligations. Here we behold in dramatic and imaginative terms the elaboration of the theme of universal absurdity.

In *The Plague,* Camus confronts this problem of faith and meaning more realistically. Once the plague strikes, the inhabitants are forced to consider the significance of time and the meaning of their life. Each one seeks to discover the reason for the catastrophe that has befallen the town. Father Paneloux preaches a sermon charging that the pestilence is a kind of retribution for the sins of the people. Doctor Rieux, however, has no patience with this hell-and-brimstone argument which maintains there is some good in the plague; the same argument could be applied to all the ills and evils that human flesh is heir to. There is no good reason for giving in to the plague. But since he does not believe in God, why does he devote himself so self-sacrificingly to the care of the stricken? His curiously revealing reply is that if he believed in God he would stop curing the sick and leave all that to the acts of God. Since the order of the world is shaped by death, he reasons that it might be vastly better for humanity not to place its trust in God. When he watches the suffering of the magistrate's boy, he wonders, Job-like, how God can justify such suffering or how man can be reconciled to it. Father Paneloux, however, concludes that suffering is a test of human faith. One must believe everything or deny everything, and who would dare to deny everything? All or Nothing!

Though he was influenced by the emotional conflicts of his age which led to the Existentialist revolt, Camus was no disciple of Sartre. Though he pictured a world steeped in absurdity, he rebelled against this knowledge of nothingness. Unlike Céline, Camus never abandoned his faith in humanity. Though the world is without ulti-mate significance, it is man that is the locus of meaning, and the meaning lies precisely in his passionate, not-to-be-denied quest for meaning. That is the only secular basis, through the mediation of suffering, for building up and strengthening the feeling of human solidarity.

The Fall, Camus's recent novel, indicates the change that had come over the writer. Restless and inquiring by temperament, he could not remain long in one spiritual home. After abandoning the philosophy of absurdity, he sought to discover a foundation on which he could build a secure body of humanistic values. For he had never been a thoroughgoing nihilist. Though he was aware of the nothingness that hems man in, he nevertheless insisted that each individual owes an obligation to his fellow-man, that the human race is knitted together by the community born of suffering and the knowledge that death comes to all. *The Fall* attempts, within the framework of fiction, to affirm those values that men must perforce live by if their life is to have any meaning at all. Thus we get the paradoxical spectacle of a nihilist who proclaims values that are essentially religious in spirit. Like the Christian mystics of the past, Camus recognized the pervasiveness of evil; he portrayed with compelling imaginative insight the absolutism of the ego, the satanic lure of selfishness, the universality of guilt.

In *The Fall* the garrulous protagonist makes clear in a lengthy dramatic monologue (the entire novel is written in this form) the transgressions of his past and the spiritual crisis he is facing at present. With ruthless honesty he bares his own spiritual condition. As a lawyer in Paris he devoted himself assiduously to helping the unfortunate, but his underlying motivation was far from being nobly altruistic. He was doing all this to magnify his insatiable ego. What he hopes to achieve lies beyond his reach: the capacity to suffer with and for others. "Yes, we shall be capable of it one day," he says, "and that will be salvation." But such a state of grace eludes our grasp. Only the experience of death momentarily awakens our fellow feeling, our unqualified love, but if people are more generous toward the dead it is because death frees them of all obligations. In these mordant reflections we behold the malady of the man of our time: he cannot love without self-love. For this unheroic hero, haunted, dejected, is driven by the need to make his self-esteem absolute, though at bottom he feels that nothing matters. He remains on the glittering surface of life, preoccupied with words and appearances, monotonously rehearsing the ritualized gestures of routine. He discovers in himself "sweet dreams of oppression," a lust for power.

This was the Caesarism that governed his conduct, but the crisis came when he could no longer demand everything and pay nothing in return. Now he begins to realize that the whole human race are his accomplices in crime. Though he knows full well his own failings, he does not detest himself, but he continues to condemn others. Finally, he perceives that the road to salvation lies in eluding judgment. But judgment is today universal. "People hasten to judge in order not to be judged themselves." No one is willing to make the effort to cleanse himself. "We lack the energy of evil as well as the energy of good."

Once the "hero" of *The Fall* gains this insight into himself, he is consumed with a feeling of scorn. Nothing human has any importance. Life seems a tiresome game, not to be taken seriously. He could never commit himself to any belief or root himself in his identity. Though he has lived among men, he has not shared their passionate interests and he could not believe in the value of the projects to which they devoted themselves so wholeheartedly. It is then that the thought of death suddenly disrupts the pattern of his daily life. Perhaps he might have to die before he had accomplished his task, but what task was that? He did not know. And how could he die without having confessed all his lies, not to God or the representatives of the church, but to men? For death sealed the lie forever. In his inner emptiness and alienation, he is tempted to make a few commitments, but he cannot fool himself. His supreme vice was that he had sought to be immortal. His debauchery was a means of transcending the fear of death, but this only robbed him of vitality and intensified his suffering. Day by day he was growing older.

He cannot forget the memory of his early betrayal: his failure to rush to the rescue of a woman who had drowned herself in the Seine. Feeling the need to confess his guilt, he now declares that "we cannot assert the innocence of anyone, whereas we can state with certainty the guilt of all. Every man testifies to the crime of all the others—that is my faith and my hope." In dwelling on this scene of "conversion" on the part of this dissolute penitent, Camus seems to be emphasizing the need for a new religion based on the universality of guilt. There is no need for religion to create guilt or pronounce sentence and hasten to impose punishment. "God is not intended to create guilt or to punish. Our fellow men suffice, aided by ourselves." Why force man to cringe in terror before the vision of the Last Judgment when he has known the judgment of others? The Last Judgment takes place every day. Jesus had to die on the cross because *"he* knew that he was not altogether innocent."

Then, too, religion has today been perverted. Christ has been transformed into a judge, and the judges of this earth presume to pass judgment in his name. The result is that no one is acquitted. "Wherefor, since we are all judges, we are all guilty before one another." Unfortunately man cannot endure judgment. Then this degraded hero announces what he considers to be the solution: the coming of the judge-penitent, one who lives among the wretched of the earth and who keeps alive in himself and in others the solidarity born of suffering. Henceforth there are to be no excuses; there is to be no granting of absolution. No man is to be allowed to clothe himself in the mantle of innocence. Every man is guilty!

For the man who is alone in the universe, deprived of the support of God, life is a dreadful burden. What shall people do now that God is dead? As the miserable hero of this novel declares: "They are free and hence have to shift for themselves; and since they don't want freedom or its judgments, they seek to be rapped on the knuckles, they invent dreadful rules, they rush out to build piles of faggots to replace churches." But the principle of causality works itself out inexorably: since man is afraid of freedom, some earthly master must take the place of heaven's law.

Though *The Fall* would scarcely qualify, in either subject matter or treatment, as a religious novel, it does voice a number of specifically religious attitudes and insights, despite the author's express repudiation of dogmatic Christianity. It is precisely his repudiation that highlights his religious concern. For here is a writer who, leaving behind him the metaphysics of absurdity, has now formulated an ethic that emphasizes the need to develop a sense of human limitations. No man is God. Camus's preoccupation with the spiritual as opposed to the theological aspects of religion is seen particularly in his rejection of the concept of meaninglessness. Whatever may be true of nature and its massive indifference to human desires, man must still devote himself to building the city of man. Since death will inevitably overtake him, he must "wake up" and surrender his drugged illusions. The unawakened or unauthentic life is a kind of life-in-death. It would be a work of supererogation to point out how closely this corresponds to some of the spiritual truths embodied in the Christian outlook. Camus in *The Fall* is saying, through his protagonist, what Christianity long ago proclaimed: namely, that we are members of one another and that we must all bear the guilt for the sins and crimes of the collectivity.

Camus's career furnishes striking evidence of the fact that the nihilist cannot plead his own cause without falling into contradiction, for why is he so fanatically bent on converting the rest of mankind to the liberating (as he hopes) truth of nothingness? It is as if, in defiance of his metaphysical first principle that nothing matters, he was impelled by a categorical imperative to rescue his fellowmen from the trap of illusion, as if he owed them a supreme obligation to reveal the light of truth. Yet he cannot have it both ways. He cannot, on the one hand, honestly maintain that all is vanity and futility, and then struggle valiantly to show mankind that this is indeed the path to salvation. The very impulse that leads the nihilist to write is in effect a contradiction of his nihilistic philosophy. The man who believes that life is absurd and who then strenuously broadcasts his evangel of absurdity—such a man is himself the victim of illusion. He is evangelical in behalf of—Nothingness.

Yet this God of Nothingness for whose sake he labors so earnestly induces in his devotees an almost religious sense of dedication. If the heart of the religious experience is uncompromising sincerity, then Camus, despite his atheistic position, was fundamentally religious, for in the absence of God, which he affirmed, he sought resolutely to impose values on the flux of existence.

Camus, despite his rejection of God, remained loyal to a standard of good which he attempted to live by. First of all, he was committed to the truth—a commitment which partakes of the sacred. Second, he denounced all those, the passive victims of time, who lead unawakened lives. The knowledge of the eternity of death, the knowledge that there will be no return, no assurance of immortality, strengthens in "the free man" the will to live meaningfully. Thus, in identifying himself with an ideal that transcends every category, he came close again to affirming a religious ultimate.

This struggle between acceptance and rejection, nothingness and the absolute, nihilism and faith, is not peculiar to Camus; it also dominates the writing of a militant atheist like Sartre. If the world is bare of meaning and if man as he confronts an inexplicable and absurd universe is reduced to the desperate expedient of saying no to life, then Nothingness emerges as an ideal of transcendence. Whereas the people of the past endeavored to establish God in the world and in the heart of man, the nihilists have seized upon Nothingness as the secret of the absolute. For Sartre God is finally dead. Having abolished the transcendental order, he is committed to nothing. But this by no means disposes of the matter.

Though Sartre declares himself to be an atheist, he finds it distressing that God does not exist, for then man stands alone in the emptiness of space, without a spiritual home, without a goal toward which to strive. Thus Sartre is bedeviled by the same dualism that tormented Camus: the need for an Absolute that cannot possibly exist. Indeed, Sartre himself in 1947 declared:

God is silent and that I cannot possibly deny—everything in myself calls for God and that I cannot forget.... As a matter of fact, this experience can be found in one form or another in most contemporary authors:

it is the torment in Jaspers, death in Malraux, destitution in Heidegger, the reprieved-being in Kafka, the insane and futile labor of Sisyphe in Camus.

All this leads one critic of Existentialism, Wilfrid Desan, to wonder if Sartre is not suffering from the refusal rather than the absence of God. Why does Sartre keep on denying that God exists?

Camus and Sartre are in a sense writing commentaries on what Pascal calls "The Misery of Man Without God." The nihilists of our time reject formal Christianity because it is not religious enough. What they seek is not dogma or ritual or the consolation of prayer but some vision that transcends them all, the truth that will render life meaningful. Thus in the very extremity of their antireligious paroxysms they express a number of traditional religious motifs. There is something "holy" in their dedication to the truth. The problems they raise in secular terms are the very ones that religious minds have grappled with in the past. The nihilists, forfeiting the promise of eternity, contend that man must shape his own destiny, since there is nothing beyond nature; the only transcendence to be achieved lies within the human sphere.

Camus is himself the rebel who blasphemes, but blasphemy is not inconsistent with a profoundly "religious" attitude. What counts to the highest degree in religion is not outward ceremonial or acceptance of dogma but the spiritual commitment, what a man does with his life, the goal of transcendence, human or divine, toward which he aspires. The key terms Camus employs in his philosophical essays and in his novels are different from those that are part of the theological debate, yet he is one with theologians in his concern with what are fundamentally religious problems: the absence of God, the relationship of a God who is all-powerful and all-knowing to the evil and the suffering that exist on earth, the contrast between the routine and boredom of life and the crisis of being lost and alone and doomed that the Existentialist hero experiences, the disruption of familiar, human reality by the knowledge of the inevitability and imminence of death, the search for the authentic life on his journey to the end of night.

PART FIVE

CONCLUSION

XIX

CONCLUSION

THE PURPOSE of this book is not to propound a thesis or to engage in polemics; its fundamental object is to examine the relation of literature to religious experience. Its aim is not to condemn those positive values of aspiration and attachment, of communion and commitment, which religion offers the believer, but to scrutinize and evaluate critically the precise conditions under which the religious consciousness, the awareness of God in all his multiple and mysterious incarnations, finds expression in the literature of our time. In short, it purports to be, in part, an exploration in the realm of aesthetics, an essay in literary criticism. It constitutes an attempt, tentative at best, to throw some light on the vexed problem of the relationship that may be said to obtain between literature and faith.

Such declarations of intention are not enough, however, to save the author from the charge that he has, in the course of his discussion, wittingly or unwittingly, introduced a number of biases. Obviously he has not composed this book in a spirit of complete detachment and neutrality. He has taken sides and disclosed frankly on a number of occasions in which direction his sympathies lie. He is bound, after all, to analyze the literary situation in the light of the truth as he sees it. In the selection of his illustrative material, as in his omissions, he is fairly certain to reveal what he considers significant and important. This cannot be helped, and he must assume full responsibility for the conclusions he has drawn and the convictions that underlie them.

It must be conceded, then, that no critic can hope to eliminate entirely the presence of bias in his work, especially when he ventures to enter such a highly controversial field as religion as it finds embodiment in poetry, fiction, and drama. If he prided himself on being scrupulously impartial in his treatment of this emotively charged and ambiguous material, then that would surely betray his intellectual blind spot. He would have to be endowed with superhuman understanding and insight to avoid all the pitfalls of partisanship. In a sense, he has to take a stand. In confronting these ultimate issues of life, he cannot afford to be either lukewarm or cautiously eclectic. When he has made all the necessary qualifications, he must finally come out into the open and commit himself. He cannot do otherwise. He can see only as far as his vision will carry him, and if he is suffering from some form of spiritual myopia his utterances will inevitably betray his infirmity. The point of view he adopts, the ideas he embraces, the examples he chooses, the way in which he analyzes the religious problem and the creative process, his strategic quotations, and his method of expression—all these are born of his past conditioning, his temperament, his basic outlook on life.

On a number of occasions we have pointed out how religion as a form of experience can and does profoundly influence the literary imagination. It has done so powerfully in the past; the influence today is still operative, though under radically altered conditions. It is a legitimate undertaking for the critic to hold up to the light the relationship that exists between the religious experience and the creative act. He is committing no sacrilege in carrying on such an investigation honestly. To define the key terms in such a relationship, to analyze a number of test cases, would in the end serve to clarify what religion, in its impact on literature, can and cannot do.

Our own assumption, or *parti pris,* has been that there is no such thing as *religious* or *political* literature. There is no such distinct genre as the religious novel or the religious poem or play. Subject matter or content is not a valid basis for literary classification. What counts is what the writer does with his material, regardless of its overt content. Is *The World's Illusion,* by Jakob Wassermann, a religious novel? Is *Moses,* by Sholem Asch, to be regarded as such? Is *Paradise Lost* a religious epic? What about *Prometheus Unbound,* by Shelley? Indeed, any piece of literature which is seriously concerned with the ultimate meaning of man's life on earth is "religious," in our sense of the term, regardless of its doctrinal orientation. Judged by such standards, *Of Human Bondage,* like *The Man Who Died,* is religious. For purposes of critical discourse, however, the scope of meaning of crucial terms must be narrowed sufficiently to permit the making of fruitful distinctions. Hence those works have been singled out for analysis in which the religious theme is dominant, in which preoccupation with religious issues plays an important role. This results at times in an arbitrary limitation of the field of inquiry, but that cannot be helped.

Only by concentrating in the main on the aesthetic dimension can we hope to steer clear of the treacherous quicksands of theological disputation, the thorny and interminable arguments over orthodoxy and heterodoxy. For example, a novel, in order to retain its specific character as a work of fiction, must present situations and characters that are credible; the only difference that emerges in the religious novel is that these must be brought into relation with the religious quest. The novelist is, of course, necessarily drawn to a consideration of the fundamental values his characters live by, the faith that moves them to action and shapes their destiny. Yet he is also pulled dialectically in a different direction, for the novel is irreducibly concrete, rooted in the quick of experience, involved in individual conflicts. Thus, in many cases, there is bound to arise a conflict of interests between the claims of religious doctrine and those of sensuous representation, a struggle between faith and art. Religion, especially in its eschatological flights, tends to become abstract and doctrinaire, while fiction derives its powers chiefly from its dramatic immediacy of presentation, its imaginative fidelity to the quality of lived experience. It is this endeavor to reconcile the two poles of devotion that often provides an internal source of tension.

Not that religious ideas and ideals are in themselves either alien or injurious to fiction; ideas make up an integral part of the literary enterprise, even though the problem of adapting them in terms congenial to the medium of fiction (or poetry or drama) remains terribly difficult. The Christian synthesis, whether the writer accepts it implicitly or fiercely rejects it, is always there in the cultural background. It cannot be discarded or ignored. The debates concerning free will, determinism, predestination, fate, God, and immortality, which loom so large on the contemporary literary scene, must be fought out, even though the writers engaged in these battles use strangely untheological weapons. Even as the writer struggles with the task of honestly portraying individual human passions, he cannot throw off the pressure of theological compulsives.

Hence the religious writer must be imaginatively gifted and uncommonly resourceful in delineating how religious beliefs work out in terms of individual destiny. The ideals that animate the characters of a novel or play cannot remain fixed in the realm of abstract thought. Sooner or later they must become controlling forces of fate. The central problem confronting the religious writer, then, is to make these religious obsessions come to life, to show precisely how they condition his dramatis personae into making the kind of choices and commitments they feel inwardly compelled to make, and yet somehow to induce the reader to feel that these characters are autonomous, free to shape their own life.

A striking and largely valid analogy may be drawn between the religious and the political novel. Just as the center of interest in a political novel cannot be the ideology in itself, so in a religious novel the center of interest cannot be theology. A novelist must wrestle with the intractable stuff of experience and integrate his material in a way that transcends ideological doctrine or theological categories. When he does that, his theological preconceptions are of necessity deeply changed by the requirements of form. What Irving Howe says of the political novelist in *Politics and the Novel* applies equally well, *mutatis mutandis,* to the religious novelist: "His task is always to show the relation between theory and experience, between the ideology that has been preconceived and the tangle of feelings and relationships he is trying to present." Since he is not writing a tract, he must devise effective dramatic means for the convincing resolution of the internal conflict. Frequently the novel (or play) may take a direction opposed to the writer's conscious intentions or his personal faith (as is true of some of Eliot's poetry), since he is under the necessity of telling the truth and deploying his material with full imaginative fidelity. The fixities and absolutes of theology are confronted by the infinite diversity of experience, the ambiguity and complexity of action, the often obscure and corrupt tissue of human motivation. A religious work is therefore to be judged in the last analysis not by its loyalty to dogma but by its depth of vision, its intensity of illumination, the degree to which intimations of the universal emerge out of the concrete. The novelist, in other words, keeps faith with a moral order which, rooted as it is in the universe of art, transcends the gravitational pull of dogma.

We are not implying that since all truth is relative, it is not possible, in investigations of this kind, to attain some measure of truth. The literary texts that communicate the religious experience are there for all to examine. Christianity is, after all, only one of the many religions that have occupied the stage of history and called forth allegiance from millions of people. Who shall say which religion is superior, which conception of God more deserving of worship? That, happily, is not within our province. We are interested primarily in analyzing those works in the Western tradition in the twentieth century, chiefly, which deal with the religious problem and in determining how the religious consciousness achieves expression in aesthetically effective terms.

It would be presumptuous and insufferable for the critic who happens to be a secular humanist in outlook to set about debunking the religious beliefs men genuinely hold. If the final truth about life in the universe were known, there would be no further need for argument. The gods would be permanently enthroned in heaven or permanently discredited. We do not, however, possess such knowledge of the final truth, despite the claims of some theologians, and the truly religious person, humble at heart, aware of his finitude and the insurmountable limitations of the intellect, is the first to acknowledge that this is so. The existence of God can neither be proved nor disproved. Since the knowledge we have of being is so radically incomplete, it would be an act of folly to rule out the religious beliefs of mankind.

Rudolf Otto, in *The Idea of the Holy,* frankly acknowledges those elements in religious experience which reach beyond the range of reason. According to him, in every religious experience, Christian or non-Christian, primitive or pagan, these elements of the irrational seem to be present. What the believer beholds and intuitively "knows" is not to be judged in terms of intellectual concepts. Nevertheless, the believer is inwardly convinced that he is communing with Something Beyond, a transcendental object. Thus man gains this numinous vision of a Being, the Wholly Other, who cannot be apprehended by the mind or the senses. God cannot be known by means of concepts and categories. The language man uses to describe God does little more than reflect his "rational" envisagement of God. If that is so, then as soon as Christianity falls into orthodoxy, it fails to furnish a true picture of the living God. What we get, instead, is the God incarnate in dogma, whereas the essence of the living God cannot be taught. He can only come to life in the heart of man in those moments when man stands awed and overpowered in the presence of a Mystery.

And who that is at all sensitive and inquiring by nature, regardless of his precise religious attitude, has not at some time stood in the presence of Mystery? In every life a time comes when man must face the ultimate meaning of his existence. A stranger in a world he never made, thrust without his volition into the maelstrom of life, he reaches during maturity a period of spiritual crisis when he confronts the absolute reality of death. Now he knows of a certainty that he will die and his body rot in the grave. It is no longer a syllogism—all men are mortal—he is formulating; he is oppressed by the knowledge that his personal death is inevitable and that it may come soon. The death by which countless generations in the past were undone, that fate will overtake him. In the light of that knowledge of the nothingness that will overwhelm him, what existential decision is he to make? Shall he adopt, as Camus does, a philosophy of absurdity, even as he protests against the final absurdity of death? What sense can he make of his brief and, alas, precarious pilgrimage on earth? What purpose shall justify his striving after fame and power? Refusing to swallow any consolatory fictions, he is resolved to find, if possible, a convincing answer, one not repugnant to reason, to the metaphysical questions his restless and unhappy mind has begun to ask. He stops suddenly in his tracks, puts aside whatever he is doing, since it is of relatively small import compared to the dreadful challenge of death, and inquires in all seriousness: "What am I doing? Where am I going?" The anguish he experiences is real, unbearably painful, for the time is growing short and death may be close at hand. As Emile Cailliet declares in *The Dawn of Personality:* "The wind of eternity strikes his face. What is the meaning of all this *for him?* Is there a meaning to it at all? Is there anywhere any ultimate sure foundation? any sense to this striving which does not seem to achieve anything final?"

The question is not one that can be postponed indefinitely, for the postponement really represents an evasion of the truth, a refusal to face reality. Plunged irrevocably into life, man, according to Cailliet, has only two options open to him: the acceptance or the rejection of God. It is not, at this point, a question of proving by means of argument that God exists. Like Rudolf Otto, Cailliet maintains that what matters is the reality of God who is not to be comprehended in metaphysical terminology.

And how, he asks, can anyone doubt that God is the reality of all realities, the creator of the universe, the fountainhead of history? The believer achieves faith without any need for further proof. As for those who call themselves atheists, Cailliet says, "They should be greatly surprised to be told that their devotion to truth, their love for beauty, their readiness to sacrifice for the sake of duty actually bears witness to the presence of God in their lives."

This is the "mystical" experience—when man stands alone with the alone and faces the world's mystery—that many writers have passed through. When their spiritual crisis reaches its peak, they must come to terms with themselves, for if life is devoid of meaning then reality takes on a sinister and oppressive aspect. Their first reaction is one of dismay or despair. How account for the appalling incidence of evil that plagues humanity? How can God be held accountable for all this suffering? And yet as the creator of all things on earth He must assume responsibility for the existence of evil. The evil is patently there; death holds all mankind in thrall. In this dilemma the writer seeks to discover a moral order that governs the universe; he needs to feel that human suffering is somehow not senseless but meaningful. The search that he undertakes is "religious" in nature, even when it does not culminate in the acceptance of God.

Lost in the infinite, the soul of man cries out for some supernatural reassurance. A Pascal, frightened by the starry spaces, broods austerely on the grandeur and misery of man. In the middle of life's journey, Tolstoy, unable to silence his doubts and yet terrified by the thought of death, grappled with the religious problem. Kierkegaard, as we have seen, affirmed the absolute by casting off the bondage of reason, the trammels of logic. Passionately drawn to Christianity and the figure of Christ, Dostoevski described himself in 1854 as the child of his age, infected with skepticism, pursued by the furies of unfaith. "How dreadfully it has tormented me (and torments me even now)," he writes in one of his letters, "this longing for faith, which is all the stronger for the proofs I have against it." Yet there were moments when God gave his troubled

soul peace, and then he was able to rise temporarily above his
infernal skepticism. Other creative spirits suffer from severe melan-
cholia, acedia, a paralysis of their will to create, an arrest of their
productive energy, even a severe nervous breakdown, until they
can arrive at some solution to this baffling mystery of life. A few
become convinced that the fate of meaninglessness is not to be
avoided and that man must learn to live with it, but if that is the
conclusion the nihilist accepts then he must make up his mind how
he is to make his peace with the years of life still left to him. Shall
he devote himself to some humanitarian cause and thus improve the
lot of posterity? To what end? Shall he stoically embrace the cult
of absurdity? Or shall he live in the moment solely for the sake of
pleasure, let death come when it will?

The nihilist must suffer the intolerable consequences of seeking
to live meaningfully in a universe that he has decided is meaningless;
he faces a future that is overclouded by a miasmal sense of futility.
When the world is stripped of ultimate meaning, then all human
suffering is without purpose. If the nihilist believes that death ends
everything, if the smell of the charnelhouse infects all of existence,
then he is stricken with a pessimism that makes life insupportable.
The perception that life is absurd fills him with despair. No age can
live without a sustaining sense of faith, even if this manifests itself
only as a determination to survive at all costs. Historians speak of
ages of faith and ages of reason, as if faith and reason were dia-
metrically opposed, but the truth is that faith is, in the best and
most stable of times, a complex process, compounded in unequal
measures of belief and doubt. It is never an assured possession.
Like all of life's most precious goods, it must be perennially rediscovered and renewed.

Everyone, of course, clings to some body of belief that helps to
guide and govern his life. That is the underlying meaning of Tillich's
statement: "The paradox of every radical negativity, as long as it is
an active negativity, is that it must affirm itself in order to be able
to negate itself. No actual negation can be without an implicit
affirmation." That is why Tillich, in that influential book, *The Cour-*

age to Be, regards the acceptance of meaninglessness as in itself a meaningful act. The difference between the religious and the unreligious person lies in the content of their beliefs. The secular humanist, like the supernaturalist, worships his "gods." Even the skeptic, if he is to be consistent in his utterance, must have faith in the validity of his method and the truth of his affirmations.

But what is the writer to do when there are no collectively sanctioned religious truths which he can share? Granted that the questions religion asks and seeks to answer are the questions that all inquiring men have raised at some stage in their lives. The trouble with the writers of our time is that they can no longer derive nourishment from the traditional religious outlook. Effectually blocked for them is the possibility of a revival of belief in the supernatural. They cannot take refuge in the irrational. Yet if vital faith of some kind is denied the writer, how can he go on living and creating? Was it not Nietzsche who, when he lost his religious faith, cried out "that God was dead and that we were trapped in a whirling Void, a meaningless chaos of being"? The function of art, he felt, was to refuse to surrender to defeat even in the midst of a doomed world. Life then is its own goal, but if that is so, all the nihilist can cling to is the brute fact of existence. When Nietzsche knew that he could not be saved, he is reported to have uttered this prophetic warning: "In crying out against the madness of God I have gone mad myself!" But even when the inner citadel of his mind was blasted, he would not recant his atheistic views. As Antichrist, he continued to proclaim the death of God and the fact that man stands alone.

It is Nietzsche, the begetter of the cult of the superman, who poignantly illustrates the tragedy of the man who went mad because he could not find rest in God. His Promethean will was torn between the twin poles of faith and skepticism, affirmation and categorical denial, heaven and hell. If his mind went under, it is because he felt the cracking of the foundations. Orphaned of God, he was left in the end without faith in man. After casting aside as spurious all that his forebears had cherished, he was left with nothing but illusion—only the illusion of self that stubbornly would not bow before the altars of God.

It is Nietzsche, furthermore, who adds a generous dash of irony to the aesthetics of literature, for if God is dead, if death is annihilation, then art, whether Apollonian or Dionysian, is a gratuitous display of superabundant energy, a magnificent form of play or make-believe. It is then that the writer must learn to laugh at art and at himself as well as at the tragicomedy of existence. He becomes, in effect, the absurd man that Camus describes so hauntingly in *The Myth of Sisyphus*. In the nineteenth century, after the decline of religion and the ascendancy of science, it was believed that art would take the place of religion. The artist was exalted as secular prophet and redeemer. But the artist in the twentieth century cannot seriously play this role; his function has been debunked.

Moreover, religion could not withstand the rigorous scrutiny and critical assaults of science. Freud, for one, challenged the fundamental assumption of religion that it could afford man any protection against the winds of adversity or the incursions of evil. Experience offered no confirmation of the belief that the good would be rewarded and the wicked punished. No providential power, Freud announced, superintended the universe and kept a strict moral account of every thought and deed. In short, Freudianism denied that human destiny conformed to any ruling principle of justice. From the writings of Freud the intellectuals appropriated the notion that religion is a form of wishful thinking designed to gain control over the world—an attempt that inevitably fails and is bound to fail. According to Freud, religion, a neurotic stage in the development of the race, would be abandoned when its fantastic claims could no longer gain assent. In the future, the intellect would triumph over instinct, reason over superstition, truth over fantasy.

Freud did not relish this work of demolition which he nevertheless carried out resolutely, without fear of the consequences, because of his devotion to the cause of truth. In one part of his iconoclastic *Moses and Monotheism* he makes this confession:

How we who have little belief envy those who are convinced of the existence of a Supreme Power, for whom the world holds no problems because he himself has created all its institutions! How comprehensive, exhaustive, and final are the doctrines of the believers compared with the laboured, poor, and patchy attempts at explanations which are the best we can produce!

The believer at least professes to know what the ideal of ethical perfection is and how best to achieve it. "We can only regret," Freud goes on to say, "if certain experiences of life and observations of nature have made it impossible to accept the hypothesis of such a Supreme Being." Freud's remarks—his regrets—are probably representative of the attitude of the vast majority of intellectuals in our time.

Freud's influence on contemporary writers has in part been neutralized by that of Jung, who feels it is justifiable to postulate a religious instinct, not unlike the theory of the libido that Freud formulated. Unlike Freud, the positivist, for whom religion was a species of infantile illusion, a kind of substitute obsessional neurosis, Jung treats religion with profound seriousness as a revelation of the tensions and needs of man's psychic life. Like the mystical poets, Jung interprets religion as the perception of the numinous in experience, the transfiguring glimpse of the divine. This is not a matter for debate or clinical diagnosis; it is simply an object of personal experience. The religious person "knows," without need for further proof, that his beliefs have changed not only his being but also the world he lives in.

Nietzsche, Kierkegaard, Dostoevski, Freud, Jung—these are some of the seminal thinkers who have helped to shape the literary consciousness of the twentieth century. One clear conclusion seems to emerge from this continuing argument over the existence of God: it is futile for man to attempt to define the nature of God. Yet the Christian mythos, whether it is accepted or rejected, is manifestly present as a potent leaven in our culture. A poet can attack it but he cannot ignore it. As we have seen, a poet like Robinson Jeffers, for example, is opposed to Christianity on the ground that it has had a morbid effect on modern life. Indeed, in his work he projects a conception of God that is close to the Buddhistic notion. If, as Jeffers feels, man must break away from his incestuous attachment to humanity and turn to the contemplation of God, this God offers no scintilla of hope, no dream of immortality, no fantasy of salvation. What is equally revealing is that Jeffers has no faith in humanitarian ideas or utopian expectations of achieving happiness or justice on earth. Giving up his narcissistic illusion that he is of any conceivable importance in the cosmic scheme, man must accept the burden of suffering. The individual perishes, Nature alone endures. The end is total darkness, the annihilation of consciousness.

That is the tragedy of the Outsider who wishes to make his life meaningful but who cannot transcend his radical negativity. He must bear this cross as long as he lives; though he affirms the futility of the human experiment, he cannot rest in a faith that is rooted in the quicksands of futility. He must find a way out; he cannot function creatively in a world that is reduced to a gigantic machine. He must perforce believe, or act as if he believed, in the freedom of the will. It is his perception of the tragic plight of man that makes him human, despite his denials, and brings him close to the authentic religious outlook. If suffering is the badge of his humanity, it is also the source of his numinous vision, even when this culminates in the Nietzschean Nemesis of negation.

His problem is how to deal with, how to rise above, the truth that his consciousness reveals. Ivan, in *The Brothers Karamazov*, is torn between the poles of affirmation and negation. Though his avowed aim was to disclose the madness to which the atheist position leads, Dostoevski portrays with remarkable insight the "Passion" of the intellectual who confronts the spectacle of universal nothingness. Yet the Outsider—one thinks of men like Heidegger and Sartre—feels that by removing all blindfolds and scrapping all anthropocentric illusions, by courageously facing the "horror" of existence, he leads a more authentic life. Like Dreiser, the Outsider stands in awe before the magnificent works of Nature but he sees in them no hint of redemptive meaning. All around him he observes the ignorant multitudes who live contentedly in a world of chimeras, infatuated with self-love, proud of their stupidly narrow power of reason, whereas the Outsider intensifies his state of defiance and willingly accepts a life of despair. Though he knows he is doomed, he keeps on asking questions while inwardly convinced that they cannot be answered. But in thus running to extremes, in candidly recognizing the contradictions of existence, he comes, like the mystic, to experience moments of luminous vision.

Though he lacks the evangelical passion which would make him attempt to convert others, he devotes himself to the relentless pursuit of truth. This is his only absolute. He will not swallow the ideological nostrums and utopian creeds of his time. Essentially the Outsider, as Colin Wilson defines him in *The Outsider,* is "he who cannot accept life as it is, who cannot consider his own existence or any one else's *necessary.*" He cannot reconcile himself to the practical necessities and petty routine that make up life for the Philistines on earth, though he realizes that whatever a man may believe about destiny, the end will be the same. Nevertheless, he is forced to rebel against this degrading human condition. That is how he is brought face to face with the religious question: if life is a useless passion, then what shall he do with himself, especially since he is convinced that life is not worth living?

But who can presume, by a tour de force of logic, to reject both life and the universe? Even as the Outsider rejects, he is urged on by a need stronger than reason to discover some solution in which he can believe and which will restore him to life. Unfortunately he is incapable of committing himself to any principle of faith. He cannot accept a religious solution that his reason repudiates. This highlights the heart of his struggle, his conflict between reason and faith, truth and intuition. If reason makes it clear that man is nothing, an atom of energy in the macrocosm, reason also forces him to suspect the conclusions of his reasoning. Here is the dilemma on the horns of which he is cruelly impaled: he cannot believe what his reason denies and he cannot believe that reason is the way to truth, for if nothing has meaning then the power of reason is itself rendered null and void. How then can the Outsider say he believes or does not believe?

In his brilliant but erratic study of the Outsider, Colin Wilson goes off the rails toward the end precisely because he insists, without regard for the requirements of consistency, on introducing a strictly religious emphasis. He speaks of the Outsider, the visions he beholds, the salvation he seeks, as if he were some sort of saint. Eloquently he dwells on the visions that come to such men as Blake, Dostoevski, Nietzsche, and Ramakrishna, but all this throws little light on the basic character of the Outsider. The mistake Colin Wilson makes lies in trying to link up the Outsider with the religious visionary, the mystic, the saint. All this tends to confound categories that are already ambiguous, if not badly confused. The truth of the matter is that the Outsider, if he is to be distinctively identified, regards it as his vocation in life to abolish religious absolutes, to eliminate the concept of God, and to emphasize that existence, all existence, is unnecessary. He is not God-intoxicated but God-emptied. To talk seriously in this context, as Colin Wilson does, of "God-consciousness" is utterly to misinterpret the fundamental outlook and motivation of the Outsider, who is the sworn enemy of the belief in God. He is the godless man who can accept no opiate illusions, no myths, no vital lies. He cannot take Christianity seriously, its sacraments and dogmas, its doctrine of original sin and its mystery of the Trinity. He applies more or less the same technique of devaluation to all the religions.

But Colin Wilson, one of England's contemporary Angry Young Men, could not remain satisfied with the "solution" he had set forth so confidently in *The Outsider*. In *Religion and the Rebel*, he seeks to formulate the religion of the future, one that will get rid of the anthropomorphic conception of God, the myth of immortality, the consolatory idea of a providence mysteriously shaping human ends. Indeed, the religion of the future, according to this young prophet, will be one without a God or gods. Modern man must make his peace with a naturalistic universe which gives no hint of a divine purpose; yet consciousness, even if that too is derived ultimately from nature, seems a phenomenon apart, that which is distinctively human, for man can contemplate his own existence and his own extinction. It is the angry and "obsessed" members of the younger generation who have become "rebels," smashers of ancient idols yet creators of the new religious vision.

They begin as rebels, but at the heart of their revolt is this steadfast need for a religion that will make life on earth meaningful. They cannot, however, gratify this need on the old terms. They cannot accept faith blindly or take the Kierkegaardian leap. How can they discover a new religion, without accepting a church or a method of organized worship? The Outsider instinctively rebels against a society that is spiritually eaten through with the cancer of meaninglessness. Though he begins as a rebellious skeptic, he usually winds up with some kind of religious conviction. If Colin Wilson does not commit himself to the existential truths of any of the historical religions, his hostility to materialism and science is not to be mistaken. He is uneasily aware of the nature of this dilemma. *Religion and the Rebel* is a badly confused book which deals only remotely with the religious problem.

Religious literature, at its best, is concerned with one fundamental theme—the fate, always problematical and mysterious, of man, the struggle in his soul between the forces of darkness and light, good and evil, nothingness and God. In this sense, perhaps all literature might be called "religious." From the beginning of time, creative man has sought to impose order on chaos, to master the confusion he perceives all around him, to discover the pattern in the carpet, to answer the riddle of the Sphinx. The quest is attended by many perils, for man in his brief sojourn on earth is surrounded by forces he can neither comprehend nor control. At any moment, his feverish search for the Holy Grail of meaning may be ended by the fall of night, the resurgence of primordial darkness. Even as he spells out his metaphysical sentences and proclaims his faith in God, he suspects that these spells are no more efficacious than the mumbo jumbo the savage chants in the jungle. Precisely because modern man is stricken with the terrifying suspicion that there is no meaning in the universe does he struggle so desperately to deny the reality of the void. All of literature, then, is in an ultimate sense an engagement with the forces that push man implacably toward the abyss, an attempt to satisfy the all-too-human need for some kind of order, rational if not providential, in the universe.

But the old order of faith has been discarded by many as no longer true. The old solutions are incapable of working their wonted magic, and man must once more endeavor to rise above chaos and old night. Where is he to find a valid principle of reconciliation between faith and denial, religion and atheism? The writer must discover anew—a stupendous task—the meaning that life has or can have, the common values that men in our age of relativism can share. Again, the existential contradictions remind him that his efforts may all be in vain. Have not men in other centuries faced the same challenge of darkness and been trapped in snares of illusion? The metaphysical, like the mystical, quest—like faith itself—represents a dangerous gamble, for there is always the possibility that there are no answers to be found. Perhaps the questions themselves are spurious. Like the traveler in Walter de la Mare's poem, "The Listeners," one may knock on the moonlit door and ask, "Is there anybody there?" Then smite upon the door a second and third time, and keep on calling in the night, with only the silence to answer his cry.

Indeed, some modern writers refrain, like the logical positivists, from raising questions that cannot be answered in operational terms. That is the measure of their tragedy. They need to pray but they cannot get themselves to believe in the efficacy of prayer, the art of verbal magic. The writers of the past, sustained by a common spiritual ideal, a belief that man must rise above the flux of passion, the pull of animal impulses, felt they were in touch with an ultimate reality that transcended the dimension of time. They dealt with a framework of transcendent values, and life was meaningful because it could always be referred to this higher reality. But having relegated the machinery of the supernatural to the scrap heap, modern man is compelled to seek his salvation in the natural and temporal order or not find it at all.

For the writer who is an Outsider this is not a matter of deliberate choice. He cannot help himself. The conditions which circumscribe his vision, the eyes with which he beholds the world, and the mind which interprets phenomena—these have already been established by his culture. He catches no hint of an ideal order outside the limits of time and space. If he cannot find his salvation in this world, his search is doomed to defeat. He is convinced that the absolute goals men in the past strove to reach were compounded of pure ghostly illusion. Outside of this brief immersion in the river of time, life has no meaning and no values, yet without some ultimate frame of reference to what viable ideal can he dedicate himself? What substitute can he find for God?

If the Outsider as poet believes that the only aim of life is life itself, that there is nothing beyond—and that is the position of humanists like Erich Fromm and H. J. Muller—how shall his work be judged? Shall religious poetry be judged by its degree of conformity to a fixed body of dogmas? That is no longer possible. For good or evil, the discoveries of science have put an end to the old conception of human nature as irremediably sinful and depraved, condemned to lifelong suffering because of the Fall. Poetry was stimulated by the advance of science to seek out new sources of experience and to explore the sensuous world in all its immediacy. The poet does not echo the findings of science; he is faithful to the scientific discipline by honestly reporting the truth of his vision. If he does not bow before the idols of science, neither does he take his theology secondhand from some authoritarian source and cease to arrive at his own independent insights. He does not, by his commitment to poetry, cut himself off from the stream of experience, the life of reason. If there are some critics who continue to measure poetry by theological standards, it is because they assume that there exists a divinely revealed higher knowledge that gives them a monopoly on the truth.

Our contention has been that this is not how religious poetry is born. The poet cannot throw off the intellectual influence of his age, the scientific values of the twentieth century; these make up an integral and inescapable part of his culture. He cannot remain productive if he roots himself in some orthodoxy, for all orthodoxy spells the death of the creative imagination and dams the free flow of the sensibility. All poetry which is dogmatic or didactic in content is rendered obsolete with the inexorable passage of time. That is the great risk religious poetry runs when it attaches itself to beliefs that have been discredited. The faith which once bore up the writers of the past is now lost; science has progressively taken over in areas where religion once flourished. There is the painful contradiction the Christian poet of our time faces: he must believe in the Incarnation as a specific historic event when his reason balks at swallowing this myth. So many myths have perished in the limbo of time. Even his efforts to utilize the myth creatively are bound to fail, for belief in myth as no more than myth, as a quickening incitement to the production of poetry, acts as a dissolvent of faith. This is the cul-de-sac in which the poet today is trapped. His skepticism militates against the spontaneous functioning of the creative spirit, and yet he cannot get himself to believe with full conviction. God as a product of myth, God as an imaginative projection, will satisfy neither the religious requirements nor the creative needs of mankind.

This does not mean that the poet, if he abandons the stay of orthodoxy, is thereby prevented from writing about the religious experience in its pure state. All of experience legitimately falls within the province of poetry. But the numinous vision can be communicated, if at all, only in negative terms. The mystical seizure is hedged round with obscurity and paradox; it blends light and darkness, yes and no, the positive and the negative, for God is both everything and nothing. Only through these ejaculatory, often delirious negations can the inspired mystic hope to convey to others some intimation of what he beholds in his vision. How else can he clothe his apprehension of the infinite? The language of religion is unavoidably shot through with contradictions. The element of paradox cannot be eliminated; it is woven into the very fabric of religious thought. The language of paradox is the identifying mark of all religion and of all religious poetry, for what religious aspiration seeks to communicate is beyond the power of words to utter. The world of being is not to be grasped within some conceptual system; like God, it eludes finite understanding. In the realm of poetry, religious paradox brings into focus the fundamental ambiguities and contradictions of life. If "existence" is to be limited to things in space and time, then obviously the postulation of an existence outside of space and time is not only inconceivable but absurd. For the man who refuses to be guilty of such an absurdity, God does not exist. But what does that prove? No religious thinker ever seriously affirms that God exists in time and space. God is everywhere and yet nowhere present.

If God is represented in a series of audacious paradoxes, if he is both immanent and transcendent, hidden yet revealed, identified with the Whole and yet somehow personal in nature, how can the believer assent to such mysteries beyond comprehension, beyond the power of reason, and how can he derive moral strength and sustenance from dependence on such a source? Inevitably, as science pictures a universe governed by invariant laws, it becomes impossible to accept statements grounded in authority or revelation. Universal determinism admits of no exceptions. Biology, too, has riddled theological assumptions full of holes. After the challenge hurled by Darwinism, nature had to be regarded, no longer as beneficent and purposive, but rather as blind and cruel, and even wasteful. Finally, psychology drove home the last nail in the coffin of supernatural theology by demonstrating the existence of determinism in the psychic as well as the physical world. Consequently the most fundamental question confronting man today is precisely the question of belief in God. The modern intellectual cannot believe in the dogmas and sacraments of Christianity. Indeed, Edmund Wilson, in *A Piece of My Mind,* feels that it runs counter to common sense to take Christianity seriously. Forthrightly he declares that the word *God* "is now archaic" and it ought to be dropped by those who do not need it for moral support. For the conception of God fails radically to fit the complex facts of modern experience, to explain why we exist, why there is a universe and not a nothing, why conditions are what they are. No one knows the final answer, but the old religious sanctions are anachronistic and absurd. To rely on God and to invoke his sacred name—that is to indulge in a species of fairy-tale magic.

George Orwell, who insisted on realistically facing the naked truth, refused to believe in what is desirable. Christianity, he argued, despite all the verbal professions of faith men make, was dead. Everyone today, he contended, regardless of his religious affiliations, *acted* (and that is what counted) as if he knew that death was the end and that this was the only world he would ever enjoy. Orwell knew well enough what the consequences would be when man lost faith in the life after death, yet he was certain that religious faith could not be restored and he did not wish to have it return. This desperate rehabilitation of the religious absolute, this surrender to the supernatural principle—that was too easy a way out of our difficulties. Orwell had no solution to offer. Suffering would always go on. One should not aim to achieve perfection on earth but should confine himself to improving as much as he could the lot of man.

An awareness of the limits of the creative imagination does not imply the death of poetry. Just as it is possible to revolt against the excesses of scientific thinking without advocating a return to Thomistic theology, so it is possible to point out the basic limitations of the poetic process without in any way underestimating its imaginative power and universal appeal. Such an aesthetic assumption simply stresses the fact that the art of poetry is not designed to "teach" a specific body of religious lessons. As for the relation of poetry to the absolute, poetry, like the vision inherent in Protestantism, renews itself perennially and retains its sense of the problematical and precarious by rooting itself in the human crisis, which never ends. The poet must remain organically situated in nature and in human culture, for that is all he possesses. That is the source and

ground of whatever vision he may hope to capture. It is human existence, this visible earth, that constitutes his sphere of endeavor, his
"religious devotion."

If the concept of reality is altered from the ground up, then
poetry, too, is bound to undergo a revolutionary transformation.
It becomes increasingly secularized. Today the crisis has grown
more acute, for the physicists penetrate to an underlying reality that
is indeterminate; the electrons engage in a vertiginous dance of
energy that only serves to reinstate the myth of nothingness. The
crisis of physics is the crisis of the contemporary soul. How affirm
meaning in the face of the nothingness that hems us in on all
sides? How can unity be achieved in a universe of unintelligible
multiplicity?

Differently put, how can the poet remain true to his vocation
when he has no faith in the ultimate triumph of meaning, the
worth of life, the values of the world he inhabits? How can he
escape the enervating metaphysical torment of the idea that all is
absurdity? Yet he must do so if he is to survive at all. Whatever
poetry does, according to Erich Heller in *The Hazard of Modern
Poetry,*

it cannot but confirm the existence of a meaningful world—even when
it denounces its meaninglessness. Poetry means order, even with the
indictment of chaos; it means hope, even with the outcry of despair.
It is concerned with the true stature of things. And being concerned
with the true stature of things, all great poetry is realistic.

Nevertheless, once the writer abandons reality, acknowledging
that it is beyond his reach of understanding, he suffers a grave
loss. He is left with a cruelly impoverished sense of the real; his
horizons are contracted; henceforth he is limited to what his senses
report. He has sacrificed the beyond, the mysterious, the transcendent, and denied the reality of the Absolute, even as a domain of the
spirit which can be symbolically explored. Once this Absolute has
perished—and it perishes if it is no longer an object of faith—
his writing is deprived of a potent source of vision: the shadow and

glory of the unknown, the visitations of the numinous, the music of the ineffable.

These, however, are the insuperable limitations of art and poetry, which are all-too-human constructions. Yet if the poet is wedded exclusively to the thing, if he must disport himself in a reality that is confirmed by the proof of the senses, he must discard those values and visions of desire which add a supernal meaning to existence. A naturalistic universe, if apprehended in the metaphor of a machine, blindly functioning, in which man is but a chemicophysical unit, soon turns into a hideous nightmare. It is then that the metaphysical challenge, religious in its extreme formulation, rings out: What is all this for? Why this magnificent outburst of energy in space? Illegitimate as the question may sound when judged by scientific standards of verification, it leaps ineluctably out of a heart (Pascal's heart) unreconciled to the myth of meaninglessness. The question may have no logical validity, it may represent sheer nonsense, but the heart has its stubborn reasons that refuse to be silenced. If there is no beyond, then the "no" is equivalent to saying there is only nothingness. The Absolute is liquidated, wiped out of the discourse of faith. Man stands alone and his destiny is at the mercy of time and fate and circumstance. He is a victim, not an immortal soul; a creature of earth and death, not a dweller in eternity; a biological organism doomed to extinction, not a child of God. If this is the naturalistic synthesis modern man has honestly worked out, how is he to live with it? For live with it he must. That is the creative problem the writer of the twentieth century faces in his struggle to affirm "religious" values in his work.

BIBLIOGRAPHY

ALDRIDGE, JOHN W. *After the Lost Generation.* New York: McGraw-Hill, 1951.

ALLEN, EDGAR LEONARD. *Existentialism from Within.* London: Routledge & Paul, 1953.

AUDEN, W. H. *Another Time.* New York: Random House, 1940.

———. *For the Time Being.* London: Faber & Faber, 1945.

———. *The Collected Poetry of W. H. Auden.* New York: Random House, 1945.

———. *The Age of Anxiety.* New York: Random House, 1947.

———. *The Enchaféd Flood.* New York: Random House, 1950.

BARRETT, WILLIAM. *What Is Existentialism?* New York: Partisan Review, 1947.

———. *Irrational Man.* Garden City: Doubleday, 1958.

BEAUVOIR, SIMONE DE. *The Ethics of Ambiguity.* Translated by BERNARD FRECHTMAN. New York: Philosophical Library, 1948.

BOBBIO, NORBERT. *The Philosophy of Decadentism.* Translated by DAVID MOORE. Oxford: B. Blackwell, 1948.

BODKIN, MAUDE. *Archetypal Patterns in Poetry.* London: Oxford University Press, 1934.

———. *Studies of Type-Images in Poetry, Religion, and Philosophy.* London and New York: Oxford University Press, 1951.

BOWLES, PAUL. *The Sheltering Sky.* Norfolk, Conn.: New Directions, 1949.

——. *Let It Come Down.* New York: Random House, 1952.

BRINTON, CLARENCE CRANE. *Friedrich Nietzsche.* Cambridge: Harvard University Press, 1941.

BRONOWSKI, J. *The Common Sense of Science.* Cambridge: Harvard University Press, 1953.

BROOKS, VAN WYCK. *The Writer in America.* New York: Dutton, 1953.

BUSH, DOUGLAS. *Science and English Poetry.* New York: Oxford University Press, 1950.

CAILLIET, EMILE. *The Dawn of Personality.* Indianapolis: Bobbs-Merrill Co., 1955.

CALVERTON, V. F. *The Passing of the Gods.* New York: Charles Scribner's Sons, 1934.

CAMUS, ALBERT. *The Stranger.* Translated by STUART GILBERT. New York: Alfred A. Knopf, 1946.

——. *The Plague.* Translated by STUART GILBERT. New York: Alfred A. Knopf, 1948.

——. *The Rebel.* Translated by ANTHONY BOWER. New York: Alfred A. Knopf, 1954.

——. *The Myth of Sisyphus.* Translated by JUSTIN O'BRIEN. New York: Alfred A. Knopf, 1955.

——. *The Fall.* Translated by JUSTIN O'BRIEN. New York: Alfred A. Knopf, 1957.

CASSIRER, ERNST. *Language and Myth.* Translated by SUSANNE K. LANGER. New York and London: Harper & Bros., 1946.

CÉLINE, LOUIS-FERDINAND. *Journey to the End of the Night.* Translated by JOHN H. MARKS. Boston: Little, Brown & Co., 1934.

CHEKHOV, ANTON. *Letters on the Short Story, the Drama and Other Literary Topics,* ed. LOUIS S. FRIEDLAND. New York: Minton, Balch & Co., 1924.

——. *The Plays of Anton Tchekov.* Translated by CONSTANCE GARNETT. New York: Modern Library, 1930.

COHEN, ELIE A. *Human Behavior in the Concentration Camp.* Translated by M. H. BRAAKSMA. New York: W. W. Norton & Co., 1953.

COMFORT, ALEXANDER. *Art and Social Responsibility.* London: Falcon Press, 1946.

————. *The Novel and Our Time.* London: Phoenix House, 1948.

————. *The Pattern of the Future.* London: Routledge & K. Paul, 1949.

————. *On This Side Nothing.* New York: Viking Press, 1949.

DESAN, WILFRID. *The Tragic Finale.* Cambridge: Harvard University Press, 1954.

DOSTOEVSKI, FYODOR. *Letters of Fyodor Mikhail Dostoevsky to His Family and Friends.* Translated by ETHEL COLBURN MAYNE. New York: Macmillan Co., n. d.

————. *The Possessed.* Translated by CONSTANCE GARNETT. New York: Macmillan Co., 1916.

————. *The Brothers Karamazov.* Translated by CONSTANCE GARNETT. New York: Modern Library, n. d.

DREISER, THEODORE. *Hey Rub-a-Dub-Dub: A Book of the Mystery, and Wonder, and Terror of Life.* New York: Boni & Liveright, 1920.

————. *An American Tragedy.* New York: Modern Library, 1956.

EISSLER, K. R. *The Psychiatrist and the Dying Patient.* New York: International Universities Press, 1955.

ELIOT, T. S. *Selected Essays, 1917-1932.* New York: Harcourt, Brace & Co., 1932.

————. *After Strange Gods.* New York: Harcourt, Brace & Co., 1934.

————. *The Rock.* London: Faber & Faber, 1934.

————. *Essays, Ancient and Modern.* New York: Harcourt, Brace & Co., 1936.

————. *The Complete Poems and Plays.* New York: Harcourt, Brace & Co., 1952.

EMMETT, DOROTHY M. *The Nature of Metaphysical Thinking.* London: Macmillan Co., 1953.

EVANS, B. IFOR. *Literature and Science*. London: Allen and Unwin, 1949.

EVERY, GEORGE. *Poetry and Personal Responsibility*. London: SCM Press, 1949.

FRASER, G. S. *The Modern Writer and His World*. London: D. Verschoyle, 1953.

FREUD, SIGMUND. *Autobiography*. Translated by JAMES STRACHEY. New York: W. W. Norton & Co., 1935.

―――. *Moses and Monotheism*. Translated by KATHERINE JONES. New York: Alfred A. Knopf, 1947.

―――. *Collected Papers*. Translated by JAMES STRACHEY. Vol. V. London: International Psycho-analytical Press, 1950.

FRIAR, KIMON (ed.). *Modern Poetry, American and British*. New York: Appleton-Century-Crofts, 1951.

FROMM, ERICH. *Escape from Freedom*. New York: Farrar & Rinehart, 1941.

―――. *Man for Himself*. New York: Rinehart, 1947.

―――. *Psychoanalysis and Religion*. New Haven: Yale University Press, 1951.

―――. *The Sane Society*. New York: Rinehart, 1955.

GRENE, MARJORIE. *The Dreadful Freedom*. Chicago: University of Chicago Press, 1948.

HARDY, FLORENCE EMILY. *The Later Years of Thomas Hardy*. New York: Macmillan Co., 1930.

HARDY, THOMAS. *The Dynasts*. London: Macmillan, 1928-29.

HARPER, RALPH. *Existentialism*. Cambridge: Harvard University Press, 1949.

HARTWICK, HARRY. *The Background of American Fiction*. New York: American Book Company, 1934.

HAVELOCK, E. A. *The Crucifixion of Intellectual Man*. Boston: Beacon Press, 1950.

HAWTON, HECTOR. *The Feast of Unreason*. London: Watts & Co., 1952.

HEIDEGGER, MARTIN. *Existence and Being*. Chicago: H. Regnery Co., 1949.

HEINEMANN, F. H. *Existentialism and the Modern Predicament.* New York: Harper & Bros., 1953.

HELLER, ERICH. *The Hazard of Modern Poetry.* Cambridge, England: Bowes & Bowes, 1953.

HEPPENSTALL, RAYMOND. *The Double Image.* London: Secker & Warburg, 1947.

HOFFMAN, FREDERICK J. *Freudianism and the Literary Mind.* Baton Rouge: Louisiana State University Press, 1945.

HOGGART, RICHARD. *Auden.* New Haven: Yale University Press, 1951.

HOLLIS, CHRISTOPHER. *A Study of George Orwell.* Chicago: H. Regnery Co., 1957.

HOLROYD, STUART. *Emergence from Chaos.* London: Gollancz, 1957.

HOSPERS, JOHN. *Meaning and Truth in the Arts.* Chapel Hill: University of North Carolina Press, 1949.

HOWE, IRVING. *Politics and the Novel.* New York: Horizon Press, 1957.

HUXLEY, ALDOUS. *Antic Hay.* New York: George H. Doran Co., 1923.

———. *Those Barren Leaves.* New York: Harper & Bros., 1925.

———. *Point Counter Point.* Garden City: Doubleday Doran & Co., 1928.

———. *Eyeless in Gaza.* New York and London: Harper & Bros., 1936.

———. *After Many a Summer Dies the Swan.* New York and London: Harper & Bros., 1939.

———. *Time Must Have a Stop.* New York and London: Harper & Bros., 1944.

——— (ed.). *The Perennial Philosophy.* New York and London: Harper & Bros., 1945.

———. *Brave New World.* New York and London: Harper & Bros., 1946.

———. *Ape and Essence.* New York: Harper & Bros., 1948.

———. *Heaven and Hell.* New York: Harper & Bros., 1956.

ISAACS, J. *An Assessment of Twentieth-Century Literature.* London: Secker & Warburg, 1951.

ISHERWOOD, CHRISTOPHER (ed.). *Vedanta for the Western World.* Hollywood: Marcel Rodd Co., 1945.

JAMES, WILLIAM. *The Varieties of Religious Experience.* New York: Longmans, Green & Co., 1902.

JARRETT-KERR, MARTIN. *Studies in Literature and Belief.* London: Rockliff, 1954.

JASPERS, KARL. *Tragedy Is Not Enough.* Translated by HARALD A. T. REICHE, HARRY T. MOORE, and KARL W. DEUTSCH. Boston: Beacon Press, 1952.

————. *Reason and Existenz.* Translated by WILLIAM EARLE. New York: Noonday Press, 1955.

JEFFERS, ROBINSON. *Roan Stallion, Tamar, and Other Poems.* New York: Boni & Liveright, 1925.

————. *Dear Judas and Other Poems.* New York: Horace Liveright, 1929.

JOHNSON, F. ERNEST (ed.). *Religious Symbolism.* New York and London: Harper & Bros., 1955.

JOHNSON, MARTIN C. *Art and Scientific Thought.* New York: Columbia University Press, 1949.

JONES, ERNEST. *The Life and Work of Sigmund Freud.* Vol. III. New York: Basic Books, 1957.

JUNG, C. G. *Modern Man in Search of a Soul.* Translated by W. S. DELL and CARY F. BAYNES. London: K. Paul, Trench, Trubner & Co., 1933.

————. *Psychology and Religion.* New Haven: Yale University Press, 1938.

————. *The Integration of the Personality.* Translated by STANLEY M. DELL. New York and Toronto: Farrar & Rinehart, 1939.

————. *Essays on Contemporary Events.* Translated by ELIZABETH WELSH, BARBARA HANNAH, and MARY BRINER. London: K. Paul, 1947.

————. *Answer to Job.* Translated by R. F. C. HULL. London: Routledge & Paul, 1954.

KIERKEGAARD, SÖREN. *Fear and Trembling.* Translated by WALTER LOWRIE. Princeton: Princeton University Press, 1941.

———. *The Concept of Dread.* Translated by WALTER LOWRIE. Princeton: Princeton University Press, 1944.

———. *Either/Or.* 2 vols. Translated by DAVID F. SWENSON and LILLIAN MARVIN SWENSON. Princeton: Princeton University Press, 1946.

KUHN, HELMUT. *Freedom Forgotten and Remembered.* Chapel Hill: University of North Carolina Press, 1943.

———. *Encounter with Nothingness.* Hinsdale: Regnery, 1949.

LANGER, SUSANNE K. *Philosophy in a New Key.* Cambridge: Harvard University Press, 1942.

———. *Feeling and Form.* New York: Charles Scribner's Sons, 1953.

LAWRENCE, D. H. *Psychoanalysis and the Unconscious.* New York: T. Seltzer, 1922.

———. *The Letters of D. H. Lawrence,* ed. ALDOUS HUXLEY. New York: Viking Press, 1932.

———. *Apocalypse.* New York: Viking Press, 1932.

———. *Phoenix,* ed. E. D. MCDONALD. New York: Viking Press, 1936.

LIEBLING, A. J. (ed.). *The Republic of Silence.* New York: Harcourt, Brace & Co., 1947.

MALRAUX, ANDRÉ. *The Psychology of Art.* 3 vols. Translated by STUART GILBERT. New York: Pantheon Books, 1949-50.

MARITAIN, JACQUES. *Art and Scholasticism.* Translated by J. F. SCANLAN. New York: Charles Scribner's Sons, 1930.

———. *Creative Intuition in Art and Poetry.* New York: Pantheon Books, 1953.

MARITAIN, JACQUES and RAÏSSA. *The Situation of Poetry.* Translated by MARSHALL SUTHER. New York: Philosophical Library, 1955.

MAUGHAM, SOMERSET. *Of Human Bondage.* Garden City: Doubleday, 1915.

———. *Plays.* 6 vols. London: Heinemann, 1934-38.

MENCKEN, H. L. *Treatise on the Gods.* New York: Alfred A. Knopf, 1930.

MEYERHOFF, HANS. *Time in Literature.* Berkeley: University of California Press, 1955.

MILES, JOSEPHINE. *The Continuity of Poetic Language.* Berkeley: University of California Press, 1951.

MILLER, ARTHUR. *Collected Plays.* New York: Viking Press, 1957.

MOTHERWELL, ROBERT (ed.). *The Dada Painters and Poets.* New York: Wittenborn, Schultz, 1951.

MOUNIER, EMMANUEL. *Existential Philosophies.* Translated by ERIC BLOW. New York: Macmillan Co., 1949.

MUIR, EDWIN. *An Autobiography.* New York: William Sloane Associates, 1954.

MULLER, HERBERT J. *The Spirit of Tragedy.* New York: Alfred A. Knopf, 1956.

MUMFORD, LEWIS. *The Conduct of Life.* New York: Harcourt, Brace & Co., 1951.

MURDOCH, IRIS. *Sartre.* New Haven: Yale University Press, 1953.

NEEDHAM, JOSEPH (ed.). *Science, Religion and Reality.* New York: G. Braziller, 1955.

NIETZSCHE, FRIEDRICH. *The Complete Works of Friedrich Nietzsche,* ed. OSCAR LEVY. 18 vols. Edinburgh and London: T. N. Foulis, 1909-13.

————. *My Sister and I.* Translated by OSCAR LEVY. New York: Boar's Head Books, 1953.

NOTT, KATHLEEN. *The Emperor's Clothes.* London: Heinemann, 1953.

O'DONNELL, DONAT. *Maria Cross.* New York: Oxford University Press, 1952.

O'FAOLAIN, SEAN. *The Vanishing Hero.* Boston: Little, Brown & Co., 1957.

O'NEILL, EUGENE. *Plays.* 3 vols. New York: Random House, 1941.

————. *The Iceman Cometh.* New York: Random House, 1946.

ORWELL, GEORGE. *Dickens, Dali and Others.* New York: Reynal & Hitchcock, 1946.

————. *Nineteen Eighty-Four.* New York: Harcourt, Brace & Co., 1949.

————. *Such, Such Were the Joys.* New York: Harcourt, Brace & Co., 1953.

OTTO, RUDOLF. *The Idea of the Holy.* Translated by J. W. HARVEY. London: Geoffrey Cumberlege, 1950.

PASCAL, BLAISE. *Pensées.* Translated by W. F. TROTTER. New York: E. P. Dutton & Co., 1931.

PATON, H. J. *The Modern Predicament.* New York: Macmillan Co., 1955.

PHILIP, H. L. *Freud and Religious Belief.* London: Rockliff, 1956.

POULET, GEORGES. *Studies in Human Time.* Translated by ELLIOTT COLEMAN. Baltimore: Johns Hopkins Press, 1956.

PRESS, JOHN. *The Fire and the Fountain.* London and New York: Oxford University Press, 1955.

RANSOM, JOHN CROWE. *God Without Thunder.* London: Howe, 1931.

RAYMOND, MARCEL. *From Baudelaire to Surrealism.* Translated by G. M. New York: Wittenborn, Schultz, 1950.

READ, HERBERT. *Existentialism, Marxism and Anarchism.* London: Freedom Press, 1949.

ROBBINS, ROSSELL HOPE. *The T. S. Eliot Myth.* New York: H. Schuman, 1951.

ROSS, MALCOLM MACKENZIE. *Poetry and Dogma.* New Brunswick: Rutgers University Press, 1954.

ROUSSET, DAVID. *The Other Kingdom.* Translated by RAMON GUTHRIE. New York: Reynal & Hitchcock, 1947.

RUGGIERO, GUIDO DE. *Existentialism.* Translated by E. M. COCKS. London: Secker & Warburg, 1946.

SANTAYANA, GEORGE. *Interpretations of Poetry and Religion.* New York: Charles Scribner's Sons, 1900.

SARTRE, JEAN-PAUL. *The Age of Reason.* Translated by ERIC SUTTON. New York: Alfred A. Knopf, 1947.

————. *Existentialism.* Translated by BERNARD FRECHTMAN. New York: Philosophical Library, 1947.

――――. *No Exit and The Flies.* Translated by STUART GILBERT. New York: Alfred A. Knopf, 1947.

――――. *The Reprieve.* Translated by ERIC SUTTON. New York: Alfred A. Knopf, 1947.

――――. *Three Plays.* Translated by LIONEL ABEL. New York: Alfred A. Knopf, 1949.

――――. *Nausea.* Translated by LLOYD ALEXANDER. Norfolk, Conn.: New Directions, 1949.

――――. *What Is Literature?* Translated by BERNARD FRECHTMAN. New York: Philosophical Library, 1949.

――――. *Troubled Sleep.* Translated by GERARD HOPKINS. New York: Alfred A. Knopf, 1951.

――――. *Existential Psychoanalysis.* Translated by HAZEL E. BARNES. New York: Philosophical Library, 1953.

――――. *Being and Nothingness.* Translated by HAZEL BARNES. New York: Philosophical Library, 1956.

SAVAGE, D. S. *The Personal Principle:* London: Routledge, 1944.

――――. *The Withered Branch.* New York: Pellegrini & Cudahy, 1952.

SCARFE, FRANCIS. *Auden and After.* London: Routledge & Sons, 1947.

SCHORER, MARK. *William Blake.* New York: Henry Holt & Co., 1946.

SCHWEITZER, ALBERT. *The Decay and the Restoration of Civilization.* Translated by C. T. CAMPION. London: A. & C. Black, 1923.

SEBEOK, THOMAS A. (ed.). *Myth.* Philadelphia: American Folklore Society, 1955.

SHAPIRO, KARL. *Beyond Criticism.* Lincoln: University of Nebraska Press, 1953.

SHAW, GEORGE BERNARD. *Six Plays.* New York: Dodd, Mead & Co., 1941.

――――. *Nine Plays.* New York: Dodd, Mead & Co., 1951.

SKELTON, ROBIN. *The Poetic Pattern.* Berkeley: University of California Press, 1956.

SLATER, ROBERT LAWTON. *Paradox and Nirvana.* Chicago: University of Chicago Press, 1951.

SMITH, H. SHELTON. *Changing Conceptions of Original Sin.* New York: Charles Scribner's Sons, 1955.

SPENDER, STEPHEN. *The Creative Element.* New York: British Book Centre, 1954.

———. *The Making of a Poem.* London: H. Hamilton, 1955.

SQUIRES, RADCLIFFE. *The Loyalties of Robinson Jeffers.* Ann Arbor: University of Michigan Press, 1956.

STRINDBERG, AUGUST. *Eight Famous Plays.* Translated by EDWIN BJÖRKMAN and N. ERICHSEN. London: Duckworth, 1949.

———. *Six Plays.* Translated by ELIZABETH SPRIGGE. Garden City: Doubleday & Co., 1955.

TILLICH, PAUL. *The Courage to Be.* New Haven: Yale University Press, 1953.

TIVERTON, WILLIAM [Martin Jarrett-Kerr]. *D. H. Lawrence and Human Existence.* London: Rockliff, 1951.

TOLSTOY, LEO. *War and Peace.* 2 vols. Translated by LOUISE and AYLMER MAUDE. New York: Heritage Press, 1938.

UNAMUNO, MIGUEL. *The Tragic Sense of Life.* Translated by J. E. CRAWFORD FLITCH. London: Macmillan Co., 1926.

USHER, ARLAND. *Journey Through Dread.* London: 1955.

VAIHINGER, H. *The Philosophy of 'As If.'* Translated by C. K. OGDEN. New York and London: Harcourt, Brace & Co., 1925.

WAGGONER, HYATT HOWE. *The Heel of Elohim.* Norman: University of Oklahoma Press, 1950.

WAHL, JEAN. *A Short History of Existentialism.* Translated by FORREST WILLIAMS and STANLEY MARON. New York: Philosophical Library, 1949.

WATTS, HAROLD H. *Hound and Quarry.* London: Routledge & Paul, 1953.

WEISINGER, HERBERT. *Tragedy and the Paradox of the Fortunate Fall.* East Lansing: Michigan State College Press, 1953.

WHALLEY, GEORGE. *Poetic Process.* London: Routledge & K. Paul, 1953.

WHEELWRIGHT, PHILIP. *The Burning Fountain.* Bloomington: Indiana University Press, 1954.

WHITE, HELEN C. *The Metaphysical Poets.* New York: Macmillan Co., 1936.

WHITEHEAD, ALFRED NORTH. *Science and the Modern World.* New York: Macmillan Co., 1925.

WHYTE, LANCELOT LAW. *Accent on Form.* New York: Harper & Bros., 1954.

WILD, JOHN. *The Challenge of Existentialism.* Bloomington: Indiana University Press, 1955.

WILLIAMS, CHARLES. *The Descent of the Dove.* London: Longmans, Green & Co., 1939.

WILLIAMS, TENNESSEE. *Camino Real.* Norfolk, Conn.: New Directions, 1953.

WILSON, COLIN. *The Outsider.* Boston: Houghton Mifflin Co., 1956.

————. *Religion and the Rebel.* Boston: Houghton Mifflin Co., 1957.

WILSON, EDMUND. *A Piece of My Mind.* New York: Farrar, Straus & Cudahy, 1956.

WRIGHT, RICHARD. *The Outsider.* New York: Harper & Bros., 1953.

INDEX